# Beyond Tomorrow

# Beyond Tomorrow

By Raymond F. Cottrell

Southern Publishing Association

Nashville, Tennessee

# Contents

*Except where otherwise noted, passages of Scripture
are cited from the Revised Standard Version.*

# What This Book Is About

FOR CENTURIES the best-laid plans of statesmen, philosophers, and other leaders of thought and action, to establish society, government, and world affairs on an enduring basis of peace with justice for all, have foundered on the cruelhearted barrier reef of human perversity, vainglory, greed, and ambition. Valorous efforts to free mankind's frail bark from the treacherous reef before the frustrating crosscurrents of history beat it to pieces have all proved unavailing. This book has been written with the earnest conviction that the only practical and permanent solution to the world's ever more complex and baffling problems is the one set forth by Jesus Christ and placed on record, by His authority, in the Holy Scriptures.

This book is written, also, in the profound belief that a fair, objective examination of all the evidence conclusively proves the Bible to be, beyond a quibble or a doubt, and in a supreme and unique sense, God's message to the human race—today in the space age as it was two thousand and more years ago in the iron age. Perhaps the most remarkable facet of the Bible

7

is that its inspired writers foretold with incredible accuracy the course history has actually taken down
through the centuries to modern times, including the
very situation that exists in the world today. More
than that, and with more than human insight, they
warned that a great global holocaust is soon to burst
upon the world, one they declare is destined to mark
the transition from the troubled world of today as we
know it, to the eternal peace and security an all-wise
heavenly Father has in store for His earthbound sons
and daughters, beyond tomorrow.

But this book is not concerned exclusively with
proverbial "pie in the sky by and by." It comes to a
focus on the practical problems of today—on what we
can believe and what we must do, in the present, to
prepare for that glorious future in a perfect world beyond tomorrow. It is written from the perspective of
history set forth in the Holy Scriptures, from which
alone we can rightly understand the events of past
centuries and the confusing crosscurrents of today,
and so prepare intelligently for tomorrow and what
lies beyond. As Abraham Lincoln said in his historic
"House Divided" speech on the eve of the Civil War,
"If we could first know where we are, and whither we
are tending, we could better judge what to do, and
how to do it."

## A Blighted Dream

Half a century ago people, generally, believed that
the world stood on the threshold of an era of universal
peace, justice, and goodwill. They expected that ignorance, crime, and war would soon be banished from

the earth, that the nations would learn to settle their social, political, and economic differences amicably in a great parliament of man, and that eventually, by the mutual consent of all peoples everywhere, the principles of the Sermon on the Mount would rule in men's hearts and regulate the affairs of earth. The prevailing mood in civilized lands was one of uninhibited and increasingly starry-eyed optimism.

And not without reason. During the nineteenth century and the early years of the twentieth, Western civilization experienced a development more profound and far-reaching than in the two preceding millenniums. Scientific discoveries and inventions, the industrial revolution, and world commerce had vastly increased the volume of wealth, and with it the standard of living for millions. Ideals of social justice were gradually improving the condition of the laboring classes and banishing poverty. Medical science was winning the agelong battle against disease and was lengthening man's span of life. Far-reaching humanitarian reforms were the order of the day, and democracy seemed destined, in time, to supplant all the old forms of tyranny everywhere.

Faith in man's supposed infinite moral perfectibility and the inevitability of his collective social progress became virtually absolute, and these twin ideas were in process of being canonized as two of the great natural laws of the universe—along with time, gravity, and the motions of the stars in their courses. Yes, the kingdom of Christ was to be set up on earth by a planned acceleration of man's moral evolution! It was confidently declared that a millennium of peace with

justice lay ahead, around but one or two more twists
and turns of the highway of time, and that Utopia—
heaven on earth—was almost within sight. Educated
and given a favorable environment, men would automatically reject all that was false and evil, and choose
the true and good. Or so the popular line of reasoning
went.

Little did our parents realize that they and their
children were about to suffer and die by the millions
in the two most disastrous wars of all time, and that
strange, sinister forces were about to dissolve that
blissful fantasy of yesteryear into a shimmering mirage. They did not foresee the rising tide of lawlessness, crime, and unconscionable conduct of all kinds
that has devastatingly shattered man's ill-founded
faith in his own supposedly infinite and inevitable
moral perfectibility.

It is a simple fact that today there is less peace,
justice, and goodwill among men than ever before in
modern times. Conflicts between class and class, race
and race, nation and nation, and ideology and ideology
are immeasurably sharper, more bitter, and more widespread than they were fifty years ago. The world is
more deeply divided by its pathetic iron and bamboo
curtains, its ugly barbed-wire fences and cinderblock
walls, and all the other barriers, tangible and in-
tangible, that men have erected between themselves
and their fellowmen. In a very real and sobering way,
intercontinental ballistic missiles equipped with hydrogen warheads leave our disillusioned, schizophrenic
generation no place in which to hide, and our vaunted
technological progress appears destined, like a Frank-

enstein monster, to engulf all of us in one colossal catastrophe instead of ushering us into that more abundant life for which we all yearn.

The present sorry state of affairs need have come as no surprise, however, had we been willing to heed the words of Christ and the prophets and apostles of old. These inspired spokesmen predicted an unprecedented accumulation of wealth in the last days and warned that as men set out to acquire what each considered his rightful share of it, irrespective of the rights or needs of others, increasingly bitter and fierce conflicts would result. They predicted an all-time low in the moral tone of society and a fearful increase in all forms of lawlessness and crime. They foretold that the accumulated injustices of centuries—with class pitted against class, race against race, and nation against nation—would reach the critical, explosive point on a worldwide scale.

## An Era of Fantastic Scientific Progress

Another noteworthy characteristic of our era is the fantastically accelerated rate of advance in all branches of knowledge, in scientific and technological progress, and in the tempo of life. Like a piece of driftwood our hapless generation is borne irresistibly forward on a flood tide of social, political, scientific, and economic change, and we find it hard to realize how different our world today is from what it was yesterday—or what it will be tomorrow. We now come into possession of more new knowledge concerning the universe about us in a day than we formerly did in a century. Rear Admiral Hyman Rickover, father of the atomic submarine, has estimated that the sum total of human knowledge doubles about every fifteen years.

Only as long ago as the time of George Washington a man's fastest rate of locomotion was the speed at which his own legs, or perhaps those of his horse, could carry him. If anything, travel was actually slower and more difficult than it had been eighteen centuries before when the Romans laced the Mediterranean world with a network of excellent all-weather highways, some of which are still in use. For instance, George Washington's first inaugural ceremony was originally scheduled to take place on March 4, 1789, but slow communications and transportation postponed the event for eight weeks, until the end of April. Yet Washington's home on the Potomac south of Washington is less than 250 miles from New York City, site of the first inaugural.

The United States' greatest land victory in the War of 1812, a quarter of a century later, took place two weeks after the peace treaty had been signed, because the British and American commanders in charge did not know that the war was over! It took the Lewis and Clark expedition eighteen months to reach the Pacific Coast from St. Louis, Missouri, and when adventurers from the great cities of the Eastern seaboard first headed for the Mother Lode country of California in the gold rush of 1849, their best route lay thirteen thousand miles by sailing ship around Cape Horn— a distance equal to halfway around the globe.

In those rugged days, scarcely more than a century ago, a person mailing a letter in San Francisco to a friend in New York City would have to allow six or eight months for a reply. A decade later, in 1860, the famed pony express between St. Joseph, Missouri—which then stood at the edge of the great American wilderness—and Sacramento, California, clipped travel time for that part of the transcontinental journey to ten days. A record run of seven days and seventeen hours in the autumn of that year carried news of Abraham Lincoln's election as President. But the pony express went out of business less than a year later with completion of the first transcontinental telegraph line.

In 1869 the famous golden spike driven into the last railroad tie at Promontory Point, in Utah, linked East and West by rail for the first time, and the journey from New York to San Francisco shrank to seven days. In 1876 a locomotive actually made the run in three and a half days. A regularly scheduled jet airliner now covers the same distance in five and a half hours.

Ocean travel has also changed greatly in the past century and a half. When launched in 1818, the S. S. *Savannah,* first ocean-going steamship, was promptly dubbed by wary travelers, "Fickett's Steam Coffin." A crew was hard to come by for the twenty-nine-day maiden voyage from Savannah, Georgia, to Liverpool, England, and it proved impossible to lure passengers aboard. For the most part, steam power was utilized only when the wind died down, because it was not possible to carry enough coal to make the entire crossing under steam. When the lookout at Cape Clear on the southern tip of Ireland sighted the *Savannah* on the horizon, he reported a ship on fire. The captain of the fast cutter dispatched to her rescue was puzzled at his inability, even under full sail, to overtake a ship proceeding, as he supposed, under "bare poles." In desperation he fired a volley over her bow, and she hove to for his inspection.

Early in 1962, a century and a half after that memorable voyage, the N. S. *Savannah,* first nuclear-powered ship designed as a commercial carrier, was launched. Her 126-pound bundle of nuclear fuel packs enough energy to keep her sailing for three years without refueling—a fabulous 270 times longer than the original *Savannah!*

Magellan's historic expedition (1519-1522) required three years to circumnavigate the globe. The opening of the first transcontinental railroad in 1869 forged the last link in steam transportation, by land and sea, completely around the world, and cut travel time to seventy-eight days. Today, making use of regularly scheduled commercial flights, a person could leave New York City after breakfast on a Monday morning, wing his way around the world, and be back in time for a late lunch the following Wednesday, two days and five hours later. An astronaut makes the circuit of the earth in an hour and a half.

Only a little more than a century ago the most rapid means of transmitting a written message was by special courier on horseback, no faster than the famed Persian postal system more than two millenniums before. Then, in 1844, the first intercity telegraph line linked Baltimore with Washington, D.C., and in 1866 the first transatlantic cable went into operation. Messages could be sent over that cable at the rate of eight words per minute. The first news it carried was of the peace treaty that ended the Austro-Prussian War. Except for the cable, the news would have required eleven days to reach the United States by steamship.

By way of contrast, a standard oceanic cable today has the capacity to transmit eighty-four messages simultaneously, at a maximum rate of 2,500 words per minute. The communications satellite Telstar, which was placed in orbit in the early summer of 1962, can transmit 600 messages at the same time, at the rate of 1,460,000 words per minute, or three times the number of words listed in an unabridged dictionary. The tiny beam of light emitted by a revolutionary device known as an optical laser, still in the experimental stage, is theoretically capable of carrying as much information simultaneously as all the radio, microwave, and television channels in the United States!

## A Sobering Paradox

When we reflect on the perplexing problems that plague our generation—the fear, the hatred, and the struggles between nations, races, and classes of society —we may at first be inclined to dismiss matters with the observation that conflicts of interest leading to murder, riot, and war have existed since the dawn of history. To be sure, but wait! In the long ago the most one man could do to checkmate his enemy was to hunt him down and engage him in personal combat. Today, one man can press a button that would loose a simultaneous nuclear attack on scores of cities half a world away and take hundreds of millions of human lives—all within a few minutes' time.

Man's former scientific and technological ignorance, the relatively primitive character of the weapons at his command, and the distance that separated him from his potential victims limited his destructive capacity and protected mankind from annihilation. Today, scientific discovery and technical prowess have placed in his hands weapons that obliterate distance and that are capable of destroying the entire human race. More destruction than was caused by all the bombs dropped by all the airplanes in World War II can now be packed aboard one airplane or submarine or intercontinental ballistic missile, and delivered on target anywhere in the world within a few minutes.

The dilemma of today is simply that while man has become a formidable giant in scientific knowledge and technological skill, he remains fundamentally the same moral dwarf he was five thousand years ago. This is the great paradox of our generation. Man's primal instinct to take every possible advantage of his fellowmen, individually and collectively, by fair means or foul, remains unchanged. The only difference now is that his inherent selfishness is more sophisticated than it used to be. Even in lands that are presumably Christian and civilized, blind passion all too often controls his heart and actions.

The bitter animosities of generations seem to have multiplied and intensified to the point where it would be literally impossible to do justice to all men, even if some miracle suddenly disposed their hearts to generosity instead of selfishness. How, for instance, could absolute justice be done to both Arabs and Jews in Palestine, or to all the Europeans and Africans in

South Africa? The best proposal for solving a difficult situation usually proves to be a compromise which leaves everyone more unhappy than before, and all too often bent on revenge. Man's collective selfishness has never been more graphically described than in the observation of a newspaper reporter covering the Versailles peace conference at the close of World War I, that if all the victorious allies—to say nothing of their defeated foes—were to be granted as much territory as each claimed, it would take a planet five times the size of ours to satisfy them all!

Proximity has only accentuated men's conflicting aspirations. In the past, oceans, mountain ranges, and deserts kept the peoples of earth at arm's length. But today, for all practical purposes, there are no oceans, mountains, or deserts. All men have become neighbors, very close neighbors in fact—as if the entire human family had moved into one vast apartment house.

Many of the residents are content to go quietly about their own business, desiring only to live unmolested lives, and willing to let others do the same. But they are constantly at the mercy of some other occupants of the house who are bent on robbery and murder. Bands of criminals lurk in dark corners and roam some of the corridors almost at will. They have devised weapons strong enough to blow up the entire apartment house. The only real deterrent to their use of these weapons is that they still have enough sense to realize that the result would be suicide as well as murder, and that the entire building would be left a shambles. This band of maniacs has already gained control of several floors, which they rule at the point of a gun, and they seem determined to extend their control over the entire building.

## What Shall We Do Next?

At this point some incurable optimist will doubtless observe that for thousands of years the world has always found a way to muddle through its problems and crises, and that somehow it will be able to do so again.

But statesmen and thinking men generally are not at all sure that, circumstances being what they are, it will be possible to do so this time. If, by some magic, men could be persuaded to scrap all their hydrogen bombs and intercontinental ballistic missiles and all the other paraphernalia of war, they would still go after each other with their fists, fingernails, and teeth. The trouble with all the proposals thus far offered is that they do not go to the heart of the problem—the sinful human heart, which the prophet Jeremiah described twenty-five centuries ago as "desperately wicked" and "deceitful above all things." The ever more strained state of international relations indicates that something great and decisive is about to take place. The pressure gauge of conflicting interests is already far over into the red, and warns that the world is on the verge of a stupendous explosion.

To change the figure, it is as if the human race were aboard a train without brakes, racing downgrade and lurching crazily along as it gathers momentum. At some point ahead it seems certain to leave the track, with disastrous consequences for all on board. There can be no doubt we stand today on the verge of solemn events of the greatest magnitude.

Fortunately, however, the situation is not as bleak and hopeless as it may appear, nor is it necessary to go whistling along wistfully in the dark. To be sure, not all is right with the world, but above the distractions of earth God still sits enthroned, and from His great and calm eternity He orders that which His divine providence sees is best. Through the sacred pages of Holy Writ light from heaven shines forth into the darkness of history, to illumine the way God would have us take from this world to the next. It is the purpose of this book to gather these precious rays of light and focus them on our pathway through the vicissitudes of today and the perplexities of tomorrow, to that perfect world beyond tomorrow.

## A Preview of the Book

Our narrative begins with the inspired record left by Daniel, greatest statesman-prophet of all time, and recounts the major episodes in his long and eventful life as prime minister of the greatest empire of antiquity. This series of incidents convinced him that the hand of God guides the destinies of men and nations in accordance with His eternal purpose. We will turn next to his account of what God revealed to him about the future course of history to the close of time, and then to Christ's own interpretation of the Book of Daniel and to the inspired comments on it penned by the inspired writers of the New Testament. We will consider at some length the present world situation in the light of Bible prophecy. The closing chapters will focus on the climax of history as set forth in the Scriptures, and on that perfect world beyond tomorrow.

This book is not written in technical theological terms, but in words everyone will find readable. Nevertheless, back of the common, everyday language is an infinitely painstaking study of the passages of Scripture considered, in the original languages in which they were written. In that study the most careful attention was given to the meaning of individual words and to the literary and historical context. A sincere attempt was made to be objective, to draw from a passage only as much as a fair reading of it in the original languages would permit.

Except where otherwise noted, passages of Scripture are cited from the Revised Standard Version, chiefly because of its rendition into modern English more intelligible to persons not familiar with the grand, but antique, language of the King James Version. All Scripture references, sources for quotations cited from other writers, and explanatory notes are grouped together at the close of each chapter, as indicated by the small, raised index numbers in the text. This will enable a reader concerned primarily with the main theme of the book to proceed without interruption. At the same time, readers who are interested in further evidence for statements made and explanations given will have ready access to the authority for them and, here and there, to additional information on the subject.

This book is sent forth with a prayer that all who read will experience a deeper appreciation of the Holy Scriptures as God's answer to the perplexing problems of life today, and will find it in their hearts to follow as God leads to that better world beyond tomorrow.

# Prisoners of War

ONE THING was certain: they were not prisoners of war by choice—Daniel, three of his personal friends, a number of their fellow countrymen, and many other young men from the great cities of Syria and Palestine. For weeks this motley procession of captives—dusty, footsore, and weary—had been marching southward along the banks of the broad Euphrates River with the ever-victorious armies of King Nebuchadnezzar. Today, it was rumored, they were but a few leagues from Babylon,[1] their destination; and from time to time their listless eyes would scan the southern horizon for a first glimpse of that fabulous metropolis of the ancient world.

For Nebuchadnezzar[2] this day's march would complete another successful campaign in the west, on the far borders of the New Babylonian Empire. As crown prince and commander in chief, he had marched forth with his resplendent legions in the early spring of that fateful year 605 B.C. For the first time his aging and ailing father, Nabopolassar, chose to remain at home, but Nebuchadnezzar was already a seasoned general himself from years of experience under his father's able tutorship. His objective on this campaign was to

destroy the bothersome Egyptian forces based at
Carchemish, in what used to be Assyria, or at least
drive them back whence they had come. Egypt was
the last major rival to be brought to heel before Babylonia could lay claim to universal empire.

It was a good five hundred miles up the Euphrates
to Carchemish, where Nebuchadnezzar met and easily
dislodged the Egyptian forces quartered there. Rem-
nants of the battered army fled toward home in great
disorder; but Nebuchadnezzar followed in pursuit,
engaged them again near Hamath, and utterly routed
them. Egypt itself lay another five hundred miles or so
to the southwest, through Syria and Palestine. Fear of
the growing power of Babylonia had led the lesser
kings of Syria and Palestine to conclude a mutual defense pact with Pharaoh-Necho II of Egypt; and since
the route to Egypt lay through their lands, it would be
necessary for Nebuchadnezzar to crush whatever minor resistance they might offer. Thus it was that he
laid siege to Jerusalem early that summer, captured it,
stripped the Temple of its choicest treasures, confirmed
the time-serving Jehoiakim on his throne as puppet-
king of Judah, and took Daniel and several other
young men of the nobility as hostages.

One day toward the close of August, however,
while Nebuchadnezzar was on the borders of Egypt
completing preparations to follow up his brilliant success by invading the ancient Nile Valley itself, a royal
messenger rode up with an urgent dispatch from Babylon. His father was dead! Secretly and in haste he
struck out directly across the vast Arabian Desert for
home, lest some usurper should claim the throne in

his absence. By forced marches he reached Babylon
about the seventh of September, found that friends had
protected his rights, had himself proclaimed king, and
then returned to Syria for a few weeks to organize the
administration of his newly conquered territories.

Thus it came about, later in the autumn, that Nebuchadnezzar, as king, and his battle-weary army were
nearing home, accompanied by a large assortment of
elite captives from the lands of the west. It was at least
eight hundred miles from Jerusalem to Babylon by
the Euphrates route, and Daniel and his fellow captives were now wan and weary from the long march,
which required from six weeks to two months.

While he was plodding along, Daniel's thoughts
doubtless went back to Joseph on his way to servitude
in Egypt a thousand years before. How alike were
their circumstances! Like Daniel, Joseph had been
snatched from his childhood home by what seemed
an evil fate. With what foreboding he, too, must have
looked forward to his lot in the strange land to which,
against his will, he was going. But in his hour of need
Joseph's thoughts had turned to his father's God, and
his hand of faith reached up to grasp the unseen hand
of Providence, in the confident belief that the God of
his fathers would be his God, too.

Then and there Joseph dedicated himself fully to
the Lord, praying that the Keeper of Israel would be
with him in the land of his exile. His soul thrilled with
the high resolve to prove himself true to God and to
act under all circumstances as became a subject of the
King of heaven. He purposed to serve the Lord with
undivided heart, to meet the trials of his lot with forti-

tude, and faithfully to perform every duty. In the long,
weary days and weeks between Jerusalem and Babylon, Daniel purposed to walk in Joseph's footsteps.

## Babylon—Metropolis of the World

As the great throng approached Babylon, they
found themselves marching through one of the most
fertile regions of the ancient world, one whose rich
harvests amazed visitors from other lands. What a
relief from the barren mountains and sterile desert
lands they had crossed! The countryside was inter-
sected with irrigation canals that carried the waters of
the Euphrates to fields for many miles on either side.
Clusters of date palms here and there testified to a
pleasant, subtropical climate.

At last the first landmark of Babylon loomed slowly
above the distant southern horizon—the famous temple-tower, *Etemenanki*. This magnificent seven-stage
tower, loftiest in all the world, rose to an imposing
height above the low-lying plain and could be seen
from a great distance. Legend had it that this stately
structure, popularly known as "the tower of Babel,"
was situated on the actual site of the original tower
that bore that name.

Two or three hours later the glistening yellow brick
walls of the city beside the Euphrates could be seen
rising majestically in the bright autumn sunshine.
These lofty walls with their crenellated parapets
stretched in a rough square a mile or more on each
side. That may seem small by modern standards, but
even so Babylon covered a greater area than most
cities of its time. During his reign Nebuchadnezzar,

who became famous throughout the ancient world as the architect and builder of New Babylon, was to enlarge the city nearly eight times by building new walls that enclosed a roughly rectangular area only a little less than three miles on a side, on both banks of the Euphrates.[3]

Soon captor and captive paused before the colorful and resplendent Ishtar Gate, at the northwest corner of the city, hard by the royal palace and the river. The Ishtar Gate was a magnificent portal in the double wall. It was 170 feet long and consisted of four tower-like structures surmounted by turrets. It was faced with sky-blue glazed bricks and ornamented in bas-relief with brilliant yellow glazed-brick bulls and mythological serpent-dragons. The bulls had decorative rows of blue hair and had green hoofs and horns; while the serpent-dragons were composite beasts with serpents' heads and tails, dragonlike bodies covered with scales, and eagles' and cats' feet. In bas-relief on the walls on both sides of the esplanade before the gate were huge glazed-brick lions, some white with yellow manes and others yellow with red manes, against a blue background. The lion was sacred to Ishtar, favorite goddess of the Babylonian pantheon.

Passing through this spectacular gateway with its massive, bronze-plated doors, the triumphant army entered the broad Procession Street, main north-south thoroughfare of the city. On the right, just inside the gate, was the royal palace, built of bright rose-colored baked bricks. Advancing southward along Procession Street to the very center of the city, the captives were ushered, at last, into the great courtyard of the *Esa-*

*gila,*[4] a vast temple complex dedicated to Bel-Marduk, the national deity. In the ancient world this great temple was second in size and fame only to Karnak, in Egypt.

The sacred tower, *Etemenanki,* three hundred feet high and three hundred feet on a side at its base, occupied a prominent position in the court area of the temple. It rose in seven concentric stages, superimposed one upon another, with each stage several feet narrower than the one below it. A shrine mounted on the seventh stage was dedicated to Bel-Marduk, Babylonian counterpart of the Baal, or "lord," of the Sidonians and Canaanites generally.

At the temple of Marduk, Nebuchadnezzar and his army gave thanks for the victorious campaign just concluded. Painful to Daniel and his friends as the ceremonies were, that which wounded their hearts most deeply was the presentation of the sacred Temple treasures from Jerusalem to Bel-Marduk, in praise of his vaunted power over the God of the Hebrews. Sadly they watched these priceless objects deposited in the god's treasure-house. This inglorious day Daniel would never forget! Following the ceremony the captive youths were escorted to quarters adjoining the royal palace, a short distance to the north of *Esagila* and its imposing tower.

## In Training for Royal Service

Daniel and his friends, then about eighteen years of age, were of noble birth, and some were members of the Jewish royal family. By the king's personal order Ashpenaz, chief eunuch of the Babylonian court, had personally selected them from among the youth of Jerusalem for their handsome appearance, cultured bearing, and evidences of intelligence, talent, and capacity to learn. Nebuchadnezzar, apparently a wise and farsighted monarch, had important plans for them and for the other captives. They were to assist him in the administration of his burgeoning empire; and to prepare them for this responsibility they were to spend three years in the imperial university studying the language, learning, and science of the Chaldeans. Then, upon graduation, they were to "stand before the king."

The Chaldeans were members of an Aramaean tribe that had migrated to lower Mesopotamia centuries before. In Daniel's time they constituted the nobility of Babylonia, and the term was now applied particularly to the scholars and counselors attached to the Babylonian court. They were masters of philosophy, astronomy, mathematics, and other exact sciences, as well as of the astrology and magic associated with Babylonian religion. They constituted a sort of royal brain trust. Chaldean, or Aramaic, was the language of culture, learning, and diplomacy. It was akin to Hebrew in somewhat the same way as English and Spanish are related to each other.

Strange as it may seem, we are indebted to these "wise men" of Babylon, for it was they who created the sciences of astronomy and mathematics, including algebra and geometry. They conceived the system of figuring by sixes and twelves, which we still use when we count by the dozen, give the number of inches in a foot or the number of degrees in a circle, or tell the time of day. They also devised the sun dial, the ecliptic, and the zodiac, and were able to calculate eclipses.

The first step in transforming this heterogeneous group of different nationalities and languages into counselors able to "stand before the king" was to give them Babylonian names. Daniel, which means "The Lord is my judge," became Belteshazzar—probably an abbreviation of *Bêl-balâtsu-usur,* which means, "May Bel protect [the king's] life." They named Daniel's friend Hananiah, meaning "The Lord is gracious," Shadrach; and Mishael, "Who is for the Lord?" they called Meshach. Azariah, "The Lord has helped," became Abed-nego, a variant form of *Abed-Nebo,* "Servant of [the god] Nabu."

The change from names reminiscent of their own God to others that identified them with the heathen deities of Babylon was the first subtle step in the brainwashing process. Nebuchadnezzar apparently made no direct attempt to change their religion. His victory over the Hebrew people, so he thought, conclusively proved the superiority of his gods to theirs, and he doubtless thought it would be only a matter of time amid the culture and learning of Babylon until these Hebrew youth would recognize that superiority. Little did he suspect that circumstances would soon force from his lips an unqualified public acknowledgment of the infinite superiority of *their* God.

## A Conflict of Loyalties

As a special token of royal favor and of concern for their welfare and progress, the king ordered that these young noblemen from foreign lands should have the same food and wine as were served at his table. But this gesture of royal goodwill confronted Daniel and his friends with a major dilemma. It was the first instance of a prolonged conflict between the customs, culture, and sophistication of Babylon on the one hand, and their own conscientious convictions on the other.

And wherein lay the difficulty? In the first place, the principles of a healthful diet revealed in the Sacred Scriptures clearly differentiate between "clean" and "unclean" flesh foods and explicitly prohibit the latter. In addition, even "clean" animals must be slaughtered in the prescribed fashion—by draining the blood.[5] Without doubt, none of the flesh food provided Daniel and his three friends would pass inspection by these two standards. In the second place, the heathen followed the practice of offering to their gods a portion of each animal slaughtered for food, thereby presumably invoking the blessing of the gods upon the remainder. To eat of such food implied faith in the power of the gods and one's acceptance of their blessing. Finally, to eat and drink of the luxurious and unhealthful viands prepared at court would violate strict principles of temperance in eating and drinking.

## Stouthearted Men

Thus, on several counts, Daniel and his three friends could not conscientiously eat of the food set before them by royal decree. They politely refused anything and everything that would in any way weaken their physical and mental powers. The other Hebrew youth seem to have decided that the king

might take offense at their refusal to eat what he had
so graciously provided. Why should they needlessly
involve themselves in further difficulty?

Daniel and his friends evidently realized that physical fitness is the result of strict adherence to the laws
of health, and an essential requirement for a staunch
character. They had dedicated their lives to the worship and service of God, out of a conviction that, despite circumstances, a divine purpose was shaping
their destiny. The result was a bold and fearless stand
for principle. Integrity of character, confidence in an
overruling Providence, and the wise improvement of
their native talents and the opportunities that came to
them—all this gave them confidence in their ability,
under God, to meet any situation and to solve any
problem with which life might confront them. They
chose to be loyal to God, to principle, to the best they
knew.

Thus it was that Daniel and his friends tactfully approached Ashpenaz, requesting permission to select
their own food. The chief eunuch must have been puzzled beyond words by these youthful slaves who refused to sit down to a table prepared by the king!
Their request made no sense to him, and he dismissed
the proposal on the pretext that he had no authority to
make an exception to the royal orders. Checkmated
on their first attempt, Daniel and his friends might
have reasoned that they had done their part. Surely,
under the circumstances, God would not hold it
against them if they took the course indicated by common sense! But Daniel and his friends were not looking for loopholes.

Next, they approached the steward immediately in charge of them, requesting a ten-day trial of their proposed menu, with the understanding that he alone should judge the results. Those ten days sufficed to convince this practical-minded steward that no harm could result from permitting these young men to have their way, foolish as it seemed to him, and he acceded to their request for a strictly vegetarian diet. Doubtless they chose this diet because it was the one God had provided for Adam and Eve in Eden. Surely the Creator knew what would be the best food for the creatures He had made, they apparently reasoned. "So the steward took away their rich food and the wine they were to drink, and gave them vegetables."

## In Partnership With God

How could ten short days make so marked a difference in the appearance of this faithful quartet, in comparison with that of the other young men, as to convince the steward that he would not endanger his own head by letting them do as they wished? Was it a miracle? Well, perhaps partly yes and partly no. It is always well to remember that God never does for a man what he can rightly be expected to do for himself —and there is much that a man can do to preserve and to promote his health.

In the first place, lifelong adherence to the revealed principles of healthful living had built into the youthful bodies of Daniel and his friends a reserve of health and vigor that gave them a tremendous initial advantage over their less-conscientious companions. The arduous eight-hundred-mile march from Jerusalem to

Babylon had doubtless been a severe and exhausting experience for these sheltered youth from the elite homes of Jerusalem. The rigors of the march had told on Daniel and his friends as well as on the others, but their basic stamina and physical reserve now enabled them to regain their usual degree of health much more rapidly than those whose bodies had been weakened by harmful habits.

Furthermore, their voluntary choice of the ideal diet originally provided by God opened the way for Him to add Heaven's blessing to their human efforts in a way that could not otherwise have been possible. A departure from principle upon this occasion would have weakened their sense of right and their abhorrence of wrong, and the other brilliant triumphs of their career in Babylon would probably never have taken place. Inspiration has recorded their loyal stand for principle as a scintillating example of the result of cooperating with God's revealed will. And what God did for Daniel, He will do for all who in this evil day choose to walk humbly in the wise pathway of His appointment.

Quickly the years of training went by. The time came for final examinations, and Nebuchadnezzar was to be chief examiner! He must have been an intelligent and wise man himself to be able to examine these youth in the various branches of Chaldean learning and science. Suffice it to say that he found the four young Hebrews not only far in advance of their fellow students, but "ten times better" than all the learned gentlemen of his realm—doubtless including their instructors! Here were promising young men indeed, men he could well use in his service. Matched with the best-trained brains of Babylon, world center of learning and culture, these youth proved to be infinitely superior to all competitors.

## Off to a Brilliant Career

The story of Daniel's meteoric rise to a position of royal favor by a course of strict loyalty to principle testifies to the superiority of the pattern of life he chose to follow. A sound mind always functions best in a sound body. The erect form, the healthy appearance, the broad knowledge, the keen comprehension of difficult problems evident in Daniel and his friends —all testified to the unimpaired vigor of their mental powers. They were graduated with the highest honors and were immediately accepted into the royal service —they "stood before the king."

For Daniel and his friends this experience marked the beginning of a long and eventful career. Little did they dream of the high destiny that was yet to be theirs. Daniel relates that he "continued" to the reign of Cyrus, first ruler of the next world empire, that of Persia. His life in Babylon thus spanned the entire seventy years of the exile.

During these years Daniel and his three friends bore a silent but eloquent witness before the heathen king and his courtiers of the goodness of God and of the wisdom of living by His revealed will. What the world needs most in our time is more men like Daniel, willing to do and dare for the right. The lives of these stouthearted prisoners of war stand forth as a brilliant demonstration of what God can and will do for those who choose to serve and obey Him. Through their loyalty to principle and unflinching courage God speaks to us today.

## NOTES

1. Babylon is from the Greek *Babulōn,* a transliteration of the Babylonian (or Akkadian) *Bâbi-ilâni,* meaning "gate of the gods," or more commonly *Bâb-ilu,* Babel. In ancient cities the gate was the place where the king and other officials transacted the public business of the city. The name Babylon implied that it was the place where the gods came down to earth to determine the fate of men and nations. It was probably the world's oldest city, having been founded by Nimrod some fifteen centuries before the time of Daniel. (Genesis 10:9, 10.) From the very first, the city and its famous tower stood as a monument of defiance against the God of heaven. (Compare Genesis 11:4 with chapter 9:1, 11.) To the Jews, Babylon became the consummate symbol of opposition to God, and because of the similarity of the shorter form of the name to the Hebrew word *balal,* which means "to confuse," they interpreted the name to mean "confusion." See Genesis 11:5-9.

2. Nebuchadnezzar is from the Aramaic *Nâbu-kudurri-usur,* which means, "may [the god] Nabu protect the [my] son." Nebuchadnezzar was son and heir of Nabopolassar, founder of the New Babylonian Empire.

3. Ancient, fabulous accounts attributing a vastly greater size to the city of Babylon have only hearsay reports as a basis, in particular one by the ancient Greek historian Herodotus. Whereas he gives the circumference of the city as about fifty-three miles, the ruins of its ancient walls, still visible today, indicate that it was actually only a little more than eleven miles in circuit.

4. The name *Esagila* means the house "that raises its head." It was the national shrine of Babylon.

5. Leviticus 11 and 17:10-14.

# A Man for the Hour

NOT LONG after Daniel and his three friends were graduated from the imperial university of Babylon,[1] a unique opportunity arose to introduce Nebuchadnezzar to the God of heaven. The king had attributed his victory over the Hebrew people to a supposed superiority of his gods over theirs, but this noteworthy experience convinced him beyond any doubt or quibble that their God was infinitely wiser than the gods of Babylon. "Truly," he admitted to Daniel after it was all over, "your God is God of gods and Lord of kings!"

In their own hearts having sworn undeviating allegiance to God, and having dedicated their talents to His service, Daniel and his three friends became Heaven's accredited ambassadors at the court of Nebuchadnezzar. Through them, God purposed to make Himself known to that great monarch, and if possible to enlist his voluntary submission to the will of Heaven. Such a course on Nebuchadnezzar's part was vital at this juncture of affairs, in view of the fact that during the Babylonian exile the fate of God's chosen people, the Jews, was largely in his hands. The experience recorded in Daniel 2 was in no sense a capricious happenstance, but wholly in keeping with God's fundamental design to acquaint the peoples of earth with His beneficent purpose for them.

Nebuchadnezzar was by all odds the most notable personality in all the Gentile world of his day; and Daniel, a man of exemplary character and unflinching loyalty to principle, was God's man for the hour. His tact, sound judgment, and judicious conduct had already won for him the respect and confidence of the king and his courtiers. Now, in one of the dramatic moments of history, God brought these two outstanding men of their time together in the remarkable encounter Daniel relates in the second chapter of his book.

## Haunted by a Forgotten Dream

The narrative bursts in on Nebuchadnezzar in the privacy of his royal bedchamber the moment he awoke from a fearful dream that was something more than the result of too much wining and dining the night before.[2] This dream, unlike so many others the king had attributed to his gods, did, in fact, come from God. Like a sudden bolt of lightning that momentarily turns night into day, it transfixed him with terror, only to vanish completely from the screen of his subconscious mind the moment he awoke. It so startled him that "his sleep left him," and as he lay awake trying vainly to recall what he had seen, he became more and more perturbed and anxious. His superstitious faith told him that the fleeting dream must be a solemn communication from the gods fraught with fearful import for him personally. He could not be at peace until he recaptured it.

Like other monarchs of his day, Nebuchadnezzar
retained as courtiers men trained in the occult arts,
men who, it was supposed, could fathom all secrets,
unravel all mysteries, and divine the future by interpreting dreams and other portents. In frustration and
fear Nebuchadnezzar turned to these professional
"wise men," whose business it was to help him out of
just such a predicament. In the dark, spectral hours
that precede the dawn he hailed them from their
slumbers to the flickering lamplight of the royal bedchamber.

In order to convince Nebuchadnezzar that this
dream was, indeed, a revelation from a God superior
to all the gods he knew, it was first necessary to demonstrate that his gods and his wise men were power-
less to provide him with the information he so eagerly
desired. Things were therefore permitted to reach a
climax in which the strongest possible incentives,
honor or death, proved unavailing. In their extremity
the wise men were finally compelled to admit that the
solution to the king's dilemma lay in the hands of a
God of whom they had no knowledge and over whom
they had no influence. Only then was the king in a
state of mind to appreciate and benefit by Daniel's
solution to the problem.

In they came, the wisest men in all his realm—"the
magicians, the enchanters, the sorcerers, and the Chaldeans"—and "stood before the king." All but Daniel,
that is. The "magicians" were masters of all magic.
The "enchanters" specialized in obtaining secret information. They divined the future by "reading" the
entrails of sacrificial animals, the flight of birds, the

pattern made by oil spreading on the surface of water, the direction an arrow would point when shaken from a quiver, the configuration of the planets—or by interpreting dreams. The "sorcerers" produced magic spells over men and beasts. The Chaldeans were the learned, elite class of Babylonian scholars, equally expert in the occult arts as well as in the more scientific branches of learning.

## The King's Wise Men Admit
## Their Ignorance

As the wise men entered, curious to learn why they had been summoned at so unconventional an hour, Nebuchadnezzar told them what had happened and frankly admitted his anxiety. "O king, live for ever," their sleepy-eyed spokesman began, addressing the king with the respect and deference required by Babylonian protocol.[3] "Tell your servants the dream, and we will show the interpretation." More than that he had never demanded of them in the past, and they felt well within their rights. They might have contrived some plausible piece of fiction to relate to him, but who could tell if this was not a clever trap, if he was not only pretending not to be able to recall his dream? How they wished they could read his mind!

Had the king been able to relate his dream, the wise men would doubtless soon have agreed upon some reasonable interpretation; but Providence had erased it from his mind in order to prevent just such deception. Heretofore the futility of their devious methods and the worthlessness of the advice formulated by such methods had not been evident, either to the king

or to the wise men themselves. They were not only
deceivers, but self-deceived by their false system. It
was a case of the blind leading the blind. The unprecedented situation that now confronted them was
providentially designed to reveal the falsity of their
pretensions—to them as well as to him.

"You have agreed to speak lying and corrupt words
before me," Nebuchadnezzar finally charged, evidently
under the impression that the wise men were tempo-
rizing, or "trying to gain time," as he put it. It did not
occur to him—yet—that they were actually as ignorant and helpless as they appeared to be. He accused
them of putting him off until they could agree on a
plausible answer, or at least until his anxiety abated.
Their evasive response to his urgent appeal made him
suspect that they actually knew the dream and its import, but were attempting to conceal this information
from him until it would be too late for him to forestall
the dread event, whatever it might be.

In his third and final appeal Nebuchadnezzar put
the wise men on the spot with the peremptory demand, "Tell me the dream, and I shall know that you
can show me its interpretation." This eminently logical request came to the crux of the matter. The wise
men protested that no king had ever made such a
difficult demand of his counselors. But when they
frankly confessed that "there is not a man on earth
who can meet the king's demand" and admitted that
"none can show it to the king except the gods, whose
dwelling is not with flesh," he was still unconvinced.

In his ill-concealed and increasing anxiety the king
offered these helpless wise men every inducement he

could think of—"gifts and rewards and great honor"
—and confronted them with the alternative of being
"torn limb from limb" and having their houses "laid
in ruins." Certainly this two-edged offer and threat
was calculated to persuade them to reveal what he
thought they were trying to conceal, if anything
could. If these extreme alternatives failed to elicit the
desired information, surely it must be because they
were party to a sinister plot against him! Was this
the explanation of their evasive tactics?

## Off With Their Heads!

As the king's fear fed on itself, his anxiety and im-
patience turned to rage. He became "angry and very
furious, and commanded that all the wise men of
Babylon be destroyed." If they were deliberately with-
holding crucial information from him, or if their
professional claims were as hollow as they now pretended, he would dispose of the whole lot of them at
one fell swoop. Thus Nebuchadnezzar's anxiety, frustration, and fear rose to a climax, and the fatal order
was issued.

Cruel reprisals such as this were common in the
ancient world, and the severity of the sentence was
quite in keeping with the customs of the time. What
king would hesitate to dispose of anyone he suspected
of conspiracy, however capable and loyal the man may
actually have been? In those rugged days a ruler's
only safety was ruthless suppression of the first signs
of intrigue. How many a royal head had rolled in the
dust because its owner's most trusted confidants had
secretly turned against him!

Thus it was that Arioch, captain of the guard, went out to arrest the hapless band of wise men and gather them in for the execution. When he came to the captives' quarters, Daniel innocently inquired, with prudence and discretion, "Why is the decree of the king so severe?" A careless word might well have brought the executioner's sword down upon his head on the spot, but the same tact Daniel had shown on former occasions now won a stay of execution for him and for all the other wise men as well. How often the presence of one whose life is guided by wisdom from above has rescued his less wise fellows from trouble and death! Disarmed by Daniel's artless and obvious sincerity, and being a reasonable man himself, Arioch "made the matter known to Daniel." Learning thus for the first time of what had happened, Daniel asked for an audience with the king.

Daniel's forthright sincerity completely disarmed Nebuchadnezzar, who could detect in it nothing evasive as with the other wise men. All the while they had seemed to be dodging the issue. Instead of excuses and an impossible demand, Daniel came with a simple and seemingly reasonable request. Would the king "appoint him a time"? If so, Daniel on his part would be ready with the information the king sought. Bold promise indeed!

Why should Nebuchadnezzar not grant Daniel time to consult his God? He liked to think of himself as a religious man, eminently reasonable withal, and Daniel's proposal appealed to him. The words of his own wise men, implying that it would be necessary for someone to get in touch with "the gods, whose dwelling is not with flesh," were still ringing in his ears, and it might be that Daniel could do just that! He seemed to radiate an atmosphere of confidence, and in times of crisis nothing can be more contagious.

## The Mystery Solved

Returning to his quarters, Daniel took Shadrach, Meshach, and Abed-nego into his confidence. After all, their lives were at stake along with his. His positive faith that God would come to their rescue in this hour of crisis was based on the certain conviction that they were where He wanted them to be, that they were cooperating as best they knew with His purpose for their lives, and that He would hear and answer prayer. The four of them, therefore, prayed the rest of that day and on into the night, as they had never prayed before.

Before another day dawned, for the first time in his life Daniel was taken off in holy vision. He saw the king tossing on his royal bed as he drifted off to sleep the night before, wondering what the future held in store, "what would be hereafter." Suddenly there flashed before Daniel's mind the very scene that had so terrified the king only the night before; "the mystery was revealed to Daniel in a vision of the night." In one brief, resplendent moment he would never forget, the dazzling vision was transfixed upon the screen of his own memory and its import revealed to him.

Daniel's first thought was of gratitude to God. "Blessed be the name of God for ever and ever," he exclaimed, "to whom belong wisdom and might. . . . To thee, O God of my fathers, I give thanks and praise." Nor did Daniel forget his companions in prayer—the credit and honor were theirs as well as his. In infinite wisdom and gracious condescension God ever chooses to work through His chosen representatives on earth, men whose lives are dedicated to Him and who reflect the principles of His character. Daniel's life in particular was a living sermon on the wisdom and power of the true God, one to which the king could not but listen.

## Daniel's Audience With the King

Early the next morning Daniel presented himself to Arioch, requesting the royal audience agreed upon the day before. Forthwith, the captain of the guard ushered Daniel in before the king with the announcement, "I have found among the exiles from Judah a man who can make known to the king the interpretation." Arioch was justified in thus taking credit to himself before the king. Had he not been sent out to slay the wise men, and was it not he who had discovered one of them who could solve the mystery?

"Are you able to make known to me the dream that I have seen and its interpretation?" the king asked Daniel, without waiting for the usual formalities. No man can do that, Daniel replied, "but there is a God in heaven who reveals mysteries." It was "not because of any wisdom that I have more than all the living" that this mystery has "been revealed to me," he admitted modestly, disclaiming all credit and honor and attributing them instead to his God. It was to *Him* that Nebuchadnezzar should look with gratitude and thanksgiving. This mystery-revealing God, Daniel went on to explain, has done what those worldly-wise men ruefully admitted scarcely twenty-four hours before they could not do.

The God of heaven, Daniel began, was about to reveal to the king what the future held in store. Ah! that was the very thing Nebuchadnezzar had been wondering about as he fell asleep.[4] His remarkable dream proved to be a revelation of the future, extending from Nebuchadnezzar's day on down through the centuries to the close of time and the establishment of God's eternal kingdom!

For two millenniums great empires such as Sumer, Akkad, Old Babylonia, and Assyria had waxed and waned in the valley of the Euphrates. Powerful leaders like Hammurabi, Tiglath-pileser III, Sennacherib, and Ashurbanipal had burst upon history like flashing meteors, only to disappear into the dark night of time. Was Nebuchadnezzar destined to share their fate? No! He resented the thought; he would be more clever than they. His empire must endure forever! Or so he thought, little realizing how many of the great and near-great before him had dreamed about the future as he did. But now, as Nebuchadnezzar listens with bated breath, Daniel, without further delay, proceeds to relate the dream:

"You saw, O king, and behold, a great image. This image, mighty and of exceeding brightness, stood before you, and its appearance was frightening. The head of this image was of fine gold, its breast and arms of silver, its belly and thighs of bronze, its legs of iron, its feet partly of iron and partly of clay. As you looked, a stone was cut out by no human hand,

and it smote the image on its feet of iron and clay, and broke them in pieces; then the iron, the clay, the bronze, the silver, and the gold, all together were broken in pieces, and became like the chaff of the summer threshing floors; and the wind carried them away, so that not a trace of them could be found. But the stone that struck the image became a great mountain and filled the whole earth."

This resplendent statue was of majestic proportions, and its dazzling metallic rainbow glistened as if burnished and scintillating in brilliant sunlight. An awesome sight indeed for one of a superstitious bent of mind who believed in the capricious power of heathen gods!

In amazement the king listened as Daniel described each detail exactly as it had been projected on the screen of his own mind two nights before. "That's right! . . . That's right!" he doubtless exclaimed again and again. As the narration proceeded, the tense lines in Nebuchadnezzar's face began to relax; and when Daniel had finished, there came from his lips a sigh of relief and an exclamation of gratitude. The most perplexing part of the mystery was solved! But Daniel was not yet through; now for the interpretation of the king's dream.

## Babylon—Queen of Kingdoms

"You, O king, the king of kings, to whom the God of heaven has given the kingdom, the power, and the might, and the glory, . . . you are the head of gold," Daniel explained. Was the face of the image Nebuchadnezzar had seen in his dream his own? Might it have been this that so terrified him? For practical purposes, Nebuchadnezzar was Babylon personified— architect alike of its stately public buildings and temples, and of its brilliant territorial conquests in lands afar.[5]

It must have come as a sobering thought to the king that Daniel's God—not Nebuchadnezzar with his consummate wisdom and skill as monarch and general —was the One to whom credit belonged for his great accomplishments. It was not his gods Bel-Marduk and Nabu, but the God of heaven! It was the God of the Hebrews, whose armies he had defeated, whose cities he had conquered, whose Temple treasures he had plundered. His kingdom, his power, his might, his wisdom, and his glory were not his own after all, nor yet the legacy of his gods, but the gracious gift of an alien God!

Incredible! But how could he deny the fact while Daniel stood before him and the vivid description of the dream reverberated through his mind? He had accepted the dream; how could he refuse the interpretation? Obviously supreme wisdom dwelt, not with his gods and his venerable wise men, but with Daniel and Daniel's God. Sobering thought indeed! In fact, it upset Nebuchadnezzar's whole philosophy of imperial authority and implied a disturbing modification of his plans for the future.

Gold was an appropriate symbol for the New Babylonian Empire founded by Nebuchadnezzar's father, Nabopolassar, twenty-three years before. In wealth, power, and extent it surpassed all its predecessors. Its capital city, Babylon, was the envy of the ancient world, and today its magnificent ruins mutely confirm the Scripture narrative. Its name became the symbol for riches and grandeur. The Greek historian Herodotus tells how lavishly gold was used, particularly in the temples of the city. Among other priceless treasures he describes is a golden image of Marduk seated upon a golden throne before a golden table and a golden altar.

## The Magnificence of Persia

But, however magnificent, Babylon was not to be the eternal city, capital of an empire Nebuchadnezzar hoped and dreamed would last forever. "After you," Daniel went on, "shall arise another kingdom inferior to you."

History records that in 539 B.C. Babylon fell to Persian forces led by Cyrus the Great, who, as Cyrus I, became the first ruler of the mighty Persian Empire, here fitly represented by the breast and arms of silver. Persia eventually controlled a considerably larger territory than New Babylonia, but as silver is inferior to gold, so this second great world empire never equaled its predecessor in splendor and magnificence.

Some have proposed that the Median kingdom should be considered the second world empire of this prophecy, and Persia the third. As an independent entity, however, the Median Empire was contemporary with New Babylonia, not its successor, yet the empire represented by the breast and arms of silver is specifically said to come "after" that of Babylon. Only Persia, which had already absorbed the Median kingdom before it conquered New Babylonia, meets this require-

ment.[6] Persia ruled the world from 539 B.C. until its
conquest, in turn, by Alexander the Great at a battle
near Arbela in 331 B.C., a little more than two centuries later.

## The Glory of Greece

For the next century and a half after the Battle of
Arbela, to the second century B.C., Greek influence
was the dominant force in the Mediterranean world
and the ancient East. Alexander was, in fact, a Macedonian, but prior to his conquest of Persia he had annexed all the little kingdoms of Greece proper,
immediately to the south of Macedonia, and it was under him that for the first time all Greece became
united. Being less civilized than the Greeks, the Mace-
donians had also absorbed Greek culture. For these
reasons Alexander is often popularly spoken of as a
Greek, and his vast domain as a Greek empire. This
"third kingdom of bronze," Daniel explained, would
"rule over all the earth." It did not actually govern the
entire world or even all the known world. Like Babylon and Persia before them and Rome after them,
Alexander and his successors bore "rule over all the
earth" in the sense that they dominated the world
scene.

Upon Alexander's death, only eight years after the
defeat of Persia, his generals carved up his extensive
domain into little kingdoms of their own. Forty years
later three of these kingdoms—Egypt, the Seleucid
Empire, and Macedonia—occupied all, or practically
all, the territory Alexander once ruled. Yet, not a man
among the three was clever and powerful enough to

win exclusive right to Alexander's throne and scepter. These successor kingdoms surrounding the eastern end of the Mediterranean were all Greek in language and culture, and this was the unifying force that bound them together in one great civilization.[7]

## The Grandeur of Rome

While Alexander marched rapidly from battle to battle and victory to victory in the East, a new nation was silently growing into power on the banks of the Tiber far to the west. This nation Daniel described as "a fourth kingdom, strong as iron," one which would "break and crush" all its competitors. History points to Rome as the power that conquered the Greek kingdoms. Like most trends of history, the transition was gradual. The process may be thought of as beginning with the Battle of Pydna in 168 B.C., when Rome terminated the Macedonian monarchy, or twenty-two years later when she annexed Macedonia outright. In 64 B.C. Rome conquered the Seleucid Empire, and in 30 B.C., Egypt. The transition from Greek to Roman power was now complete, and all the major fragments of the extensive empire of Alexander the Great became Roman provinces.

Iron was an appropriate symbol for the Roman Empire. Her famed legions ranged at will over the entire Mediterranean world and over practically all of western Europe and much of western Asia as well. As Daniel had predicted, Rome literally crushed all other nations.[8] By the second century of the Christian era the Roman Empire extended from Spain and Britain in the west to the Euphrates River in the east, and from

Germany on the north to the Sahara on the south—by all odds the largest and strongest empire the world had ever known.

## Five Fateful Words

A human historian would have been tempted to forecast another and still greater empire to be built upon the ruins of ancient Rome. But not so the prophet Daniel. Following the fourth empire, he said, there was to be "a divided kingdom," whose fragments could never again be permanently reunited. History tells of successive waves of barbarian invaders from the north sweeping over the Roman Empire like the fierce blasts of a hard winter. In A.D. 476 the Heruli deposed the last Roman emperor, Romulus Augustus, and for a century and a half thereafter the barbarian tide surged relentlessly southward until the process of inundation was complete. Today, after nearly a millennium and a half, the grand empire that was Rome remains "divided," exactly as God told Daniel it would be.

In the statue Nebuchadnezzar saw in his dream, the fragments of the Roman Empire are represented by "feet and toes partly of potter's clay and partly of iron." This, Daniel explained, meant that some of the fragments would be "strong" and some "brittle," an apt description of the nations that have occupied the former territory of the Roman Empire down to our day. Whether the ten toes of the image were intended to represent ten divisions, no more and no less, Daniel does not say. In view of the fact that the prophecy is silent on this point, it is safe to conclude that the toes represent *division* into many parts, rather than any specific number of divisions.

As the feet and toes of the image were a mixture of iron and clay, so, said Daniel, the rulers of these successors to ancient Rome would "mix with one another in marriage" in an endeavor to achieve unity, but still be unable to "hold together." Down through the centuries repeated attempts have been made to unify the nations of Western Europe, both through intermarriage and by military might, but never with more than temporary success. Charlemagne set out to do so about A.D. 800; Charles V, about A.D. 1500; and Napoleon Bonaparte, about A.D. 1800. Kaiser Wilhelm II's pursuit of a similar mirage led to World War I, and that of Adolph Hitler to World War II. To a man they all failed, as God had said they would —midget men matching their puny wills against that of the Most High!

Between the two world wars the League of Nations vainly strove to persuade the nations of earth to cooperate, but national ambitions dragged that body down to oblivion. After World War II the victorious powers founded the United Nations, in the vain hope of attaining "one world," but that organization has enjoyed little more success than its ill-fated predecessor at persuading the restless nations to work together in harmony.

The old power struggle for the control of Western Europe continues unabated. The fateful words of the prophet, "they will not hold together," are as accurate a description of the fragments of ancient Rome today as they were fifteen centuries ago. Modern political technology has found no way to fuse the iron and clay of Nebuchadnezzar's image together.

## God's Eternal Kingdom

Thus the divisions of the metallic image correspond precisely to the various universal empires that have arisen in the past, and to the nations of Western Europe as we see them today. But was this state of disunity to continue forever, or would there eventually be another great world empire? Neither, Daniel told a spellbound Nebuchadnezzar. "In the days of those kings [the rulers of the successor kingdoms to ancient Rome] the God of heaven will set up a kingdom." As Nebuchadnezzar watched, "a stone was cut out by no human hand" and, careening like a mammoth boulder toward the base of the cliff, struck the colossal statue on its feet. Then, like a stone roller crushing sheaves of grain on an ancient threshing floor, this stone ground the metals of the image to powder resembling chaff, which the wind scattered until not a trace of them could be found. As the king looked on, the stone grew and grew until it "became a great mountain and filled the whole earth." This picturesque scene Daniel interpreted as representing the end of all human governments and the inauguration of God's kingdom.

Some have supposed that the kingdom of God to which Daniel here referred came into existence at the first advent of our Lord, two thousand years ago. But in the dream "not a trace" of earthly kingdoms was to remain when God sets up His kingdom. It is destined to "bring them to an end," not to exist side by side with them. "The stone that struck the image," we read,

"became a great mountain and filled the whole earth."
When our Lord came to earth the first time, He explicitly declared that His kingdom was yet future and
would be set up only when He Himself should return
to earth in person to judge the living and the dead.[9]
This transition is destined to come about, not gradually by a process of moral evolution, but cataclysmi-
cally, even as the stone in Nebuchadnezzar's dream
shattered the statue and so completely ground it to
powder that "not a trace" of it "could be found." Then
and only then, Daniel explained, would the "stone"—
Christ's kingdom—become "a great mountain" and
fill the earth.

How accurately the twenty-five intervening centuries have confirmed every detail of Daniel's inspired
interpretation! No human genius, whether of his age
or ours, could have foreseen so exactly what was to be.
The wise men of that far-off day ruefully admitted that
no one "except the gods, whose dwelling is not with
flesh," could reveal these things. Little did they realize
how truly they spoke! The inexorable march of time
has confirmed every word down *to* the very last, climactic event, and on the solemn authority of God's
own word, the next great fact of history is to be the
setting up of Christ's eternal kingdom.

No more accurate word picture of conditions in the
world today could be painted than the description of
"the time of the end" given by Daniel and the other
inspired writers of old. Everything they foretold about
the state of the world in the last days is already true or
in visible process of fulfillment. A thoughtful perusal
of the Scriptures will suffice to convince any honest-

minded reader that this is so. According to the sure word of prophecy, the coming of our Lord draws near. We are rapidly approaching the midnight of human history, and but a few moments, as it were, remain before the glorious dawn of Christ's eternal reign.

## A King Worships His Slave

King Nebuchadnezzar was profoundly impressed as Daniel reconstructed the forgotten dream and explained its meaning. Full well he knew that no mere human being could possibly tell what he had dreamed, especially since he himself had forgotten it. Yet Daniel reproduced it all, vividly and accurately in every detail, exactly as the king had seen it. It is to Nebuchadnezzar's credit that he accepted Daniel's interpretation instantly and without reservation. Had he not threatened his own wise men only the day before, "Tell me the dream, and I shall know that you can show me its interpretation"? To the king, Daniel's narration of the dream was conclusive proof of the accuracy and reliability of the interpretation given. To us today the equally accurate fulfillment of his interpretation in history is convincing evidence that both the dream and the interpretation originated with God.

Little wonder that "King Nebuchadnezzar fell upon his face, and did homage to Daniel," and then ordered "an offering and incense" to be offered up to him as if he were a god like Bel-Marduk! Think of it—monarch of the greatest nation on earth prostrating himself before a youthful captive he had brought back to Babylon from a remote province of his vast empire! Whether Daniel accepted these acts of worship without protest, the record does not state. The Scriptures elsewhere consistently reject the idea of worship being addressed to mere human beings. Daniel's explicit and repeated ascription of credit to God, and his categorical denial of any superior wisdom himself, strongly imply that he either refused the king's acts of worship or accepted them only in the name of his God, as if offered to God and not to himself.

Like a little boy peering out into the fog of a murky night, Nebuchadnezzar had been curious to know what the future held in store; yet the dream and its interpretation were not given simply to gratify royal curiosity. God sought Nebuchadnezzar's intelligent cooperation with His infinite purposes in the present. Only the man who takes tomorrow into consideration can make intelligent choices today.

In gratitude and recognition of Daniel's distinguished service, the king awarded him "high honors and many great gifts, and made him ruler over the whole province of Babylon." An honor indeed for a foreign slave hardly more than twenty years of age, a youthful prodigy whose only goal in life was to be true to the best he knew! Prince at heart that he was, Daniel chose to share the honors of the day with his three friends—Shadrach, Meshach, and Abed-nego— whom the king, upon his request, assigned to administer the province of Babylon. Daniel himself, however, "remained at the king's court" as "chief prefect over all the wise men of Babylon." But far above any human honor or reward, he was God's man for the hour.

## NOTES

1. According to Daniel 1:5, the course of training lasted "three years," and according to chapter 2:1, the episode of the king's dream came in the "second year" of his reign. Nebuchadnezzar became king in the late summer of 605 B.C., and according to Babylonian custom reckoned his first regnal year from the Babylonian New Year's Day in the spring of 604 B.C. to that of 603 B.C. His second regnal year would thus be from the spring of 603 to 602 B.C., spring to spring. In specifying the length of the course of training as "three years," Daniel follows the system known as inclusive reckoning, as did all Bible writers and ancient peoples generally. According to this system of reckoning, any parts of the first and last units of time are reckoned as whole units. Thus the first of these "three years" extended from the autumn of 605 B.C., when Daniel arrived at Babylon, to the spring of the following year; the second year, from 604 to 603 B.C.; and the third year, during which he was graduated, from 603 to 602 B.C. Accordingly, Daniel was graduated during the second official year of Nebuchadnezzar's reign, and the incident of chapter 2 thus came within a few months of his graduation.

2. Daniel 2:1, 3, 31.

3. From this point in the narrative onward to the end of chapter 7 the language used is Aramaic, the official language of Babylonian royalty. The rest of the Book of Daniel has come down to us in Hebrew.

4. Daniel 2:28, 29, 45.

5. Babylonia of the time of Nebuchadnezzar is known as Neo-Babylonia, or New Babylonia. An ancient civilization had flourished there more than a thousand years earlier, but the city had usually been ruled by foreign kings from the time of Hammurabi in the eighteenth century B.C. until the time of Nabopolassar, Nebuchadnezzar's father and founder of New Babylonia. This is the Babylon of the Book of Daniel.

6. See pages 106-109.

7. The Greeks called themselves *Hellas*. The classical period of Greek history is known as the Hellenic Age. The term Hellenistic refers to the period from the death of Alexander the Great to the time when Rome became supreme in the eastern Mediterranean. During that time Greek influence was dominant.

8. In his *History of the Decline and Fall of the Roman Empire* (ed. by J. B. Bury), Volume 4, page 161, the famed English historian Edward Gibbon wrote: "The arms of the republic, sometimes vanquished in battle, always victorious in war, advanced with rapid steps to the Euphrates, the Danube, the Rhine, and the Ocean; and the images of gold, or silver, or brass, that might serve to represent the nations and their kings, were successively broken by the *iron* monarchy of Rome." (Emphasis his.)

9. Matthew 16:27 and 25:31.

# Fireproof Men

SOME NINE years had passed since the startling dream of the metallic statue. Time gradually erased its vivid impression from the king's mind, and imperceptibly its lesson faded from his memory. As success crowned one military campaign after another, he forgot that his kingdom, power, and glory were a gift-in-trust from the God of heaven, and that it was only by divine consent that he ruled over his vast domain. He forgot his own solemn declaration about Daniel's God being "God of gods and Lord of kings."

Great had been the mortification of the Chaldeans at their dismal inability to reconstruct and interpret Nebuchadnezzar's troublesome dream, and then at Daniel's brilliant success in doing so. They were the professional wise men of the realm and he was a mere fledgling among the experts, yet he had soundly defeated them at their own game. They could never forget that the king had ordered his executioners around to slaughter them as if they had been dumb brutes, and then lavished upon Daniel praise and adoration ordinarily reserved for the gods! True, they owed their lives to him, but they resented the thought and hated him the more on that account.

To top it all, the king had added lasting injury to the gross insult of the moment by promoting Daniel to be "chief prefect" over them, and then had ordered the elevation of Shadrach, Meshach, and Abed-nego over the province of Babylon on the magic carpet of Daniel's coattails. For nine years now these crestfallen Chaldeans had reluctantly worn the galling yoke this hated band of foreigners had so cleverly forged—or so they surmised—for them. All this time they had been plotting revenge and scheming to recoup their lost prestige and influence with the king.

As explained in the preceding chapter, the metallic statue in the king's dream represented the divine blueprint for history and, in particular, revealed to Nebuchadnezzar his role in that plan. His appointment of Daniel as prime minister—presumably to advise the king in accordance with the divine purpose communicated in the dream—implies that for a time Nebuchadnezzar must have been inclined to cooperate with what had been so graciously revealed to him by the God of heaven.

Smarting under defeat, the Chaldean wise men naturally resented a national policy oriented toward cooperation with the God of the Hebrews, and must have sought to steer the king away from it. Eventually they proposed that Nebuchadnezzar reassert his personal leadership by initiating a new imperial policy with Babylonian nationalism as its keynote, and that he erect a golden colossus to symbolize the new policy. All the officials and vassal rulers of the realm would be summoned to participate in its dedication, and would be required to reaffirm their allegiance to Nebuchadnezzar by prostrating themselves in worship before the towering image.

## The Significance of the Image

At first glance this clever proposal had the superficial appearance of intent to cooperate with the message of the dream. But *this* statue was to be of gold from head to toe, not a succession of baser metals—a clever hint that Babylon, merely the head of gold in the image of the dream, was to continue forever. By making his image all of gold Nebuchadnezzar thus rejected the idea that his kingdom must someday yield to another and his royal line become extinct. Other nations might come and go, but Babylon must go on forever. Accordingly, the erection of the statue was an official act of defiance against God's purpose in history. Such had likewise been the intent of the first builders of Babel when they founded the city and erected its original tower fifteen centuries or more before.[1]

Perhaps the old gods, though slumbering, might be awakened, the wise men assured their king. Was he not master of the world? What evidence did the king have that Yahweh, the God of the Hebrews, could interfere if he reasserted his own authority? Yahweh had not been able to protect His own people against the might of Babylon; how could He help the Babylonians? Babylon was none of His business. Oh, the God of the Jews might be wise, but His wisdom was evidently not of the sort that would be useful or effective in international politics.

On the other hand, events had shown Nebuchadnezzar to be *both* wise and strong, and proved the wisdom and power of Nabu and Bel-Marduk. Was not the presence of Jehoiachin, king of Judah, in Babylon tangible evidence of all this? Perhaps in his anxiety the king had overestimated Daniel's God, they urged, and Nebuchadnezzar would do well to honor the Babylonian gods who had given him victory over the Hebrews and their God. So it was, believing what he wanted to believe and doubting what he wished to forget, that the king finally agreed to go ahead with the erection of this colossal replica of the image of his dream.

## The Great Colossus

Daniel gives the height of Nebuchadnezzar's magnificent statue as sixty cubits and its width as six, which would be approximately one hundred feet tall and ten broad—a ratio of ten to one. The average human body, however, is something less than five times as tall as it is broad, and a statue of these dimensions would appear altogether out of proportion. It is plain, therefore, that the sixty-cubit measure includes the pedestal on which the statue evidently stood as well as the statue itself, thus allowing a height of fifty feet or so for each.[2] The majestic golden image here described would have felt completely at home among Nebuchadnezzar's many superlative architectural and engineering masterpieces.

The colossal statue was obviously not of solid gold, as one of that size would require at least two thousand tons of the precious metal, nor does Daniel say that it was. It is known, however, that Nebuchadnezzar did make lavish use of gold. The Greek historian Herodotus tells of a golden image of Bel-Marduk more than twenty feet in height in one of the temples of Babylon. Nebuchadnezzar's statue was probably of brickwork overlaid with gold, and thus had the appearance of being solid gold.

Daniel does not tell what, or whom, the statue represented, if anything. It might have been an image of Bel-Marduk or Nabu, both favorite deities of Nebuchadnezzar, or a replica of the image the king saw in his dream, or possibly a likeness of the king himself. Who knows? He does say, however, that it was erected on the plain of Dura, apparently near Babylon, but just where is not known. A small tributary of the Euphrates still bears that name, as do also some neighboring hills.

## Strike Up the Band!

The day finally arrived for the dedication; and all "the satraps, the prefects, and the governors, the counselors, the treasurers, the justices, the magistrates, and all the officials of the provinces" assembled before the image that King Nebuchadnezzar had set up. Somewhere in that throng stood Shadrach, Meshach, and Abed-nego, administrators of the Babylonian province, complying with the king's requirements as far as they could without compromising religious principle. Where was Daniel? He does not say and we need not speculate. Except for Daniel, however, everybody who was anybody was there, regally attired in colorful costumes, with retinues of slaves and attendants.

Towering above them all, and resplendent atop its lofty pedestal in the bright Babylonian sunshine, was

the rich gold of the majestic statue silhouetted against
the burnished blue dome of the sky, an imposing symbol of the wealth and power of the greatest empire
the world had ever known. When all was ready, trum-
peters announced the arrival of the king, and every
eye followed him as he ascended the royal dais erected
near the foot of the statue. As the tumult of conversation subsided into muffled whispers, another flurry of
trumpets summoned all to give ear to the herald as he
read the royal proclamation:

"You are commanded, O peoples, nations, and languages, that when you hear the sound of the horn,
pipe, lyre, trigon, harp, bagpipe, and every kind of
music, you are to fall down and worship the golden
image that King Nebuchadnezzar has set up; and
whoever does not fall down and worship shall immediately be cast into a burning fiery furnace."

As the herald spoke in stentorian tones, all eyes
turned furtively in the direction of the furnace, belching forth its fire and smoke. But furnace or no furnace,
who would dare defy the king to his face? Who was
so naïve as not to know that life, limb, and position
alike depended upon his goodwill? The furnace was
simply an impressive way of saying that he meant
business.

The idea of having the furnace—perhaps a convenient brickkiln—all stoked and blazing away, also
doubtless originated with the Chaldeans. Its murky
smoke curling ominously up through the still morning
air into the blue sky was a portent of Nebuchadnezzar's determination that all men everywhere should
acknowledge Babylonian supremacy—forever! Full

well they knew that the three Hebrews would not bow
down to it, and with the furnace ready for use they
could maneuver the king into disposing of the troublesome trio ere he should change his mind, or the heat
of his anger should abate. With all Babylonian officialdom looking on, he would have to act—then and
there. To hesitate would be fatal.

The whole affair seems to have been cleverly staged
from start to finish, and apparently the only part of
the plan that went awry was Daniel's unexpected absence. All the while the Chaldeans kept a wary eye on
Shadrach, Meshach, and Abed-nego. They well knew
that it would take a good pretext to convince the king
to do away with able and trusted public servants whom
he had personally elevated to high office. But today,
they consoled themselves, their humiliation of yesteryear would be avenged, and *they* would stand forth
again as the defenders of the king and his realm.

Then the royal musicians began to play. Some instruments, with their queer names and exotic tones,
were evidently from faraway lands. The orchestra had
an international flavor appropriate to the occasion.
Wind instruments and stringed instruments and per-
cussion instruments of all kinds joined together in
what was perhaps the national anthem of New Babylonia. Entranced, for a moment the assembled officials
forgot to prostrate themselves, but another glance at
the roaring furnace reminded them of their duty; and
in a trice satraps, governors, and magistrates of every
rank and nationality fell prostrate to the ground.

No one noticed the fleeting and almost impercepti-
ble smile of satisfaction that passed across the king's

face as he watched the undulating wave of compliance that swept over the assembled multitude like a gust of wind across a standing field of wheat ready to harvest. Thus it would be—must be—with all the decrees with which his royal messengers hastened to the farthest corners of the realm, and men everywhere bowed in submission!

## Treason!

But suddenly Nebuchadnezzar was aware of a commotion behind him. Ah! those bothersome Chaldeans again. They had a way of interrupting him at the most inopportune moment. Why weren't they flat on their faces paying homage to the great image? No matter; here they are bowing before him personally. What is that? There are some who dare defy the king's decree? Who are they, and where? "See, over there," say the wise men, pointing innocently in the direction of Shadrach, Meshach, and Abed-nego. Yes, there they were, the three of them, stark upright, apparently in brazen defiance of his command—as if they knew full well what they were doing and were proud of it. Yet it might be that they had misunderstood; fetch them here. Out rang the order, and a guard went to bring them.

"All along," the Chaldeans now reminded the king, "we have noticed something of which you have apparently not been aware. These Jews do not serve your gods. In fact, during all their years here in Babylon they have never once so much as paid any of our gods the least token of respect. They seem to hold the entire pantheon of Babylonian deities in contempt, despite the fact that you, O king, have set them over the affairs of the province of Babylon. Apparently they do not appreciate the favors you have lavished upon them.

"We have long suspected," the Chaldeans continued, "that these men are poor security risks. Here they are in public defying you to your very face. If this overt act of insubordination should go unpunished, what can you expect from these hundreds of officials when they get back to the provinces, far from your watchful gaze? How far do you think your national policy will get if a group of your highest officials in the imperial capital can ignore it publicly at the very outset? Either a public example of them, O king, or the whole plan will fail." Nebuchadnezzar saw the point, of course.

Here they come, now, the three Hebrews. All eyes are riveted on them as they stand respectfully at attention before the royal dais. The king has appreciated their loyal service over the past nine years; they have been his most trustworthy public servants. What can be wrong now? Did they misunderstand his orders? He will explain things personally and offer them another chance. This initial lenience is evidence that the dedication ceremony and the fiery furnace were no trumped-up scheme of *his*. Absolute monarch that he was, he would need no excuses to justify his decision to get rid of them, had such been his purpose.

"Is it true, O Shadrach, Meshach, and Abed-nego," he asks, "that you do not serve my gods or worship the golden image which I have set up? Now if you are ready when you hear the sound of the horn, pipe, lyre, trigon, harp, bagpipe, and every kind of music, to fall down and worship the image which I have made, well and good; but if you do not worship, you shall immediately be cast into a burning fiery furnace; and who is the god that will deliver you out of my hands?"

Resolutely but tactfully the three Hebrews replied: "O Nebuchadnezzar, we have no need to justify ourselves before you in this matter. It is simply that we cannot serve your gods or worship the golden image which you have set up. Our minds are made up, and another test will be unnecessary." There was no further explanation to give, no excuse to offer, no apology to make. It was simply that his imperial will had come into collision with their conscientious convictions. If he chose to force the issue, they were content to leave the outcome up to the God of heaven.

"Contrary to what you may think," they declared with fireproof faith, "our God whom we serve is able to deliver us from the burning fiery furnace, and for that matter we are confident that he will deliver us out of your hand, O king." There was no need to strike up the band again to experiment with their faith. They had counted the cost and were ready to pay the supreme price, if necessary, rather than be untrue to their God.

## Through the Fire

"Then Nebuchadnezzar was full of fury, and the expression of his face was changed against Shadrach, Meshach, and Abed-nego." Their calm but resolute refusal to bow to his wishes was more than even Nebuchadnezzar knew how to pass by. If they still obstinately refused to cooperate, he would have to

give the assembled officials an object lesson of the fate
that awaited any who dared ignore his decrees. There
was no room for such men anywhere within the con-
fines of his vast empire—except in the fiery furnace.

To make the lesson more impressive, and to make
sure that the God these three seemingly defiant young
men professed to serve would not interfere in their
behalf, as they implied, Nebuchadnezzar ordered the
furnace to be heated "seven times more than it was
wont to be heated." He then summoned "certain
mighty men of his army" to toss the three youths into
it. He would take no chances. But the greater the heat
the more impressive the miracle.

The Babylonians were adept at making a hot fire.
With all the burnt brick needed for the great building
enterprises of Babylon, they had had a great deal of
experience with brickkilns. For fuel they used straw,
and along with it generous quantities of oil or tar
from the petroleum pits that still abound in the region.
Yes, they knew how to make a hot fire, and in a few
moments the roar of the furnace testified to the intense
heat within. Stalwart soldiers then marched the three
martyrs to the front of the furnace, bound them hand
and foot, and hurled them inside—only to die of the
heat themselves at its threshold.

An object lesson indeed, as the eyes of all Babylonian officialdom froze on the great furnace belching
out smoke and writhing flames.

But look! What's that? There the men are, walking
around in the flaming inferno as if there were no fire
at all. The king rubbed his eyes and blinked as he
counted out loud, "One, two, three—four! Arioch!

how many men did you toss into the furnace?" "Three, O king," came the reply. "But I see four men loose, walking in the midst of the fire, and they are not hurt. Who is that fourth man? He's not one of the Hebrews, nor yet one of my soldiers. What a stately person he is! Arioch, did you cast in one of my high officials by mistake? But none of my officials look like that. The appearance of the fourth is like a son of the gods!" exclaimed the king.

Nebuchadnezzar's gold-plated folly, which to this moment had been the center of attention, was instantly forgotten by king and subjects alike. The nobles standing nearby saw Nebuchadnezzar's face turn pale as he started from the throne, eyes riveted on the furnace. Hastening down unceremoniously from the dais, he rushed to the door of the furnace and called out above the roar and crackle of the flames, "Shadrach, Meshach, and Abed-nego, servants of the Most High God, come forth, and come here!"

Out they came, these three fireproof men, "and the king's counselors . . . saw that the fire had not had any power over the bodies of those men; the hair of their heads was not singed, their mantles were not harmed, and no smell of fire had come upon them." They had not dashed out of the furnace as soon as the tongues of flame gnawed them free from the cords that bound them hand and foot. The king had placed them there, and it was up to him to call them out. They were still his loyal servants, ready to comply with any reasonable command he should give. When he called, they came forth. The flames had loosed and burned the cords that bound them, but nothing more.

In the presence of the Lord of heat and cold, the flames had lost their power to consume.

Of what do you suppose Shadrach, Meshach, and Abed-nego thought as they walked calmly over the incandescent fagots of what was supposed to be their funeral pyre? Perhaps of the promise penned by the prophet Isaiah more than a century before, "When you walk through fire you shall not be burned, and the flame shall not consume you."[3] The word of the Lord was their insurance policy, and in their minds no doubt lingered but that God would honor His promise. They knew He could. They believed He would. And He did. Their incandescent faith had made them fireproof!

## An Honest Admission

Confronted by the Hebrew trio who had walked unharmed through the fire, Nebuchadnezzar could not deny that a miracle had taken place—right before his eyes and in the presence of all the assembled officials of his empire. Nor could he well avoid a public acknowledgment of the fact. "Blessed be the God of Shadrach, Meshach, and Abed-nego," he exclaimed, "who has sent his angel and delivered his servants, who trusted in him, and set at nought the king's command, and yielded up their bodies rather than serve and worship any god except their own God." How news of what had happened would spread throughout the empire as the officials returned to their respective provinces! Hot news it would be indeed. No stranger tale had ever before been told, and this had happened in broad daylight.

Nebuchadnezzar spoke of the divine being he saw walking about in the furnace as an "angel"—literally a "messenger"—and attributed the deliverance of the three Hebrews to His presence. Was this not the "angel of the covenant," God's own Son?[4] God had countermanded his order for their execution and honored them for their trust and loyalty. But the king went even further: "Therefore," he continued, "I make a decree: Any people, nation, or language that speaks anything against the God of Shadrach, Meshach, and Abed-nego shall be torn limb from limb, and their houses laid in ruins; for there is no other god who is able to deliver in this way." This decree effectively silenced the Chaldean conspirators and prevented the instigation of further cruel attacks upon the faithful Hebrew officials.

Nebuchadnezzar is to be commended for not commanding his subjects to worship the God of the Hebrews. His decree was intended simply to prevent any further indignity or offense being offered to the God of heaven. This, he doubtless reasoned, would at least forestall a possible visitation of divine judgment upon the nation.

The penalty here threatened was the same Nebuchadnezzar had intended to inflict on the Chaldeans when they proved unable to relate his dream a few years before. To us this penalty seems unreasonable and cruel, but judged by the standards of that far-off time it was not unusual. In those days the individual had no rights; life and limb were his own only at the whim and mercy of the king. The civil liberties free men enjoy today are a direct result of applying Bible principles to relations between the state and the individual citizen.

## Keep Church and State Forever Separate!

The courageous Hebrew trio's close brush with death is a grim reminder of the universal fact that whenever government, with its coercive powers, sets out to enforce religious observances by law, persecution inevitably follows. The only safe relationship for church and state to maintain is for the two to remain forever and completely separate, each content to function in its own sphere and to rely on its own legitimate means of securing allegiance and cooperation. God never intended that secular government should either impose religion, even the true religion, upon men's consciences or penalize men for practicing the religion of their choice. In attempting either, the state interposes its purely human authority and power between men and their Creator, and this is repugnant alike to the authority of God and the dignity of man.

The legitimate function of civil government is to regulate a man's conduct in relation to his fellowmen, so that each person may have an opportunity to realize the worthwhile and legitimate objectives intended for him by his Creator, and conversely to restrict him when his conduct imperils the same rights for others. It has no mandate to meddle in any way, direct or indirect, with any man's relationship to God.

Man is infinitely more than an intelligent animal with gregarious instincts; he is a rational, moral being created in the likeness of God, animated by the spark of God-given life, and endowed with personality and the capacity to develop character. The Creator has never delegated to any man the right to intervene, under any pretext whatever, between Himself and His creatures, whether individually or collectively. That relationship is preeminently sacred.

Down through the ages, however, rulers, sometimes on their own initiative and sometimes in response to ecclesiastical pressure, have usurped this divine prerogative and have set out to govern men's consciences as well as their conduct in society. They have done so either by establishing a state religion or less directly by legislation of a quasi-religious nature that has the effect of denying to some the free exercise of religion and of imposing civil disabilities upon them because of it. Nebuchadnezzar's gold-plated folly was one such attempt, and the result was persecution. Centuries later, certain Roman emperors who set out to impose the imperial cult on Christians reaped a gory harvest in the blood of thousands of martyrs who refused to comply.

During the Middle Ages, and even in more recent times, a misguided church has deliberately manipulated the authority and power of the state to enforce conformity with its wishes, and those who have paid with their lives because of a conscientious refusal to conform can be counted in the millions. Let us not deceive ourselves into thinking that all men who would perpetrate such atrocities are dead. Strange as it may seem to people living in lands where religious liberty now prevails, in some nominally Christian countries this unholy alliance between church and state still produces a fresh crop of martyrs each year, to say nothing of those regions of earth where atheism is the state religion.

In this age of liberty we are prone to forget that our precious legacy of civil and religious freedom was won only at the price of the blood of martyr and patriot. Let us cherish these hard-won liberties, ever aware that evil and unscrupulous forces are stealthily but actively at work, even in this land of liberty, to deprive us of religious freedom. The potential threat to religious freedom in the United States is greater now than at any time in history, and eternal vigilance is still the price of liberty.

Now, as never before, all who cherish liberty of conscience should make their own the immortal words of Thomas Jefferson chiseled in stone on the memorial erected to him among the flowering cherry trees beside the Tidal Basin in Washington, D.C.: "I have sworn upon the altar of God eternal hostility against every form of tyranny over the mind of man." Church and state are as surely bound before God to apply the Golden Rule in their corporate relationship to individuals, as the latter are obliged to do so with respect to one another.

## Tried and True

Nebuchadnezzar's dream had convinced him that the God of the three Hebrews was infinitely wiser than all the gods and the wise men of Babylon. Their deliverance from the fiery furnace now persuaded him that God is not only wise, but able to intervene in behalf of those loyal to Him. Perhaps it also caused him to be more considerate of all the exiled Jews.

Instead of resulting in the demotion and execution of the three Hebrews, as the Chaldeans had intended, the fiery furnace had precisely the opposite effect, for "the king promoted Shadrach, Meshach, and Abed-nego in the province of Babylon." Their supreme act of loyalty elevated them to a more favorable position than before, where they could bear an even more effective witness to the infinite superiority of the worship and service of the true God. Those today who purpose in their hearts to be loyal to the best they know, God—and sometimes men—will similarly honor.

Today, as in Daniel's day, "the greatest want of the world is the want of men,—men who will not be bought or sold; men who in their inmost souls are true and honest; men who do not fear to call sin by its right name; men whose conscience is as true to duty as the needle to the pole; men who will stand for the right though the heavens fall."[5]

The God of Shadrach, Meshach, and Abed-nego still lives and is still able to make those who honor Him "fireproof."

## NOTES

1. Genesis 11:1-9.
2. In Aramaic literature the word here translated into English as *statue* or *image* is used to describe an upright stone shaft, only the top portion of which was carved to represent a human body. The stone Colossi of Memnon at ancient Thebes in Upper Egypt, sculptured statues representing Amenhotep III—carved out of solid rock about 1400 B.C. and still standing—are sixty-four feet in height. The ruins of a similar statue of Ramses II (1250 B.C.) indicate

that it originally stood about fifty-seven feet tall. The famed Colossus of Rhodes, representing the Greek god Helios, built about 300 B.C. with sheets of metal over a supporting framework, reached the dizzy height of 105 feet. By way of a modern comparison, the Statue of Liberty in New York harbor is 111 feet tall and its pedestal 194 feet. The dimensions Daniel gives for Nebuchadnezzar's golden image show that the author was familiar with Babylonian mathematics. The Babylonians invented and made use of what is known as the sexagenary system of counting, based on the number 60. This system has at least one advantage over the decimal system, in that 60 is divisible evenly by twelve factors, whereas 100 is divisible by only nine. The dimensions 60 and 6 thus give the narrative an authentic Babylonian flavor.

3. Isaiah 43:2.

4. The Hebrew word translated *angel* means "messenger." The messenger or angel of the covenant mentioned in Malachi 3:1 is generally considered to be the coming Messiah. Christ came to this world as the messenger of God's love and grace.

5. Ellen G. White, *Education,* p. 57.

# Shock Therapy for a Power-Crazed King

A T A LEISURELY Oriental pace the sundials of Babylon marked off the passing days and years, and Nebuchadnezzar gradually settled down to works of peace. With plans for the most ambitious urban renewal project of all antiquity, he practically rebuilt Babylon and doubled its size. On countless thousands of bricks his name still testifies mutely to his architectural ambitions and achievements, and it is little wonder that he became inordinately proud![1] But the city's golden age came just before the sunset.

Of the last seven or eight years of Nebuchadnezzar's reign nothing definite is known save for the inglorious episode recorded in the fourth chapter of Daniel. Over these mysterious years the cuneiform tablets have drawn a discreet and unanimous silence, and not without good reason. The unusual character of the episode is reflected in its unique form, a royal proclamation which gives, in the king's own words, an account of what took place.

As chief counselor to the king, Daniel naturally had access to this remarkable document, which he reproduces, possibly with explanatory comments of his own here and there. The two contrasting before-and-after word portraits Nebuchadnezzar gives of himself reveal, first, a proud heathen monarch standing at the very pinnacle of success, and then a humble, submissive servant of the God of heaven, content in a knowledge of His infinite goodness, mercy, and justice. The proclamation is addressed "to all peoples, nations, and languages, that dwell in all the earth," and commences with a declaration of royal goodwill: "Peace be multiplied to you!"

Nebuchadnezzar announces as the theme of this royal rescript, "the signs and wonders that the Most High God has wrought toward me." This providential experience was a "wonder" in the sense that it was a supernatural occurrence, or miracle, and a "sign" in that it was designed to teach the king an important lesson. Now he shares the experience and its lesson with all his subjects. How human of Nebuchadnezzar to want to relate what had happened to him! That it was not in the least complimentary to him personally made no difference. He told everything just as it took place, embarrassing as it all was:

"I, Nebuchadnezzar, was at ease in my house and prospering in my palace," he begins. He was secure on his throne, and no perplexing problems ruffled the serenity of his reign. Nearly forty years had slipped by since the death of his father, and he was enjoying the fruits of his brilliant conquests and basking in the splendor of his magnificent architectural triumphs. All was well throughout his vast domain, and Nebuchadnezzar sat in his magnificent palace—"at ease."

Faded and forgotten, however, were the lessons of the great image of his dream three or four decades before, and of the fiery furnace a few years after that. Forgotten, also, were his own ascriptions of honor to the God of heaven upon those two awesome occasions. "Truly, your God is God of gods and Lord of kings, and a revealer of mysteries," he had declared after the first. "Blessed be the God of Shadrach, Meshach, and Abed-nego, who has sent his angel and delivered his servants, who trusted in him, and set at nought the king's command, . . . for there is no other god who is able to deliver in this way," he had proclaimed following the second.

Ah! there was the root of the trouble. He had forgotten God's providential dealings with him in years gone by and the practical lessons of past experiences. Like the foolish rich man of Christ's parable he was sated with prosperity and success. He forgot that like the grass of the field he was here today but would be gone tomorrow. He forgot that his splendid accomplishments were not really his own, that he was accountable to the God of heaven for the wisdom and skill that produced his brilliant military, architectural, and administrative triumphs. Out of how many a present predicament a less perverse memory might save us; yet how short, often, is our recollection of things we would prefer to forget!

## Another Dream—and What a Dream!

"I had a dream which made me afraid," relates the king. Another dream! But, like the ancients generally, Nebuchadnezzar took dreams seriously; and, even as many years before, a dream proved to be the most impressive means by which the God of heaven could reach him. God ever speaks to men by the means best adapted to penetrate the callous self-interest that encases their minds and hearts. Once more the king awoke with a start, but this time, unlike the last, he found the dream still vividly etched on his memory. So vivid was it, in fact, that the more he turned it over in his mind, the more perplexed and alarmed he became trying to imagine what its import might be.

His distress finally reached such a pitch that he summoned his wise men, some of whom were the very men who had let him down forty years before under similar circumstances, but upon whom he nevertheless still relied for counsel. Doubtless they wondered at the peremptory summons, and perhaps on their way through the eerie shadows of the palace courts to the royal bedchamber they commented among themselves on that hair-raising experience of long ago. What was on the king's mind this time?

So in they came again, the wisest men in all the realm, bowing reverentially before their king and then waiting in deference before him. As Nebuchadnezzar began to relate the dream, a furtive sigh of relief, undetected by the king, must have passed from one to another and vanished out into the stillness of the Babylonian night. In rapt concentration they listened. What a dream!

"I saw," the king began, "and behold, a tree in the midst of the earth; and its height was great. The tree grew and became strong, and its top reached to heaven, and it was visible to the end of the whole earth. Its leaves were fair and its fruit abundant, and in it was food for all. The beasts of the field found shade under it, and the birds of the air dwelt in its branches, and all flesh was fed from it.

"I saw in the visions of my head as I lay in bed, and behold, a watcher, a holy one, came down from heaven. He cried aloud and said thus, 'Hew down the tree and cut off its branches, strip off its leaves and scatter its fruit; let the beasts flee from under it and the birds from its branches. But leave the stump of its roots in the earth, bound with a band of iron and bronze, amid the tender grass of the field. Let him be wet with the dew of heaven; let his lot be with the beasts in the grass of the earth; let his mind be changed from a man's, and let a beast's mind be given to him; and let seven times pass over him. The sentence is by the decree of the watchers, the decision by the word of the holy ones, to the end that the living may know that the Most High rules the kingdom of men, and gives it to whom he will, and sets over it the lowliest of men.' "

## Wise Men in a Quandary

As Nebuchadnezzar related his dream, the glint of professional complacency that lit the faces of the wise men gradually vanished. Increasingly worried glances passed back and forth from one to another as the tale unfolded. The trouble, this time, was that the meaning of the dream was all too obvious, and they feared that if they confirmed the obvious, they would pay for it with their lives. After all, it could possibly be a trap, and they were not going to put their feet into it. It would be better to profess ignorance than to risk the king's displeasure at what he would consider an act of disloyalty, if not treason. The wise men remembered only too well his peremptory decree forty years before, to have off with their reluctant heads.

History is replete with examples of courtiers who deliberately falsified information rather than risk giving bad tidings to their king. Seldom at a loss for an explanation that would make an evil omen out to be a good one, on this occasion the wise men were unable to contrive a favorable interpretation, and they concluded that no interpretation at all would be preferable. Any subterfuge would have been so patent that Nebuchadnezzar could certainly discern their duplicity. The king remembered his dream all too well! Let him figure it out for himself!

Instead of issuing another edict for the decapitation of his wise men, however, Nebuchadnezzar dismissed them in disgrace and confidently summoned Daniel. "I know that the spirit of the holy gods is in you," he commended his prime minister, "and that no mystery is difficult for you." Then he retold the dream, admitting to Daniel as he did so, "All the wise men of my kingdom are not able to make known to me the interpretation, but you are able, for the spirit of the holy gods is in you." The general import of the dream was clear enough, and Nebuchadnezzar realized only too well that it was a harbinger of adversity to come, that it boded something most unwelcome to him personally. While relating his dream, the king must have been watching Daniel's face closely, and felt his own fears confirmed as he saw Daniel's consternation.

Daniel, too, saw the meaning of the dream at once. In fact, he too was startled and "dismayed for a long time, and his thoughts alarmed him." In his mingled astonishment, perplexity, and embarrassment he was speechless. Seeing the effect of the dream on Daniel, Nebuchadnezzar sought to put him at ease. "Let not the dream or the interpretation alarm you," he said. He knew that Daniel felt nothing but the highest personal loyalty toward him.

Who could be so naïve as to *mis*understand the dream? The amazing tree—its colossal size and its bounteous provision for every need of beast and bird —could represent no one but Nebuchadnezzar and his illustrious reign. He alone could be said to reach to heaven, and his majesty and authority to be "visible to the end of the whole earth." Its fair leaves and abundant fruit were a perfect figure for Babylonian wealth, culture, and civilization. That much was beyond question. In one of Nebuchadnezzar's building inscriptions he himself refers to the Babylonian Empire as a great spreading tree.

## What Fate Held in Store

Up to this point Nebuchadnezzar had already figured out the meaning of the dream. But what of the watcher who came down from heaven, obviously with a message from the gods—or, more accurately, from God? What fearful fate was foreshadowed in the ominous decree, "Hew down the tree and cut off its branches, strip off its leaves and scatter its fruit; let the beasts flee from under it and the birds from its branches"? He trembled at these portentous words.

Daniel, too, hesitated in dumb amazement, but he could not stand there silent forever. Speak he must. At last, with the king's reassurance and his own usual tact he found a way to tell the truth without offending his sovereign. "May the dream be for those who hate you and its interpretation for your enemies!" he finally exclaimed, passionately. Then, regaining his self-composure, he went on: "Yes, O king, you are that tree. You have become strong. Your greatness reaches to heaven, and your dominion to the ends of the earth." It was flattering to the king to reflect that even God in heaven recognized what he knew so well himself—that he stood without peer in all the earth. How Daniel wished that the rest of the dream might be reversed! Yet he dare not evade the solemn duty of revealing to Nebuchadnezzar the nature of the divine judgment that was about to humble his pride and arrogance once and for all.

From a human point of view there was no reason why the splendid tree should not flourish forever, but God saw sufficient cause why it should be cut to the ground. Nebuchadnezzar was not to sit upon his throne permanently, accepting the tribute of subject kings and receiving the flattery of his servile courtiers. "You shall be driven from among men," Daniel began, "and your dwelling shall be with the beasts of the field; you shall be made to eat grass like an ox, and you shall be wet with the dew of heaven." Fearful thought! From supreme monarch of all men he was to be reduced to the society of dumb beasts, to eat as they eat, and to lodge with them under the open sky. Before this any sane man would cringe.

But wait! There is respite. True, the tree is to be hewn down, but the heavenly messenger continues with the divine decree: "Leave the stump of its roots in the earth, bound with a band of iron and bronze . . . till seven times pass over him." Daniel says nothing further about the bands of iron and bronze; if anything, they presumably symbolize preservation—the tree would not be left altogether to the mercy of the elements. Almost without exception ancient translators and expositors of Daniel understand the Aramaic word here translated *times* to mean "years." For instance, Josephus, a Jewish historian of New Testament times, specifically explains it as meaning seven *years*.[2]

And what was to happen to the king during those fateful seven years? The king himself had already quoted the heavenly watcher as saying, "Let his mind be changed from a man's, and let a beast's mind be given to him." Not only was he to live with the beasts, to eat with the beasts, and to take on their unkempt appearance, but his brilliant intellect was to be reduced to the instinctive processes of their dim minds. Could pride take a greater tumble? The king found his troubled spirit clinging desperately to that forlorn stump standing alone out in the field, wet with the dew of heaven, as Daniel hastens to reassure him, "Your kingdom will be sure for you. Your reason will be restored, and you will return from the haunts of the beasts to the realm of men—yes, you will also return to your throne."

Earnestly hoping, even yet, to avert the impending calamity, Daniel pleads, "O king, let my counsel be acceptable to you; break off your sins by practicing righteousness, and your iniquities by showing mercy to the oppressed, that there may perhaps be a lengthening of your tranquillity." If he will but mend his ways, the evil sentence pronounced upon him can yet be turned aside.[3]

## One Quiet Summer Evening

What Nebuchadnezzar's immediate reaction to Daniel's admonition may have been we are not told. From what we know of the king we may imagine that he courteously thanked his prime minister and dismissed him, but without making any personal commitment in response to Daniel's earnest appeal. As weeks and months sped by and nothing happened, the initial impact of the dream gradually faded from his thoughts. His empire remained intact, and the tribute that trickled in from all parts of his realm automatically kept his coffers full to overflowing. His court officials were as deferential as ever, and he had never seemed more secure on his throne. Doubtless, too, he was busier than ever with this building project or that, some new palace or temple or wall or fortification. He had what amounted almost to a mania for stately architecture. Then, before he realized it, twelve months had passed.

One quiet summer evening the king leisurely strolled from terrace to terrace of his famous Hanging Gardens, whence his eye could take in all the splendid temples and palaces and walls of Babylon.[4] Precious little of what Nebuchadnezzar saw that evening had been there before his day! The evening shadows mounted the walls of Marduk's temple a little to the south of the palace, and the last lurid rays of the setting sun struck athwart the upper stages of the lofty temple tower. The fishermen tied up their fragile craft on the murky banks of the Euphrates below. In the deepening shadows of night the king's lips moved in silence: "Is not this great Babylon, which I have built by my mighty power as a royal residence and for the glory of my majesty?" Yes, the greatest city of antiquity lay at his feet in the gathering twilight, a tribute to *his* wealth, wisdom, genius, and skill! The world, too, lay at his feet, and his magnificent accomplishments infinitely surpassed those of all who had gone before him.

Hardly had the unuttered words formed on his lips when a fateful voice fell like a clap of thunder from the cloudless sky above, an imperative voice to which he could not turn a deaf ear. He listened. He had to listen. In the slow, solemn tones of a judge rendering a verdict, the same holy watcher who had appeared to him in the dream announced: "The kingdom has departed from you, and you shall be driven from among men, and your dwelling shall be with the beasts of the field; and you shall be made to eat grass like an ox; and seven times shall pass over you, until you have learned that the Most High rules the kingdom of men and gives it to whom he will."

One fearful cry, and instantly, like a stage curtain falling at the close of a dramatic act, insanity descends upon the brilliant mind of the king, obliterating everything. Reason departs; the mental faculties fail. The light of intelligence fades from his eyes, and in its place there remains nought but the blank, glassy stare that marks the dumb brute, and with it a primordial desire for a few blades of grass to eat and a pile of straw on which to spend the night. No longer does Nebuchadnezzar envision himself as the builder of Babylon and the ruler of a vast empire whose borders touch the ends of the earth. He is an ox! *Sic transit gloria mundi!*[5]

Startled beyond words, courtiers waiting in the shadows rushed to his side. With considerable difficulty they ushered him to his quarters and summoned the royal physicians and counselors. Among the latter, of course, was Daniel, who recounted the king's dream. They remembered it all too well, but probably neither Nebuchadnezzar nor Daniel had told them its interpretation. Now, before their incredulous eyes, their revered sovereign was acting out its astonishing fulfillment!

## When Time Stood Still

At Daniel's suggestion the wise men apparently set up a regency to conduct the royal administration until the king should return from the far land to which he had gone. The brickmakers, the brickkiln operators, the brick glazers, and the bricklayers all ceased from their labors, and time stood still in Babylon. Time stood still for Nebuchadnezzar too. "He was driven from among men, and ate grass like an ox, and his body was wet with the dew of heaven till his hair grew as long as eagles' feathers, and his nails were like birds' claws." Whether Nebuchadnezzar's courtiers kept their beastly king in some secret enclosure within the palace walls, where, unmolested, he could lead the leisurely and uncomplicated life of an ox, or whether they spirited him far away from the city to some Babylonian Shangri-la, we do not know.

No cuneiform secretary cut the story of the king's fate on his clay tablets. Ancient scribes could never have been persuaded to record anything but the valorous deeds and glorious achievements of their lord. It would be unthinkable to pass on a tarnished memory of their revered sovereign to future generations! Later, upon his return to sanity, the king did not hesitate to promulgate a decree recounting his experience and explaining its import, but he too would never have considered placing a record of it in permanent form among the imperial archives of Babylon. Why should he deliberately detract from the luster of his reign and ask to go down in history as the mad monarch? Who wants to be remembered by posterity for his blunders and the embarrassing episodes of his life? No one—certainly not one of the most renowned of the ancient kings.

From the brief description given, no precise medical diagnosis of Nebuchadnezzar's insanity can be made. Some have called it *zoanthropy,* a form of insanity in which a person believes he is an animal and acts like one. Of the fact that he was insane there can be no doubt, for the angel had specified that his mind would be changed into that of a beast; and furthermore, when the seven years had passed, the king himself declared, "My reason returned to me." While the court officials watched and waited, their king was blissfully unaware of the passing of the "seven times"

foretold by the heavenly watcher. For him, time stood
still for seven full years.

## The Return to Sanity

With the approaching expiration of the seven years
Daniel and the other wise men must have watched
eagerly for the return to sanity. The moment came.
The last rational thought to flash across his royal con-
sciousness had been the divine decree sentencing him
to live with the beasts. As intelligence returned, he
doubtless gazed for an incredible moment at his in-
human appearance and turned to ask his courtiers
what had happened. But the question died on his lips,
half spoken, as he remembered that fateful voice from
heaven. God had taken away his intelligence; now
God had restored it. For the first time in all his life the
humility of true wisdom dawned in his inmost soul,
and he began to understand.

Appropriately, the first thing Nebuchadnezzar did
the moment his reason returned was to lift his eyes
heavenward, whence the voice had come seven long
years before, and "blessed the Most High, and praised
and honored him who lives for ever; for his dominion
is an everlasting dominion, and his kingdom endures
from generation to generation." Seven years of insanity had taught him more true wisdom than an entire lifetime. Vainglorious pride had been his besetting
sin, and oppression of his fellowmen its inevitable
harvest. How many children of the poor were weeping
for bread, and how many a slave had fallen under the
lash to rise no more! Drastic remedy, indeed, but how
effective it was!

The king's first official act upon the restoration of his intelligence was a proclamation extolling the Eternal One. His rescript closes with one of the most exalted ascriptions of praise to God that any man, king or commoner, ever composed: "Now I, Nebuchadnezzar, praise and extol and honor the King of heaven; for all his works are right and his ways are just; and those who walk in pride he is able to abase."

Remarkably, this admission of humility only added to the luster of the twilight years of Nebuchadnezzar's brilliant reign, as the king himself testified: "The glory of my kingdom, my majesty and splendor returned to me. My counselors and my lords sought me, and I was established in my kingdom, and still more greatness was added to me." They accepted him once more as their lord, and everything went on as it had before the seven years of divine shock therapy stopped the clock and changed the king's outlook on life, duty, and destiny.

This experience evidently came very late in Nebuchadnezzar's life, probably not long before the close of his reign, but these were doubtless the happiest and most serene years of his brilliant career. This public proclamation acknowledging God's justice, mercy, goodness, and supreme authority is the last recorded act of his life. He had learned, the hard way, "that the Most High rules in the kingdom of men," even as the watcher from the skies had said.

## NOTES

1. Nebuchadnezzar seems to have wanted to be remembered more as a builder than as a conqueror.

2. Josephus, *Antiquities* x. 10. 6.

3. See Jeremiah 12:14-17; 18:1-10; Ezekiel 18:21-24.

4. Nebuchadnezzar's famous Hanging Gardens were a sort of penthouse park four floors above the street level—one of the Seven Wonders of the ancient world. He built this elevated, tree-studded pleasure garden to please a Median wife, who pined for the wooded hills of her native land.

5. Latin for "Thus passes the glory of the world."

# Point of No Return

A FTER a long, notable reign of forty-three years Nebuchadnezzar died, in peace, in October, 562 B.C. Twenty-three years and a staccato succession of incompetent rulers later, the mighty Babylonian Empire itself passed the point of no return and followed its architect into oblivion. On the night of October 13, 539 B.C., only two days after the main Babylonian army had disintegrated before the Persians at Opis, about thirty miles to the north, Belshazzar entertained the aristocracy at a sumptuous state banquet.

The Southern Palace, Belshazzar's official residence, was situated on the east bank of the Euphrates immediately inside the great Ishtar Gate. In the center of the palace area was an immense hall, the ruins of which can still be seen, and it was here that formal state ceremonies were usually held.[1] In all probability this was the place where Belshazzar banqueted "a thousand of his lords" that last fateful night of his life, for no other hall in the city was large enough to accommodate so many guests. The ancient Greek historian Xenophon relates that the night the Persians took the city "a certain festival had come round in Babylon, during which all Babylon was accustomed to drink and revel all night long."[2]

A century or so ago nothing was known about Belshazzar aside from what Daniel tells about him in the fifth chapter of his book. Bible critics used to point to this uniform silence as conclusive evidence that Belshazzar never existed, that the account of the great feast of Daniel 5 was fictitious, and consequently that the Book of Daniel was not reliable history. Today, however, the fact that Belshazzar was the last Chaldean to occupy the throne of Babylon has been established to the complete satisfaction of the entire scholarly world. In fact, the conclusive identification of Belshazzar is one of the outstanding triumphs of Biblical archeology. On the basis of evidence now available, it seems probable that Belshazzar was a grandson of Nebuchadnezzar.[3]

The people of Babylon are said to have believed that the city could withstand a twenty-year siege. Its fortifications were supposed to be impregnable, and about the city was a system of irrigation canals whose waters could be released to flood the surrounding countryside, and thus counted on to check an approaching army. Apparently all this gave Belshazzar and his guests a false sense of security. Even so, it seems almost incredible that he should have staged this gala entertainment at a time of national disaster, especially in view of the fact that the vanguard of the Persian army was rapidly approaching the city.

All the lords and ladies of society were there dressed in their Babylonian best, and among them were Belshazzar's wives and concubines. During the course of the feast the king "drank wine in front of the thousand," and "when he tasted the wine"—when he was "under the influence," as we would say—he called for the sacred gold and silver goblets his grandfather Nebuchadnezzar had taken from the Temple in Jerusalem, and drank from them.

This drunken caprice was apparently in mockery of the God of Israel. Had the king been in command of his reason, he would probably not have given the order, inasmuch as it was uncommon for Orientals to desecrate sacred objects of other religions. It may be that use of these sacred goblets, which commemorated a past Babylonian victory, was intended to fortify the courage of the guests in view of the recent defeat at Opis and the imminent arrival of the Persian vanguard. By drowning their fears in wine, they at least diverted their minds from the present danger. As king and courtiers drank, they "praised the gods of gold and silver, bronze, iron, wood, and stone." Bel-Marduk, they believed, could surely be counted on to protect his own city!

## Handwriting on the Wall

While the king and his courtiers were drinking in mockery from the sacred goblets, which should never have been touched to profane lips, silently and unannounced "the fingers of a man's hand appeared and wrote on the plaster of the wall of the king's palace, opposite the lampstand." Transfixed with fright and terror, Belshazzar and his guests watched as the mysterious apparition wrote a cryptic message in dazzling letters of fire. In the wink of an eye the king's "color changed." His face became ashen white, consternation gripped his heart, "his limbs gave way, and his knees knocked together." Gone was his bravado, gone his vainglorious boasting. Like an irresistible magnet the moving hand riveted the gaze of two thousand eyes, from one end of the hall to the other, to the wall opposite where the king sat. The riotous merrymaking and boisterous revelry subsided to a deafening silence, and a thousand faces took on a deathly pallor.

Regaining his voice, the king called out for "the enchanters, the Chaldeans, and the astrologers," and in they came. With hand unsteady from wine and fright he pointed to the letters of fire and solemnly swore, "Whoever reads this writing, and shows me its interpretation, shall be clothed with purple, and have a chain of gold about his neck, and shall be the third ruler in the kingdom." The cryptic writing must first be *read,* and then deciphered. In that far-off day the art of writing and reading was considered a highly specialized skill, and few besides the priests and wise men were able to do either. Few in that great hall, perhaps not even the king, could read.

The royal purple, a deep purplish red sometimes called crimson, would be a token of kingly favor. The chain of gold was the ancient counterpart of a medal awarded to public servants the king wished to honor for distinguished service. The successful wise man would also be promoted to be "third ruler in the kingdom." Belshazzar was only second in command because his absent father Nabonidus still ranked first. Third place would thus put the lucky wise man next to Belshazzar, one step from the throne.[4]

But not one of the wise men even offered to read the writing, to say nothing of being able to reveal its fearful import. Ordinarily adept at contriving auspicious interpretations of the most untoward circumstances, this time they petrified into silence under the steady glare of the burning letters on the wall. Mystified and baffled, they stood as helpless as a row of wooden idols before their king.

The words on the wall were doubtless in Aramaic, the language of culture and government; but there were only three words, consisting of fourteen letters altogether, and in ancient Aramaic as in Hebrew only the consonants were written out. Each of the three words might have a different meaning, or shade of meaning, depending on the vowels that the reader supplied to the consonants, and also on the context in which the word was used. But this cryptogram provided no context to indicate which meaning was intended! Even with a knowledge of the correct meaning of each word, however, the reader could not be certain of the import of the message as a whole, and the mere reading of the words would thus not solve the mystery. A puzzler indeed, even for the shrewdest mind. The inability of the wise men to decipher the fiery cryptogram left the king even more "greatly alarmed" than before. Obviously this message had come from the gods and must be a portent of evil, but not a man in the kingdom could unlock the mystery it concealed.

## "There Is a Man"

Affairs had thus reached an impasse, or so it seemed, when in came "the queen, because of the words of the king and his lords." Had a shout of fear and consternation from the half-intoxicated nobles reverberated through the palace area and aroused her? From at least as far back as the time of Josephus, a Jewish historian of New Testament times, commentators have usually considered this queen to have been the king's mother or grandmother.[5] She could hardly have been Belshazzar's own wife, for his own "wives, and his concubines" were already among the revelers in the great hall.

"O king, live for ever!" the queen mother addressed her royal son as she came before him. "Let not your thoughts alarm you." Her personal knowledge of Daniel and of his close relationship to Nebuchadnezzar was such as the king's daughter might be expected to have, and she evidently remembered much that the younger generation never knew or had already forgotten. Upon Nebuchadnezzar's death, probably, the policy for which Daniel had stood at court fell into disfavor, with the result that he retired from public service. The king's greeting to Daniel, "I have heard of you," implies such a retirement before Belshazzar began to reign. The further fact that he was called into service again by the Persians soon after the events of this fateful night implies that his earlier retirement had not been due to ill health or advanced age. Furthermore, his stern censure of Belshazzar, in verses 22 and 23, reflects a sharp clash in policy. Under any circumstances Daniel was now nearly eighty years of age, an elder statesman who had apparently dropped out of sight years before.

"There is in your kingdom a man in whom is the spirit of the holy gods," the queen mother went on to explain, in the very words she had doubtless heard her father Nebuchadnezzar describe him.[6] "In the days of your father light and understanding and wisdom, like the wisdom of the gods, were found in him, and King Nebuchadnezzar, your father, made him chief of the magicians, enchanters, Chaldeans, and astrologers, because an excellent spirit, knowledge, and understanding to interpret dreams, explain riddles, and solve problems were found in this Daniel, whom the king named Belteshazzar. Now," she concluded confidently, "let Daniel be called, and he will show the interpretation."

Daniel was summoned forthwith to the banquet hall. The king greeted him as "one of the exiles of Judah whom the king my father brought from Judah," and said, "I have heard that you can give interpretations and solve problems." He then repeated to Daniel the queen mother's glowing tribute and the promise of great reward he had made to the wise men only moments before. In a state of shock that produced silence and inaction, the inebriated lords and ladies watched in suspense as Daniel scanned the writing on the wall, still glowing as if etched by a blazing stylus in letters of fire. Could *he* read it?

## Guilty!

Daniel promised to read the cryptic message and to explain its meaning, but declined the royal gift Belshazzar offered him. This disclaimer was doubtless genuine, for honors from a Babylonian king were soon to become worthless, perhaps even a liability. The Persians might look upon such honors as proving what would appear to them to be guilt by association.

But his refusal was also rhetorical, for according to verse 29 he accepted the honors.

Before turning to read the blazing words on the wall, however, Daniel recounted a lesson from the past which Belshazzar had, it appears, deliberately chosen to ignore. "O king," he said, "the Most High God gave Nebuchadnezzar your father kingship and greatness and glory and majesty; and because of the greatness that he gave him, all peoples, nations, and languages trembled and feared before him; whom he would he slew, and whom he would he kept alive; whom he would he raised up, and whom he would he put down.

"But when his heart was lifted up and his spirit was hardened so that he dealt proudly, he was deposed from his kingly throne, and his glory was taken from him; he was driven from among men, and his mind was made like that of a beast, and his dwelling was with the wild asses; he was fed grass like an ox, and his body was wet with the dew of heaven, until he knew that the Most High God rules the kingdom of men, and sets over it whom he will.

"And you his son, Belshazzar, have not humbled your heart, though you knew all this, but you have lifted up yourself against the Lord of heaven; and the vessels of his house have been brought in before you, and you and your lords, your wives, and your concubines have drunk wine from them; and you have praised the gods of silver and gold, of bronze, iron, wood, and stone, which do not see or hear or know, but the God in whose hand is your breath, and whose are all your ways, you have not honored."

Stern indictment indeed, and a most unusual way for a slave to address his king! Under other circumstances Belshazzar would have called upon his executioner to make reply. But Belshazzar was now in a receptive mood. Yes, even in his inebriated state he remembered something about Nebuchadnezzar's remarkable experiences and of his high esteem for Daniel. But he had wished to forget, and now the sacred gold and silver goblets from Jerusalem lay scattered about the banquet tables in mute testimony that Belshazzar, too, chose to defy the God of heaven. He knew that all Daniel said was true, and he stood speechless before the bar of divine justice, his sentence etched on the wall for all to see. King and kingdom had alike been weighed in the balances of heaven and found wanting. Both had passed the point of no return.

## Deciphering the Mysterious Words

Then Daniel turned toward the fateful, cryptic message and read solemnly and deliberately, "MENE, MENE, TEKEL, and PARSIN."[7] MENE means "numbered" or "counted," TEKEL means "weighed" or "measured," and PARSIN means "pieces." The whole inscription could be translated, "Counted, Counted, Weighed, Pieces." Obviously the cryptogram would not make sense unless it was known *what* had been counted, weighed, and broken into fragments. Guided by inspiration and with his background of knowledge and experience in God's dealings with the nations— as set forth in the messages to the earlier prophets and as demonstrated so forcefully in His former dealings with Nebuchadnezzar—and now with the scene in the banquet hall before him and his knowledge about the advancing Persian armies, Daniel went on to interpret for the king and the terrified banqueters the mysterious message:

"MENE, God has numbered the days of your kingdom and brought it to an end; TEKEL, you have been weighed in the balances and found wanting; PERES, your kingdom is divided and given to the Medes and Persians." The word *MENE* was written twice, apparently for emphasis—as if to indicate that a careful checking of the figures had been made and that the sum was without error and therefore to be accepted as final. In the divine ledger the account with Babylonia was closed; the empire was morally bankrupt and ready for receivership. The consonants of the word *PERES* also stand for Persia and the Persians, who were even then at the gates of Babylon. This might be understood as implying that the shattered "pieces" of the once-great Babylonian Empire were at this time given to the advancing Medes and Persians.

That was it; Belshazzar could not argue his case with the departed apparition, and furthermore sentence had already been pronounced. It was too late to do anything about it now, except to carry out his promise to Daniel. That, Belshazzar did not forget. His courtiers brought the royal purple robe and placed it about Daniel's shoulders, and they hung the golden chain around his neck. Then before all the lords and ladies of Babylon Belshazzar issued his last decree, which promoted Daniel to be "the third ruler in the kingdom"[8] of Babylon.

## A Gloomy Anticlimax

This tragic episode closes with the notation that, that very night, "Belshazzar the Chaldean king was slain. And Darius the Mede received the kingdom." The head of gold gave way to the breast and arms of silver.[9] The story of the great feast is the only narrative Daniel relates that did not have a happy ending, and it makes gloomy reading indeed.

As Daniel finished speaking and left the hall, a group of Persian officers entered, having found their way into Babylon, it is thought, through the river gates in the wall along the Euphrates, which flowed diagonally through the city. The Greek historians Xenophon and Herodotus report that the Persians had diverted the river from its usual channel through the city by turning its waters, momentarily, into the many irrigation canals upstream.[10] As a result, these sources report, the water level was lowered sufficiently to permit the Persians to wade downstream into the very heart of the city. If so, the Persians may have known that friends would open the gates for them. But whether the gates were left open through carelessness, or were deliberately opened by the influential pro-Persian party in the city is not known. Possibly the guards were as intoxicated as their king. Had they been sober they would surely have noticed the receding waters of the river and raised an alarm.

As it was, the Persian vanguard was able to enter the city and take it intact, without a pitched battle. According to Xenophon, the Persian generals Gadatas and Gobryas went directly to the palace, found Belshazzar "standing with a drawn saber" by his throne in the banquet hall, and quickly cut him down, on the very spot where he had been when the heavenly watcher pronounced sentence against him.[10]

Had the fateful words of fire faded from the wall by the time the Persians entered? No one knows, nor does it matter. Xenophon reports also that the guards in the citadel, hard by the palace, held out a little longer, but that with the coming of daylight they realized that the rest of the city had fallen to the Persians, and they too surrendered. The golden empire of the Chaldeans was at an end, and Darius the Mede became king over the province of Babylon, under the general suzerainty of Cyrus, supreme ruler of all Persia.

The Apostle Paul declares that God has appointed a day when He will judge all men. Evidently, like Belshazzar, we too must stand one day, each of us, before the bar of divine justice.[11] What will the great Judge of all men say on that awful day when my name, and yours, pass in review before Him? Will we be "numbered, weighed, and found wanting," or will He say to us, "Well done, good and faithful servant; . . . enter into the joy of your master"? There is no higher court to which appeals can be made from the decisions of the Chief Justice of the universe.

## NOTES

1. Robert Koldewey, *The Excavations at Babylon,* translated by Agnes S. Johns, pp. 103, 104.

2. Xenophon, *Cyropaedia* vii. 5. 10, 13, 15, 16, 26-30; Vol. 2, translated by Walter Miller, Loeb Classical Library, pp. 265, 267, 269, 271, 273.

3. See Daniel 5:1, 11, 13, 18, 22. For information on

the dramatic series of discoveries which proved that Belshazzar really existed and that he reigned jointly with his father Nabonidus, see Raymond Philip Dougherty, *Nabonidus and Belshazzar,* pp. 11-13, 38, 43, 59, 60-63, 70, 93-97, 105-107, 134, 135, 193, 199, 200; R. H. Pfeiffer, *Introduction to the Old Testament,* pp. 758, 759. Bible writers commonly use the words *father* and *son* in the sense of *ancestor* and *descendant,* two or more generations apart. For instance, Achan, great-grandson of Zerah, is called Zerah's "son." (Joshua 7:18, 24.) Jehu, grandson of Nimshi, is called Nimshi's "son." (2 Kings 9:2, 14; compare 1 Kings 19:16.) The same is true of Azariah the great-great-grandson of Zadok. (1 Kings 4:2; compare 1 Chronicles 6:8-10.) Numerous other instances might be cited.

4. Dougherty, *Op. cit.,* pp. 136, 137.

5. Josephus, *Antiquities* x. 11. 2.

6. See Daniel 4:8, 9, 18.

7. In ancient Hebrew and Aramaic only the consonants were written. The reader had to supply the vowels as he read. The context would usually make clear what vowels should be supplied, but in some instances various vowel combinations were possible, and the meaning would vary accordingly. In this instance there was no context to indicate what vowels should be supplied. Also, anciently, words were not spaced as they are today. If the same procedure were followed with the English words *numbered, counted,* and *pieces,* the result would be: NMBRDCNTD and PCS. Obviously, someone attempting to read this combination of consonants without any clue as to the words intended would be quite at a loss to decipher the cryptogram, and even when he had identified the words he would not know *what* was "numbered," "counted," and broken to "pieces."

8. Dougherty, *Op. cit.,* pp. 136, 137.

9. Daniel 2:32, 38, 39.

10. Xenophon (see note 2, page 104), *Herodotus* 1. 191; translated by A. D. Godley, Vol. 4, *Loeb Classical Library,* pp. 239, 241.

11. Acts 17:31; Matthew 25:31, 32.

# It Pays to Be Insured

IN THE rugged Zagros Mountains three hundred miles to the northeast of Babylon was Media. Closely related to the Medes were the Persian tribes immediately on the south. The rough, mountainous country in which the Medes and the Persians spent their lives made them a healthy and vigorous people, and their warriors were accustomed to hardship and privation.

The Persian tribes had long recognized the general suzerainty of the Medes. During Nebuchadnezzar's reign in Babylon a young prince of one of these tribes married a Median princess. Their son, Cyrus, succeeded in uniting the various Persian tribes under his personal authority, rebelled against his Median overlord and own grandfather, and fell heir to all Media. Thus it came about that Persia, which heretofore had been considered a province of Media, henceforth became the dominant force within the empire.

Despite this change in political fortunes, however, friendly relations continued between the Persians and the Medes, and the latter were eligible to high office and often served as officers in the Persian army. Foreigners commonly spoke of "the Medes and Persians," and more often than not when they used a single term it would still be "the Medes." Even Persian documents refer to the Persians as "Medes," and their realm as that of the "Medes and Persians," as does the Bible. These same documents designate various Persian kings by the title "king of the Medes," as well as by the more common title "king of Persia."

Cyrus, later called "the Great," proved to be one of the most remarkable rulers of all history. He was tolerant, farsighted, and an able organizer. During his lifetime he pieced together what was by far the largest empire the world had ever seen up to that time, one that extended from India and central Asia on the east to the Aegean Sea and Europe on the west. The empire he founded endured for more than two centuries— twice as long as New Babylonia—until Alexander the Great decisively defeated the Persians near Arbela in 331 B.C.

## The Conquest of Babylonia

In a few years Cyrus succeeded in bringing much of western Asia under his control, thereby doubling the extent of his territory, and built up a formidable army, which he hoped would someday be a match for the Babylonians. Not yet ready for a direct attack on Babylon itself, whose excellent fortifications made it theoretically impregnable, he began to whittle away systematically at the border regions of the outlying provinces. By 540 B.C. he had consolidated these conquests and felt ready for the big test of strength. The next year he breached the famed Median Wall Nebuchadnezzar had erected to protect against incursions from the east and decisively defeated the main Babylonian army at Opis on the Tigris River, about thirty miles north of Babylon. Organized resistance ceased, and all Babylonia suddenly lay open before Cyrus without the need for another pitched battle.

The Persian vanguard wheeled southward in pursuit of Belshazzar, who retired behind the walls of Babylon, where he expected to be able to hold out indefinitely. But on the fateful night of October 13, only two days after the battle at Opis, the Persian vanguard entered Babylon by strategem. Two weeks later Cyrus himself arrived and was roundly welcomed by the populace. For all practical purposes he was now master of the world.

The people of Babylon hailed Cyrus as their liberator, as did also the Jewish exiles, who of course looked upon the Chaldeans, their captors, as archfoes. With what joy and hope the Jews must have watched Cyrus's meteoric rise to power and his conquest of Babylonia, in view of the fact that a century and a half before the prophet Isaiah had identified Cyrus by name as the one who would set them free and who would decree the rebuilding of Jerusalem.[1]

Cyrus proved to be not only a great military leader, but a remarkably wise and tolerant ruler as well, one who knew how to win the peace as well as war. Whereas the Assyrians and Babylonians destroyed the cities they captured and engaged in the wholesale transplanting of their peoples, Cyrus not only spared cities he took but restored previously displaced peoples to their homelands and assisted them in the work of reconstruction. Persian administrative documents show that as a rule they retained the former officials of conquered territories. The change of government in Babylon proved to be no exception, for Cyrus took over the city and its administrative machinery intact. Persian soldiers guarded the temples and public buildings to prevent looting and the destruction of property, and to guarantee the orderly continuation of the daily life of the city.

The resentment conquered people usually feel toward their conquerors did not develop. This was due in part to the generous policy of Cyrus and in part to the deep dislike of the native Babylonians for their Chaldean overlords. Furthermore, Babylon was the seat of an ancient and venerable civilization, and the Persians had high respect for its learning and culture. Cyrus declared himself "king of Babylon" and honored the city by making it one of his capitals. He let the Babylonian people follow their own customs.

## "Darius the Mede"

Daniel relates that upon the fall of Babylon to the Persians "Darius the Mede received the kingdom, being about sixty-two years old." According to Daniel's introductory statement to the ninth chapter, this Darius was "the son of Ahasuerus, by birth a Mede, who became king over the realm of the Chaldeans." He was thus a Mede and not a Persian; he was advanced in age; and he was "king," not over the entire Persian Empire, but over what had formerly been "the realm of the Chaldeans," probably the home province of Babylonia. Apparently he reigned but a short time, for his first regnal year only is mentioned. Cyrus had already ruled all Persia and Media for at least twelve years and was yet to reign for another nine. The conquest of Babylon thus came a little beyond the midpoint of his career as king.

Cyrus appointed this Darius over the city and province of Babylon, and here Darius ruled as king. Of his own fortunes after the fall of Babylon, Daniel relates that he "prospered during the reign of Darius and the reign of Cyrus the Persian."[2] Apparently the two reigns were concurrent. As we have already noted, great rulers of antiquity often followed the practice of appointing subkings to rule over parts of their domain. Nebuchadnezzar's appointment of Jehoiakim and Zedekiah as kings of conquered Judah is a case in point.[3]

This "Darius the Mede" is unknown to secular history. No contemporary documents mention his name. Probably he went by another name prior to being elevated to the kingship, and "Darius" was his reigning title. A king's reigning title is commonly different from his private name. The fact that Darius's reign was so brief, possibly not much more than a year, as Daniel implies, may account for the fact that documents giving his regnal title have thus far not been found.

## A Clever Plot

Darius the Mede, so Daniel relates, "set over the kingdom a hundred and twenty satraps," or local governors, to administer its affairs, and over these satraps "three presidents, of whom Daniel was one." As might be expected, Daniel was soon "distinguished above all the other presidents and satraps, because an excellent spirit was in him." His obvious sincerity, integrity, faithfulness to duty, and gracious personality won the confidence and trust of the Medes and Persians as it had that of the Chaldeans. Many years had passed since Nebuchadnezzar commended Daniel for having "the spirit of the holy gods," and at the great feast the night of Babylon's fall the queen mother similarly praised him.[4]

When it became known that Darius planned to set Daniel "over the whole kingdom," the other two presidents and the 120 satraps became jealous. They resented the idea that a Jewish exile should be promoted to authority over them. Another complaint some of these officials may have had against him was that his own scrupulous honesty made it inconvenient for them to line their own pockets with the royal revenue. It was embarrassing to have a man like that looking over their shoulders all the time. Perhaps, also, they could not believe that Daniel was actually as honest as he appeared to be, and they may have suspected that he was simply a more clever operator than they.

Accordingly, the presidents and the satraps launched a secret investigation, looking for irregularities in Daniel's administration which they could make the basis for accusing him to the king. But "they could find no ground for complaint or any fault, because he was faithful, and no error or fault was found in him." There was not a shred of evidence they could twist one way or the other to make him even appear to be slack or dishonest. His administrative record was beyond reproach.

The self-constituted investigating committee next turned to Daniel's personal life. Daniel, they noted, never went with them to the temple to worship, and never participated in their religious ceremonies. Furthermore, as a devout Jew he was absent from his office every Sabbath, as prescribed in "the law of his God."[5] They finally concluded, "We shall not find any ground for complaint against this Daniel unless we find it in connection with the law of his God." How right they were! So they set about to contrive some way by which to turn Daniel's unbending loyalty to his God onto a collision course with the laws of the Medes and the Persians, which were, theoretically at least, equally inflexible. Perhaps in a conflict of loyalties Daniel could yet be mortally injured.

Thus it was that Daniel's foes seized upon his allegiance to God as the only means to their ignoble end. If he had no vices, they would make his virtues his undoing! But knowing Darius's high esteem for Daniel, they would have to camouflage their plot well in order to succeed.

One day the presidents and the satraps came tumultuously into the royal audience chamber, as if on business they considered of utmost importance. Perhaps they chose a Sabbath morning for this unscheduled audience, knowing that Daniel would not be present to foil their plans. Their business? asked the king. Ah! they have ready for his signature the draft of an edict designed to solidify the loyalty of Darius's Babylonian subjects to the new administration. A dramatic gesture such as this was just the thing needed to give the new regime a firm basis in public support, they claimed. The sly rascals doubtless also reasoned that it would be flattering to the ego of Darius to become a recipient of honors usually reserved for the gods alone.

"We are all agreed," they said, "that the king should establish an ordinance and enforce an interdict, that whoever makes petition to any god or man for thirty days, except to you, O king, shall be cast into the den of lions." The document was all ready for his royal seal, and once this had been affixed to it, "according to the law of the Medes and the Persians," it could not be revoked.[6] Darius obligingly affixed his seal to the decree, and out the unscrupulous schemers went in triumph.

The ruse had worked out exactly as the plotters had planned that it should! It is not difficult to imagine their exclamations of triumph once they were out of the king's hearing. At last they had Daniel in their trap! Oh, the priests of Bel-Marduk would doubtless protest when they heard about the edict, but they could be persuaded to cooperate—for a month. Had the king not already showered royal favors upon them? Now let them reciprocate.

## Springing the Trap

Under the circumstances a smart man might have decided to conduct his personal devotions in secret. But not Daniel. He made no display of his devotion, but neither did he attempt to conceal it. It was his custom to retire to his prayer room, an "upper chamber" or cupola atop his flat-roofed house, at the regular morning and evening hours of prayer and also at noon.

He would continue to do precisely that. Doubtless having observed this practice during the course of their investigation, the plotters now posted some of their number to watch Daniel's rooftop retreat, and sure enough, out he came on schedule.

It is worthy of note that Daniel "got down upon his knees" when he prayed, an example all who approach God in prayer today might well follow. The windows of Daniel's prayer room were "open toward Jerusalem," reflecting no doubt the fact that his thoughts and his petitions were also oriented in that direction. It was at about this time that Daniel offered the importunate prayer recorded in Daniel 9:4-19, in behalf of the beloved city and its Temple, both of which still lay in ruins.

Pretending to be horrified, the presidents and the prefects and the satraps and the counselors and the governors all went at once to the king and reported what they had observed. "O king! Did you not sign an interdict, that any man who makes petition to any god or man within thirty days except to you, O king, shall be cast into the den of lions?" "Yes," the king promptly replied, "the thing stands fast, according to the law of the Medes and Persians, which cannot be revoked."

That was all they needed. The king had affirmed the law and pronounced it inviolate. Triumphantly, now, they accused Daniel, "one of the exiles from Judah" and thus a foreigner, of sedition. "Daniel . . . pays no heed to you, O king, or the interdict you have signed, but makes his petition three times a day." The law is on the books, and it is too late, O king, to be concerned about Daniel. He has defied you, and the integrity of Persian law is at stake. Thus the jaws of the trap sprang shut, with Daniel securely inside, the victim of malicious jealousy.

## Out to the Lions' Den

Instantly Darius saw through the plot, but now he, too, was caught fast in the trap, and there was no escape. The purpose of the new law was not to honor him after all, nor was its aim the security of the realm. It had but one motive—to deprive him of his most trusted friend and reliable public servant. The king "was much distressed, and set his mind to deliver Daniel," and "labored till the sun went down" to find a loophole in the law, but all to no avail. The dignity of Median and Persian law, once enacted, was such that it could not be altered even by the one who had promulgated it.

At sunset the unscrupulous officials reminded Darius that the sentence must be executed that very day. They doubtless feared that if there were further delay, Daniel might yet escape from their clutches, and that must not be permitted to happen.

Therefore the order was issued, and Daniel was ushered into Darius's presence for the fatal sentence. Accompanied by the king himself, the officials took him to the den of lions, opened the door, and triumphantly tossed him in. In deep emotion the king pleaded, "May your God, whom you serve continually, deliver you!" Then the stone door was rolled back into place, and the king's own seal and the seals of his officials were affixed to it. This would prevent Daniel's escape or his rescue should the lions chance not to be hungry at the moment, and it would also be a guarantee to the king that none of these scheming scoundrels could tamper with the door during the night and do away with Daniel by some other foul means if this one should fail.

It was dark when Darius returned to the palace and retired to his bedchamber. But sleep would not come. It was the worst night of his life. At dawn he hastened back to the lions' den and "cried out in a tone of anguish, . . . 'O Daniel, servant of the living God, has your God, whom you serve continually, been able to deliver you from the lions?'" Breathlessly he awaited a reply from the recesses of the cavern. Daniel respectfully called back, "O king, live for ever! My God sent his angel and shut the lions' mouths, and they have not hurt me, because I was found blameless before him; and also before you, O king, I have done no wrong."

Quickly Darius broke the seals, and when Daniel was brought up, "no kind of hurt was found upon him." All his life Daniel had carried what we might call lion insurance, and this time he collected on his policy.

Darius now hailed the ringleaders of the plot and confronted them with their victim, alive and uninjured—a living miracle none of them could gainsay. The conspirators were speechless. When able to talk again, they doubtless accounted for the miraculous deliverance with the facetious explanation that the lions had not been hungry. Nevertheless, the requirements of the royal decree had been met and Daniel was safe. After all, the law had not specified that he must remain there until the lions were ready for their next meal!

## The Punishment Fits the Crime

Now the king remembered another section of Persian law, one the conspirators had apparently forgotten in their haste to dispose of Daniel. Their complicity was now evident—they had conspired to do away with the king's favorite counselor, and the miracle had proved him innocent. Ancient legal codes commonly provided that false accusers should suffer the same penalty they sought to have inflicted upon anyone who proved to be innocent of the charges made against him.[7]

So Darius gave the order, and the ringleaders of the plot, together with their entire families, as was the custom, were consigned to the same fate they had contrived for Daniel. Cruel and repugnant as this practice is when measured by modern ideas of justice, it was wholly in keeping with the standards of the day. Did Darius, with mock concern for their welfare, taunt the ringleaders as he herded them into the den with the suggestion that the lions were probably still not hungry? They would soon find out. But the lions suddenly developed a ravenous appetite, and before the culprits reached the bottom of the den, "the lions overpowered them and broke all their bones in pieces." These charlatans did not carry lion insurance, and Marduk sent no angel to rescue them from their fate.

Returning to the palace, Darius issued an imperial rescript decreeing that all men within his dominion should "tremble and fear before the God of Daniel, for he is the living God, enduring for ever. . . . He delivers and rescues," the king went on, "he works signs and wonders in heaven and on earth." This was evident from the fact that He had saved Daniel from the power of the lions. This edict does not necessarily mean that the king gave up his polytheistic beliefs and practices. Like Nebuchadnezzar before him, he simply acknowledged what he had found to be a fact —the power of the God of heaven. The intent of his decree was to avert the possibility that anyone under his jurisdiction should offend Daniel's God and thus bring down the wrath of Heaven upon the realm.

It pays to be insured. The same policy that protected Daniel is still available today, and the rates have not changed. Are you fully covered?

## NOTES

1. Isaiah 44:24 to 45:6.
2. Daniel 6:28.
3. 2 Kings 24:1; 2 Chronicles 36:13.
4. Daniel 4:8; 5:12.
5. By the word *law* Bible writers generally mean the revealed will of God as contained in the Sacred Writings, particularly the first five books of the Bible, traditionally credited to Moses.
6. Compare Esther 1:19; 8:8.
7. See Deuteronomy 19:18-21. Compare the penalty for false accusation in the Code of Hammurabi, Laws 1-4, in J. B. Pritchard, *Ancient Near Eastern Texts*, p. 166.

# *A Light in the Dark*

I N THE SERIES of remarkable episodes found in the first six chapters of the Book of Daniel the curtain that separates the infinite from the finite has been drawn aside by an inspired hand. These chapters present a dramatic view of God at work behind the scenes of history, silently, patiently working out the counsels of His own will. The providential incidents here recorded assure us that, through all the play and counterplay of human interests and power and passions, a master hand is at the helm.

With chapter 7, however, the narrative abruptly changes, and in the latter half of the book the prophet Daniel relates what he was shown and told by the angel Gabriel in a series of four great visions, during the later years of his eventful life. He was now a grand old man well above the Biblical threescore years and ten, yet still in command of much of his youthful vigor of body and mind.

In this series of visions the Infinite One, who knows the end from the beginning, gave His faithful ambassador at the court of Babylon a dramatic preview of the future. Here we find revealed also a knowledge of the experiences through which we must yet pass prior to the inauguration of His eternal, righteous reign. In these chapters strange, symbolic beasts march solemnly across the prophetic stage, and in language that is often obscure to us today the angel who attended Daniel in vision explains their unusual actions.

Our first encounter with these puzzling scenes and sometimes mystifying explanations is likely to leave us with the impression that they are utterly unintelligible. Have you ever looked at a picture so out of focus that everything was a hazy blur, one in which even the faces of your best friends were scarcely recognizable? When you first sit down to read the prophetic passages of the Book of Daniel with a sincere desire to understand them, you may feel somewhat the same way. You may be tempted to conclude that everything is a hopeless, confused blur, and turn away with a sense of frustration and futility. But wait! As with a camera or a pair of binoculars, it is possible to bring everything into sharp focus.

## What Bible Prophecy Is

What is Bible prophecy? The word *prophet* means "spokesman." A prophet speaks for, or in behalf of, someone else.[1] The prophets of the Bible were God's spokesmen, men through whom He chose to communicate a knowledge of His infinite purpose to His people on earth. The messages they bore for God we call *prophecy.* These messages consist of counsel, reproof, and warning, and of instruction concerning the past, present, or future. We here use the word *prophecy* in the latter sense. Bible prophecy is thus light from heaven shining forth amid the darkness of this world, to illumine our way from this world to the next.[2]

As we have said, the prophetic messages of Daniel constitute an inspired preview of the divine purpose as it was to unfold in events then still in the future, particularly events relating to God's plan for the salvation of man and the eventual inauguration of His eternal kingdom on earth. These messages contain information designed by God to help us understand the outworking of that grand purpose in history, thereby confirming our faith and enabling us to cooperate more intelligently with His infinite purpose for us. They also provide us with an inspired preview of momentous events that are yet to take place.

## Is It Reasonable to Believe in Bible Prophecy?

At this point someone is sure to ask what reason there is for believing that the Bible writers had any greater insight into the mystery of the future than the ancient Babylonian wise men could obtain by observing the planets or than a gypsy fortune-teller can secure by gazing into a crystal ball. What objective reasons are there for believing that the prophecies of Daniel are actually what they claim to be, a genuine revelation of the future?

As a matter of fact, the question of the authenticity and reliability of Bible prophecy is but one facet of a larger problem—the authenticity and reliability of the Bible as a whole. The two stand or fall together. The question thus becomes, What reasons are there for believing that the Bible as a whole is what it claims to be, a supernatural revelation of the infinite purposes of God and a record of human events in relation to that purpose, and not an ordinary human document? Let us briefly consider five major points of evidence that the Bible is, indeed, a supernatural book deserving of our supreme trust and confidence.

## Bible History Is Authentic and Reliable

The Bible frequently mentions important persons, places, and events associated with great nations of antiquity such as Egypt, Assyria, Babylon, Persia, Greece, and Rome, as well as many of lesser importance. It is now possible to check the accuracy of a great many of these Bible statements by comparing them with official contemporary records inscribed on stone, baked clay tablets, papyrus, parchment, and other writing materials of antiquity. Scores of ancient cities painstakingly unearthed by archeologists have yielded a wealth of additional information which, added to their written records, provides us with a most remarkable knowledge about the remote past.[3] Prior to these discoveries we were dependent almost exclusively on hearsay reports by Greek and Roman writers, most of whom usually had no way of verifying information. Their accounts are often an uncertain mixture of fact and fancy, of history and legend.

More than a century ago, however, the scholarly world was almost wholly dependent on these secondary accounts for information about ancient times, and accepted them as authoritative. Where the Bible accounts differed, scholars declared it to be in error; and where it gave information not mentioned by the classical writers of Greece and Rome, they wrote it off as either legend or deliberate fiction.

Then came the great discoveries of which we have spoken, one hard upon the heels of another. These discoveries have completely revolutionized the attitude of scholars toward the Bible as history until, today, they acknowledge it to be the most authentic and reliable record that has come down to us from ancient times.[4] Point by point, over the years, the historical accuracy of the Bible writers has been astonishingly vindicated.

The Bible stands out as a uniquely authentic and reliable source of information. This consistent, invariable accuracy is an impressive testimony to a divine hand that evidently protected its writers from making the mistakes all other ancient historians made, and creates a formidable presumption that should lead honest, intelligent readers to a serious examination of its claim to being a supernatural book.

## Amazing Unity and Remarkable Preservation of the Bible

The unity and harmony of the Bible constitute another impressive witness to its divine origin. Written in three different languages over a period of fifteen centuries, by some forty kings, prophets, generals, fishermen, shepherds, teachers, preachers, philosophers, and doctors—men from all walks of life—its fundamental point of view and basic teachings are the same throughout. The basic unity and harmony of the Bible writers can be accounted for only on the basis that one mastermind inspired them all.

The remarkable preservation of the Bible for thousands of years before the invention of printing, much of the time with only a few handwritten copies in existence, also testifies to a divine, protecting hand. This is all the more impressive in view of repeated attempts by enemies to destroy it. Its custodians, the Jews, were repeatedly scattered in exile and their city Jerusalem reduced to a pile of rubble. The succession of tragedies that overtook their nation should, in the normal course of events, have resulted in the complete destruction of their sacred literature, yet miraculously it has come down through the centuries intact. No other book in all history has survived so many perils.

Furthermore, the text of the Bible has, for all practical purposes, come down to us unchanged, despite the fact that the earlier portions of it were copied laboriously by hand for twenty-five centuries before the invention of printing. Recently discovered manuscripts of various books of the Old Testament more than two thousand years old read practically word for word like the copies that have come down to us through the centuries. Copies of parts of the New Testament almost as old testify similarly to the accuracy with which it has been preserved. This providential preservation of the Scriptures, both from destruction and from any significant change in the text, is impressive evidence of the fact that a supernatural hand has been over it.

## Morality of the Bible

In unique contrast with all other ancient peoples, the Jews believed in one true God—holy, righteous, and infinite. They believed that, as Creator of all things including man, He is deeply and personally interested in man's happiness and well-being. In sharp contrast, other peoples of antiquity worshiped many gods, to whom they attributed human emotions and passions and who were supposed to be guilty of every form of immoral conduct, including falsehood, revenge, murder, theft, and adultery.

But the Bible stoutly condemns all such practices and summons man to the very highest conceivable moral conduct. Surely this exalted concept of morality was not in any sense a product of bright minds of that or any other age. It could not have originated with men, because it is so contrary to man's natural tendencies. Even the Jewish nation itself was in constant revolt against the lofty moral ideals set forth in their own Scriptures. It cannot be said that the morality of the Bible reflects their natural inclinations, for they often rejected, mistreated, and murdered the men who dared thus to reprove their conduct.

The only reasonable way to account for the lofty morality of the Bible, which is diametrically opposed to man's natural instincts, is to recognize that it originated, as its writers consistently claim, with God. Its moral teachings thus constitute another formidable witness to the supernatural origin, and thus the authenticity and reliability, of the Bible. Its principles are the only permanent things our world knows.

## Influence of the Bible

Closely related to the intrinsic moral teachings of the Bible as an evidence of its supernatural origin is its impact on the lives of those who read and accept it for what it claims to be. Here is a book that appeals

to men of every race, nation, age, and station in life—
in the twentieth century as well as in the first. In
whole or part, it has been translated into nearly twelve
hundred languages, and people of every country on
earth claim it as their own.

The final chapters of the Bible were penned nearly
nineteen centuries ago, and its first chapters another
fifteen hundred years before that. Yet it is as perfectly
suited to man's needs in the space age as it was in the
iron age—as attested to by the fact that it continues
to be the world's best seller and most popular book,
outselling its nearest competitor by millions of copies
every year.

Children still like to hear its stories, philosophers
still reflect on its sublime truths, and countless thousands of the world's best scholars are, even today, de-
voting their lives to understanding it more perfectly.
More volumes have been written about it than about
any other book—perhaps than all other books together. It is equally at home and appreciated in the
humble dwellings of the poor and in the mansions of
the rich. It still comforts the sick and suffering and
brings solace to those who mourn.

The Bible's salutary influence on men's lives has
been constant down through the centuries, irrespective
of race, culture, tradition, or educational background.
It stimulates physical health and vigor, and sharpens
the intellect. It refines and polishes the character and
personality. It transforms thieves into men of integrity, murderers into benefactors of their fellowmen,
sharp dealers into generous givers, cannibals into
Christians, barbarians into peaceful, law-abiding citi-

zens. Those who accept its authority and apply its principles to the problems of life prove to be the best adjusted, most stable and consistently useful members of society.

Down through the centuries the Bible has won the absolute self-surrender of countless millions of people all over the world and inspired them to passionate, self-sacrificing service for their fellowmen. Millions have willingly laid down their lives rather than be untrue to its principles or deny their faith in it. It has spurred untold thousands of men and women to leave loved ones, friends, and lives of comparative luxury to go out to the far corners of the earth to endure hardship, toil, and dangers of all kinds, to live in unpleasant, unhealthful, and even hostile surroundings—with the sole motive of telling strangers about the better way of life set forth between its covers. What other book can lay claim to influence such as this?

Applied to government, Bible principles result in freedom and an orderly state of society, with justice and equal opportunity for all. Applied to social problems, the Bible produces considerate employers and faithful employees; it inspires care for the poor and needy, and the humane treatment of criminals and enemies. Applied to business relations, it produces honesty and fairness in all transactions. It has inspired the founding of a majority of the world's universities, colleges, hospitals, orphanages, and countless other philanthropic enterprises. It inspires charity at home and abroad, and brings help for people everywhere in time of disaster or war.

The Bible's influence has been uniformly the same in every age and country where it has had an opportunity to condition men's thinking and their way of life. Nations where this influence has been most marked are the very ones that have enjoyed the most stable political and economic conditions, and that, generally speaking, aim at making the Golden Rule their guide to international relations. The great fundamental moral and ethical standards universally recognized by civilized nations today were derived from the Bible.

There is but one adequate explanation of all this—something far above and beyond mere human ideals and experience inspired the men who wrote this Book. It continues to inspire those who read it, accept it, and give it an opportunity to mold their lives.

## The Significance of Fulfilled Prophecy

The Bible is thus a unique book and comes to us with many convincing evidences that it is authentic, that it is what it claims to be—God's Book. Still another category of evidence for its supernatural origin is fulfilled prophecy. The Bible records hundreds of predictions, some of which were made centuries in advance of the events foretold. The exactness with which these predictions have been fulfilled testifies to their supernatural origin. Sometimes critics of the Bible claim that these predictions were actually made *after* the events had taken place, and cite the predictions of Daniel as a prime example. To demonstrate the fallacy of this claim, let us examine briefly one set of predictions that no one claims were made after the

# Babylon--A Metropolis in Daniel's Time

When Daniel and the other Hebrew captives first saw Babylon, it was an imposing sight—the seven-stage temple-tower, Etemenanki; the glistening yellow brick walls with their crenellated parapets; the colorful and resplendent Ishtar Gate, 170 feet long; and broad Procession Street, along which captors and captives paraded.

But this square-shaped city of approximately a mile on either side was to be enlarged under Nebuchadnezzar by nearly eight times. By careful planning and beautifying, it would become the showplace of the ancient world.

It was here that God revealed much of the future to His servant Daniel.

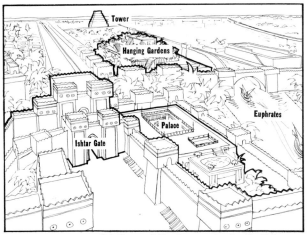

Painting on following opening by Jim Padgett

Robert Ayres, Artist

**King Nebuchadnezzar was profoundly impressed as Daniel
reconstructed the forgotten dream and explained its meaning.
(Read "A Man for the Hour," page 35.)**

Robert Ayres, Artist

"Then Nebuchadnezzar was full of fury, and the expression of his face was changed against Shadrach, Meshach, and Abednego." (This gripping story begins on page 58.)

Clyde Provonsha, Artist

**Through the inspired preview of the future revealed to Daniel
in the long ago, God speaks imperatively
to us in the space age.**

Clyde Provonsha, Artist

**Pagan Rome's persecution of Christians pales into insignificance when compared with what followed. (Read "History's Greatest Hoax," page 219.)**

Lester Quade, Artist

**Fulfilled prophecies of God's Word tell us where we are in the stream of time; those relating to the future tell us where we are going. ("The Coming Crisis," page 270, introduces these prophecies.)**

Robert Ayres, Artist

**The Apostle John made a Scriptural record of the vision showing "the holy city, new Jerusalem, coming down out of heaven from God." (See page 361.)**

Jim Padgett, Artist

Revelation 12 is a dramatic word picture of the Christian era. With the sky for a stage, a noble, virtuous woman symbolized the early church. (See page 205.)

Jim Padgett, Artist

In Revelation 17, apostate religion is symbolized by a woman
without virtue, "sitting on a scarlet beast" that "had
seven heads and ten horns." (See page 215.)

Jim Padgett, Artist

**For more than twelve centuries the Bible was a household item at the peril of the possessors' very lives. (Read "History's Greatest Hoax," page 219.)**

Clyde Provonsha, Artist

As the last sands of time fall through God's hourglass, men and women everywhere are aware that something great and decisive is about to take place.

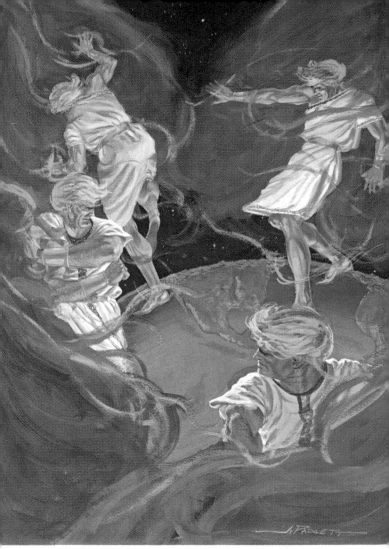

Jim Padgett, Artist

**Prophecy shows (in Revelation 7) four angels representing divine restraint that holds back universal strife and confusion threatening the earth. (Read "Grapes of Wrath," page 333.)**

Jim Padgett, Artist

**John figuratively pictures Christ (Revelation 19) as riding forth from heaven on a white horse as Commander of "the armies of heaven." (See page 358.)**

Purified by fire, and with the blight of sin removed forever, the earth will be restored to its Edenic beauty and perfection.

event—the Old Testament prophecies concerning the life and mission of the Messiah.[5]

Centuries before the Messiah actually appeared, Old Testament writers foretold that He would be a divine-human being, that He would be of the tribe of Judah and the family of David, that He would be born in Bethlehem, that He would begin His ministry about A.D. 27, that He would labor chiefly in Jerusalem and Galilee, that He would heal the sick and teach the good news of salvation, that He would die a vicarious death for men's sins, that He would triumph over death, and that He would intercede for sinners.[6]

All that is necessary to determine whether these and countless other predictions met their fulfillment in the person, life, and teaching of Jesus Christ is to read the New Testament. The precise fulfillment of these predictions is surely sufficient evidence that the prophetic messages of the Bible are, indeed, divinely inspired, and that they merit the sober attention of intelligent men and women today.

## Human History As Seen by Bible Writers

To the inspired writers of the Bible, our planet is the great cosmic battleground on which the agelong conflict between the forces of good and evil is being waged, and they see all human history as the story of that conflict. According to the Book of Revelation, last book of the New Testament and counterpart to Daniel in the Old, that conflict began in heaven in the remote past when Lucifer, an exalted angel, defied God and led many of his fellow angels in open re-

volt.[7] The prophet Isaiah declares that Lucifer aspired
to usurp divine authority in the universe, apparently
with the intention of securing to himself the allegiance
of its myriad inhabitants.[8] John, author of the Book
of Revelation, relates that "war arose in heaven," but
that Lucifer and his rebel angels were defeated and
expelled. Following the creation of this world, as recorded in the Book of Genesis, our first ancestors cast
in their lot with this fallen archrebel, and as a result
the conflict was transferred to our little world.[9]

But God did not abandon the human race to its
fate. Instead, He set in operation a plan to thwart
Satan's devices by demonstrating, within human history, that the divine government is based on principles of love and justice, and that the happiness and
well-being of all can be secured only through voluntary cooperation with these principles.[10] The Creator
originally endowed His creatures with the capacity to
choose between good and evil, and provided them with
sufficient information on which to base an intelligent
choice.[11]

God's ultimate objective has ever been to make the
entire universe, including our fallen world, a place
where righteousness, justice, peace, and harmony prevail, and where each individual can attain to the high
destiny intended for him by his Creator. This goal
can be achieved, however, only when all created beings understand and appreciate His infinite wisdom
and goodness, and individually choose to cooperate
with His plan for their lives because they realize that
His way is best. To the Bible writers the individual
lives of all who have ever lived, and their collective

history as nations, are all part of this great demonstration of the relative merits of good and evil, of loyalty to God or to Satan.

## The Cross the Central Fact of History

The divine plan for the salvation of the world called for God's own Son to be "born in the likeness of men" and to live among them, as one of them. By His own perfect life He was to provide them with an example of how they ought to live. He would also reveal to them the infinite goodness of their heavenly Father and the wisdom of walking in His ways. Then, "being found in human form," the Apostle Paul continues, "he humbled himself and became obedient unto death, even death on a cross."[12] He died the death we deserve to die because of our sins, in order that we may receive the eternal life He came to impart; and to all who accept this gracious gift He accords the right to become "children of God."[13] His vicarious sacrifice proved that "the wages of sin is death," but that "the free gift of God is eternal life in Christ Jesus our Lord," and made provision that "whoever believes in him should not perish but have eternal life."[14]

Beyond any lingering doubt the cross proved Satan to be a liar and a murderer.[15] It vindicated God's justice in requiring obedience to the principles of heaven, and His mercy in granting forgiveness to all who are truly repentant. At the cross the arrogant pride of a created being who sought to usurp the Creator's rightful place as ruler of His own universe, came face to face with the infinite goodness of the Creator, who was willing to humble Himself and to die in order to restore to divine favor those who had rebelled and gone astray.

But that was not all. The Saviour triumphed over death, rose from the tomb, and a few days later ascended to the Father, where He now administers the divine merits of His vicarious sacrifice, and where all who come to Him in faith "may receive mercy and find grace to help in time of need."[16] When "this gospel of the kingdom" has been "preached throughout the world, as a testimony to all nations," then "the end will come," and "the kingdom of this world" will again "become the kingdom of our Lord," and "he shall reign for ever and ever."[17]

## The Setting of Daniel's Prophecies

The great conflict between good and evil is fought out to a conclusion on the battleground of each human heart. The issue is simple—a choice to do as we please, or to accept God as our Father, His Son as our Saviour, and the Holy Spirit as our guide and teacher. This same conflict between the principles of good and evil also goes on among the nations today, as it has since the dawn of human history. Anciently, when God was working out His plan for the salvation of the world through the Jewish nation, Satan's primary effort to thwart His beneficent purpose was naturally directed at the Jews as custodians of His revealed will and as His appointed representatives on earth.

In Christian times Satan has waged this same battle against the church, that is, against those in every land who choose in their hearts to be true and loyal to God, and against the church as His appointed agency for the salvation of the world. But, according to Daniel and other Bible writers, the crucial battle of this agelong conflict will come at "the time of the end," as Daniel calls it, just before the final and complete triumph of good over evil and the inauguration of God's eternal reign.[18] It is in this overall setting that the prophetic messages of the latter part of the Book of Daniel must be studied and understood.

## The Importance of Daniel's Message for Our Day

The prophecies of Daniel look forward to the time when "the God of heaven will set up a kingdom which shall never be destroyed," and which is destined to "break in pieces" all earthly kingdoms and "bring them to an end." Repeatedly Daniel uses such expressions as "the time of the end," "the latter end," and "the latter days," with the clear import that the events foretold reach down to, and climax in, the transition from this age to the age to come.[19] Obviously, these solemn events are yet future, and as we shall see, not far in the future. It is therefore of supreme importance in our day to know what God has revealed about these momentous events, in order to be prepared for them and to meet our Lord in peace.

The messages of Daniel and the Revelation, in particular, were designed to enable us to understand the climactic events soon to take place, in order that we may stand firm and remain loyal to the Captain of our salvation, and lest we be surprised and discouraged by the severe trials through which we must pass, and surrender our faith. The presence of Daniel's cryptic

messages in the Bible is sufficient evidence that God
intended them to be understood. God would not capri-
ciously reveal something to us that we are incapable
of understanding.

Let us diligently heed the light God has given to
illumine the pathway by which we must journey from
this world to the next.

## NOTES

1. The Hebrew word for *prophet, nabi'*, probably means
"one who proclaims a message." The Greek word *prophētēs*,
from which our English word *prophet* comes, means "one
who speaks for [someone else]."

2. 2 Peter 1:19.

3. Two great libraries containing more than 10,000 numbered clay tablets were unearthed at ancient Nineveh. One
of these tablets contains the Babylonian story of creation
and another tells about the Flood. Another great library
consisting of 16,000 clay tablets was found at Khattushash,
the ancient Hittite capital.

4. James T. Shotwell, *An Introduction to the History of
History,* p. 80; W. F. Albright, *The Archaeology of Pales-
tine and the Bible,* pp. 124-127; "The Bible After Twenty
Years of Archaeology," in *Religion in Life,* Vol. 21, Au-
tumn, 1952, p. 550; "The Biblical Period," *The Jews; Their
History, Culture and Religion,* p. 3.

5. Every essential fact about the life and ministry of
Christ, as the Messiah of the Old Testament, was foretold
centuries in advance. The remarkable fulfillment of these
prophecies provides one of the strongest evidences that
Jesus of Nazareth was indeed the promised Messiah. See
Luke 24:27, 44.

6. On Jesus' deity and humanity, see Isaiah 7:14 and 9:6,
7; on His lineal descent, Genesis 49:10 and Isaiah 11:1; on
Bethlehem as His birthplace, Micah 5:2; on the time of His
ministry, Daniel 9:24-27; on the place of His ministry,
Isaiah 9:1, 2 and Zechariah 9:9; on the nature of His minis-

try, Isaiah 61:1-3; on His substitutionary death, Isaiah 53:4-6; on His triumph over death, Isaiah 53:11; on His intercessory ministry, Isaiah 53:12.

7. Revelation 12:5, 7-9.

8. Isaiah 14:12-14.

9. See Genesis 3.

10. See Isaiah 1:17-20.

11. That our first parents had the capacity to choose between good and evil is evident from the story of the Fall, as recorded in Genesis 3. Again and again the Bible writers declare that God has revealed His will to men, thereby giving them all the information necessary on which to base an intelligent choice. See Deuteronomy 30:19; Joshua 24:15; 2 Timothy 3:16, 17; etc.

12. Philippians 2:6-8; Hebrews 2:14-17; see John 3:1-17.

13. John 3:16; compare 1:12.

14. Romans 6:23; John 3:16.

15. The Jewish leaders introduced false witnesses into the trial of Jesus in the hope of condemning Him. (Matthew 26:59-66.) Jesus declared the devil to be "a liar and the father of lies," and said that he was "a murderer from the beginning." John 8:44.

16. Hebrews 4:16.

17. Matthew 24:14; Revelation 11:15.

18. Daniel 7:21, 22; 12:1; Revelation 12:17; 13:11-18.

19. Daniel 8:17, 19, 26; 10:14; 12:4, 6, 13.

# *Panorama of Prophecy*

T HE FOUR VISIONS Daniel records in the last
six chapters of his book trace the future from
his day forward to the end of time and the
inauguration of God's eternal reign of righteousness,
with emphasis on the great climactic events destined
to take place in what Daniel calls "the time of the
end." Each of the visions presents the subject from a
slightly different point of view. Daniel names Gabriel
as his angel attendant while in vision. In the first two
visions Gabriel presents this information in the form
of an animated motion picture, with symbolic animals
acting out the roles of nations on the stage of history,
and then explains to Daniel the meaning of what he
has seen. The third and fourth visions constitute a
further, literal explanation of the subject.

## A Bird's-eye Preview of the Four Visions

Let us begin with a brief bird's-eye preview of each
of the four prophetic narratives. The first vision is
recorded in Daniel 7. Here Daniel tells of seeing four
beasts emerge, one after another, from the waters of
the great sea. The first resembled a lion with eagle's
wings, the second was a bear, the third a leopard with
four wings and four heads, and the fourth a nonde-

script creature even more terrifying than its predecessors. The latter had ten horns, among which Daniel saw another rise up, replacing three of them.

The angel explained that the four beasts represented four great kingdoms that were to arise, one after another, on the stage of history. The ten horns on the fourth beast stood for the fragments into which the fourth kingdom would eventually break up, and the horn that came up last represented a persecuting power that was to wage war to the death against God's people on earth. Eventually, however, "the Ancient of Days" would sit in judgment on this persecuting tyrant, annihilate him, and assign universal and eternal dominion to His own loyal people.

In the second vision, recorded in Daniel 8, the prophet was shown another animated motion picture, in which a two-horned ram came charging out of the east in all directions and overcame all opposition. Then he saw a he-goat flying at fearful speed out of the west attack the ram and utterly defeat him. Like the legendary unicorn, this goat had a prominent horn between its eyes. Soon after its victory over the ram the great horn was broken, and in its place four other horns grew out toward the four points of the compass. Out of one of the four sprouted still another horn, one that, in time, "grew exceedingly great."

The angel specifically identified the ram as representing Persia, the he-goat as Greece, the conspicuous horn as the "first king" of Greece, the four horns that replaced it as his successors, and the little horn as the persecuting tyrant.[1] In the figurative language of the prophecy, this "horn" was to invade "the glorious land," subdue "the host of heaven," and overthrow the "sanctuary" and ban its ritual service for 2300 "evenings and mornings." Then deliverance would come.

By the time of the third vision the close of the seventy years of exile in Babylon foretold by the prophet Jeremiah was at hand, and Daniel was praying earnestly for the release of his people. One day while he was praying thus, Gabriel came to assure him that the expected decree for the return of the Jews to their homeland and for the rebuilding of Jerusalem and the Temple would soon be issued. But, the angel explained, in the distant future the great persecuting power already mentioned in the two preceding visions would again level the city and its sanctuary, which was then to remain desolate until God intervened and destroyed the tyrant. This prayer and the third vision are recorded in the ninth chapter of Daniel.

Two years later, Gabriel appeared to Daniel for the fourth and last time. On this occasion he gave a lengthy and detailed narrative of events that would transpire between his day and the close of time. After mentioning Persia and Greece briefly, the angel introduced two warring powers he called "the king of the north" and "the king of the south." He then traced the process by which the former eventually triumphs over the latter and proceeds to crush God's people, to obliterate their religion, and to establish his own apostate form of worship. "At the time of the end," however, God delivers His people and establishes His eternal kingdom. Chapters 10 to 12 record this vision, with chapter 10 standing as an introduction and the latter part of chapter 12 as a postlude to it.

Let us now examine each of these visions in more detail, down to the rise of the persecuting tyrant and the period of severe persecution.

## The Vision of Chapter 7

"I saw in my vision by night," relates Daniel, "and behold, the four winds of heaven were stirring up the great sea. And four beasts came up out of the sea, different from one another. The first was like a lion and had eagle's wings. Then as I looked its wings were plucked off, and it was lifted up from the ground and made to stand upon two feet like a man; and the mind of a man was given to it."

The lion was followed by "another beast, a second one, like a bear. It was raised up on one side; it had three ribs in its mouth between its teeth; and it was told, 'Arise, devour much flesh.'" Third in line came "a leopard, with four wings" and "four heads; and dominion was given to it." Then "a fourth beast" emerged, "terrible and dreadful and exceedingly strong; and it had great iron teeth" and "claws of bronze." It "devoured and broke in pieces, and stamped the residue with its feet. It was different from all the beasts that were before it; and it had ten horns."

Four great beasts of prey: a lion with eagle's wings that learned to stand on its feet like a man, a bear in whose mouth were three ribs, a four-winged leopard, and a nondescript beast with iron teeth, bronze claws, and ten horns! Our first reaction may be that all this sounds more like a nightmare than an intelligible revelation of truth from heaven, and that it conceals more than it reveals. If this is, indeed, an important communication from heaven, why did God conceal its message in cryptic symbols such as these?

## Why Symbols Are Used in Bible Prophecy

In the first place, symbolic prophecy is like an animated cartoon. Now, a cartoon is a most effective method by which to convey certain kinds of information—a political problem or a humorous social situation, for instance—far more quickly and effectively than would be possible in mere words. It commands immediate attention, it is interesting, it is easy to understand, and it makes a vivid and lasting impression. Symbolic prophecy thus constitutes a most effective method for revealing truth. Modern cartoonists use animals in much the same way as did the angel of prophecy. For instance, in cartoon language a bald eagle represents the United States, a lion stands for England, a dragon for China, a bear for Russia, a rooster for France, and so on. Cartoonists usually picture these animals acting out contemporary events or policies the cartoonist attributes to the governments thus represented.

Strange to say, however, symbolic prophecy at the same time effectively conceals information from those for whom it is *not* intended, those who might use the information in an attempt to thwart God's purposes. From this point of view symbolic prophecy is like coded messages a government uses to communicate with its diplomatic and military representatives, yet at the same time conceal it from all for whom it is not intended. Daniel's visions may thus be thought of as a set of secret instructions from God to His army on earth, the church. In fact, the angel Gabriel specifically told Daniel, "None of the wicked shall understand; but those who are wise shall understand."[2]

## The Symbols of Daniel 7 Explained

In his explanation the angel told Daniel the meaning of each symbol. "These four great beasts," he said, "are four kings who shall arise out of the earth. . . . As for the fourth beast, there shall be a fourth kingdom on earth, which shall be different from all the kingdoms, and it shall devour the whole earth, and trample it down, and break it to pieces. As for the ten horns, out of this kingdom ten kings shall arise." The terms *king* and *kingdom* are here used synonymously, as a comparison of verse 17 with verse 23 makes evident. In fact, several ancient translations of the Bible read "kingdoms" instead of "kings."

Daniel saw these four beasts emerging, one after another, from the sea, the waves of which were being whipped up by turbulent winds. According to Revelation 17:15, the waters of the sea symbolize "peoples and multitudes and nations and tongues," and doubtless the same is intended here. The symbol is appropriate, for the roar of ocean waves breaking on the shore resembles the confused noise of a large throng of people all talking at once. The winds stirring up the ocean waves are a fit symbol of the political and military strife that usually accompany the rise and fall of earthly kingdoms. In the Bible, wind is often used figuratively of such strife and commotion.[3] "Four winds" would be wind from every point of the compass, and thus general strife and confusion.

A brief review of the high points of the dream of Daniel 2, which we have already considered, helps to clarify the vision of chapter 7. Despite the two completely different sets of symbols, a point-by-point comparison of the two makes their identity of subject matter and scope unmistakable. There is general agreement among Bible scholars that the two visions cover the same events and span of history, from Daniel's day forward to the end of time and the inauguration of God's eternal kingdom. To show this relationship, let us list the symbols of Daniel 2 and those of chapter 7 side by side:

## The Visions of Daniel 2 and 7 Compared

### The Great Metallic Image of Daniel 2

1. The head of GOLD, identified by Daniel as Babylonia. Verses 32, 37, 38.[4]

2. The breast and arms of SILVER, identified by Daniel as Babylonia's successor —Persia. Verses 32, 39.

3. The belly and thighs of BRONZE, identified by Daniel as "a third kingdom" that would "rule over all the earth"—Greece. Verses 32, 39.

4. The legs of IRON, identified by Daniel as "a fourth kingdom, strong as

### The Great Beasts of Daniel 7

1. A LION, identified by the angel as the first of four great kingdoms. Verses 4, 17.

2. A BEAR, identified by the angel as the second of four great kingdoms. Verses 5, 17.

3. A LEOPARD, identified by the angel as the third of four great kingdoms. Verses 6, 17.

4. A TERRIBLE BEAST, exceedingly strong and having great iron teeth; identi-

iron," one that would crush all competitors—Rome. Verses 33, 40.

fied by the angel as a fourth kingdom that would "devour the whole earth." Verses 7, 17, 19, 23.

5. The feet and ten toes of mingled IRON AND CLAY, identified by Daniel as successors to the fourth kingdom, or the fourth kingdom in a divided state—the nations of western Europe since the fall of Rome. Verses 33, 41-43.

5. THE TEN HORNS, Identified by the angel as "ten kings," or "kingdoms," that would arise out of the fourth great kingdom. Verses 7, 20, 24.

6. "A STONE . . . cut out by no human hand" demolishes and obliterates the image, identified by Daniel as an act of God that would "break in pieces all these kingdoms and bring them to an end." Verses 34, 35, 44, 45.

6. THE ANCIENT OF DAYS sits in judgment over the fourth, ten-horned beast and destroys it. Verses 9-11, 26.

7. The stone becomes a "GREAT MOUNTAIN" that fills the whole earth, identified by Daniel as the universal, eternal kingdom ultimately to be established by God. Verses 35, 44.

7. Sitting in judgment, the Ancient of Days awards universal and everlasting DOMINION to the "son of man" and to "the saints of the Most High." Verses 13, 14, 18, 22, 27.

## The Babylonian Lion

The lion was an appropriate symbol for ancient Babylon. In fact, as archeologists have found, the lion was its favorite decorative symbol. Furthermore, Babylonian art often combined the king of beasts and the king of birds into a composite creature, usually a lion with eagle's wings, and sometimes an eagle's claws and beak as well. A lion is noted for its strength and an eagle for its powerful wings and swift flight, a fit allusion, here, to Nebuchadnezzar's brilliant conquests. Various Bible writers refer to him as a "lion."[5]

Daniel then saw this lion with its wings plucked. This is an apt description of Babylonia in its weakened condition after the death of Nebuchadnezzar. He also saw it "lifted up from the ground and made to stand upon two feet like a man" and given a man's "mind," or "heart," as the Aramaic reads literally. When we call a man lionhearted, we ascribe to him unusual boldness and courage. Conversely, a man-hearted lion would be timid and cowardly. In its enfeebled state Babylonia proved to be no match for the armies of Persia under Cyrus. The lion's wings had been clipped; it could no longer fly upon its prey.

## The Persian Bear

The second beast, the bear, stood for Persia, which followed Babylonia. Daniel saw it "raised up on one side." This unusual posture is doubtless a reminder of the historical fact that the Persian Empire was, in truth, a union of Media and Persia, though by the time Babylonia fell to Persian arms, Persian influence had become dominant and that of Media gradually vanished. Daniel also saw "three ribs in its mouth between its teeth," which spurred it on to "devour much flesh." It has been suggested, appropriately, that these three ribs represent conquered countries such as Babylonia, Lydia, and Egypt.

Each new victory naturally spurred the Persians on to ever greater conquests, until eventually their empire extended from central Asia to Egypt and from India into Europe—3,300 miles from east to west and 1,500 from north to south. It is less than 2,500 air miles from New York to San Francisco. Persia certainly did "devour much flesh," far more than any nation that was before it.

## The Greek Leopard

As the bronze of the metallic image of Daniel 2 followed the silver, so the leopard of chapter 7 follows the bear. Daniel identifies Greece as the nation that followed Persia,[6] not Greece of the classical period, which was contemporary with Persia, but of the time of Alexander the Great and after. Alexander decisively defeated the Persians at the Battle of Issus in Asia Minor and again near Arbela, in upper Mesopotamia. During the next few years his splendid Macedonian phalanxes marched over much of the heartland of Asia and even down into India. The leopard itself is a swift beast, but the lightning speed and unprecedented extent of Alexander's conquests called for the addition of four wings to the symbol to make it complete. His rapid and successful campaigns are unique in ancient history.

No sooner, however, had Alexander settled down at Babylon, which he made his capital, than he died, in the prime of life, from "swamp fever"—probably malaria—following a drunken debauch in 323 B.C. He conquered the world but failed to subdue himself. For the next two decades his generals sparred for control of his far-flung dominions, but not a man among them proved strong enough to weld the parts together again. The Battle of Ipsus in 301 B.C. reduced the number of competitors to four: Cassander in Greece and Macedonia, Lysimachus in Thrace and Asia Minor, Seleucus in Syria and Mesopotamia, and Ptolemy in Egypt and Palestine. Twenty years later, with the elimination of Lysimachus, the number was reduced to three. Eventually, Seleucus gained control of the region on the north of Palestine, and Ptolemy all on the south of it.

Despite Alexander's premature death, his ambitious plan to unite the diverse peoples of the ancient world by Greek language, thought, and civilization became a reality for the next two centuries, which are known in history as the Hellenistic era.[7] Even today, after the passing of two millenniums, the language, literature, art, architecture, philosophy, and culture of the ancient Greeks still permeate Western civilization with grace, charm, and beauty. Our own orators, poets, sculptors, and philosophers are heavily in debt to their Greek counterparts of the long ago. Political unity there was not, but cultural unity prevailed, and Greek became the principal language of the ancient world.

## The Fearful Fourth Beast—Rome

In the metallic image of Daniel 2 the iron followed the bronze. Here in Daniel 7 "a fourth beast, terrible and dreadful and exceedingly strong," follows the leopard. As every schoolboy knows, the next great world empire after the Greek era was Rome. Daniel's description of this fourth beast is singularly appropriate to ancient Rome. "It had great iron teeth," he relates—reminiscent of the iron in the metallic image of Daniel 2. Daniel 2 also made special mention of the fact that as iron "breaks to pieces," "shatters," and "crushes" all things, so this fourth world power was to "break and crush" all others.

The fourth beast of Daniel 7 similarly had "teeth of iron and claws of bronze" with which it "devoured and broke in pieces," and then stamped "the residue with its feet." A more fitting figurative description of the invincible Roman legions marching to and fro over Europe and the Mediterranean world could hardly be imagined. No other nation of antiquity so appropriately matches the description here given.

The transition from Greece to Rome was gradual. The first part of Alexander's former dominions to be absorbed by the Romans was Macedonia, his homeland. At the Battle of Pydna in 168 B.C. Rome terminated the Macedonian monarchy and annexed it outright twenty-two years later. The Greek historian Polybius, who was an eyewitness of the battle, and the Roman historian Livy both date the end of Alexander's empire with this battle,[8] which made Rome sovereign in the eastern Mediterranean. The conquest of Macedonia, Alexander's homeland, by the Romans, and the end of the Macedonian kingdom in 168 B.C. make that year as appropriate as any for dating the transfer of sovereignty from Greece to Rome. The fall of Syria in 63 B.C. and Egypt in 30 B.C. completed the transfer.

## The Kingdoms That Replaced Rome

As the iron legs of Daniel 2 blended into the two feet and ten toes of the image, so the sovereignty of the fourth beast of chapter 7 passes to the ten horns, which Daniel identifies as ten kingdoms. To the Hebrews, originally a pastoral people, horns became symbols of strength and power, and thus of nations as instruments of power.[9]

Daniel numbers the four great beasts consecutively, in the order of their appearance on the prophetic stage. He states specifically that the third beast arose "after" the second, and the fourth "after" the third.[10] In contrast with the four great empires, which are consecutive, the ten successor kingdoms to the fourth world empire are subdivisions of that kingdom, which the vision thinks of as continuing to exist along with them and in them, and the ten are clearly contemporary with one another. Of the four beasts, Daniel envisions only the fourth as still in existence, at least in a sense, at the time of the great final judgment.

History records that the Roman Empire was invaded and partitioned by some twenty Germanic tribes that pressed irresistibly down from the north and became the founders of the great nations of modern Europe. This process of fragmentation took nearly two centuries, from about A.D. 378 to 554. Whether the ten toes of the image and the ten horns of the fourth beast represent ten particular tribes, or whether ten is here simply a round number denoting all the fragments of the ancient Roman Empire, is not certain nor does it matter.[11] Among these, the Ostrogoths, Visigoths, Franks, Vandals, Suevi, Alemanni, Anglo-Saxons, Heruli, Lombards, and Burgundians were the more important and are best known today. Some include the Huns, a horde of invaders from the steppes of central Asia that ravaged Europe for a time.

The remainder of Daniel 7 deals with the persecution of God's people and their eventual deliverance from all oppression. These two aspects of the vision are to be considered in the following chapter. We turn now to Daniel 8.

## The Vision of Chapter 8

In this vision Daniel saw a ram with two long horns, of which "one was higher than the other, and the higher one came up last." He then saw the ram charging off in all directions, "westward and northward and southward." No other beast was able to "stand before him, and there was no one who could rescue from his power." After this had been going on for a time, Daniel saw "a he-goat" that "had a conspicuous horn between his eyes" coming "from the west across the face of the whole earth, without touching the ground." Approaching the ram, the goat "ran at him in his mighty wrath . . . and struck the ram and broke his two horns; and the ram had no power to stand before him, but he cast him down to the ground and trampled upon him; and there was no one who could rescue the ram from his power." Therewith the ram disappeared from the scene. When the he-goat became strong, his "great horn was broken, and instead of it there came up four conspicuous horns toward the four winds of heaven."

In explaining the vision to Daniel the angel Gabriel told him that the ram with its two horns represented "Media and Persia," and the he-goat Greece. The Medes were stronger at first, but Persia eventually became the dominant force within the empire, which is more commonly known simply as Persia. The directions in which the ram charged—north, west, and south—are the very directions Persian conquests took, their main thrust being generally westward.

Then came the Greeks under Alexander the Great, the "conspicuous horn" Gabriel specifically declared to be their "first king." Daniel saw the great horn "broken" almost as soon as the goat became "strong," and it is a simple fact of history that Alexander died soon after his conquests were completed. Like the four heads of the leopard beast of Daniel 7, the four horns which then arose toward the four points of the compass represent the divisions of Alexander's empire.

## Visions of Daniel 7 and 8 Compared

| The Great Beasts of Daniel 7 | The Great Beasts of Daniel 8 |
| --- | --- |
| 1. A BEAR. Verses 5, 17. | 1. A RAM specifically identified by the angel as Persia. Verses 3, 4, 20. |
| 2. A LEOPARD. Verses 6, 17. | 2. A HE-GOAT, specifically identified by the angel as Greece. Verses 5-8, 21. |
| 3. The leopard's FOUR HEADS. Verse 6. | 3. The he-goat's FOUR HORNS, specifically identified by the angel as the divisions of the Greek empire. Verses 8, 22. |

Babylonia is conspicuously absent from the vision of Daniel 8, probably because the Babylonian Empire was soon to disappear from the stage of history. Although the symbols of chapter 8 are altogether different from those of chapter 7, the correspondence between the two is so close as to leave no doubt that the ram and he-goat of the one are the counterparts of the bear and leopard in the other. In chapter 7, for instance, the bear was "raised up on one side," whereas in chapter 8 the higher of the two horns on the ram came up last. Also, the four heads of the leopard correspond exactly with the four horns of the he-goat. The fulfillment of these symbols in history is too close to require further extended comment here. We will consider the remainder of the vision, dealing with the great future period of tribulation, in our next chapter.

There is no clear counterpart in Daniel 8 for the fourth, fearful beast of Daniel 7. It seems that the "little horn" of chapter 8 plays the combined roles of both the fourth beast and the little horn of chapter 7.[12] Inasmuch as the vision of chapter 9 deals almost exclusively with what was, in Daniel's time, a future persecution of God's people, none of the four universal empires being mentioned, discussion of that vision will also be reserved for our next chapter.

## The Vision of Daniel 10 to 12

By the time of this vision Persia had fallen heir to Babylonia and had become the dominant power in world affairs. This vision is not symbolic like those of chapters 2, 7, and 8, but a detailed, literal narration of the historical events to which it looks forward. At first the language seems ambiguous and confusing, but to a large extent careful study makes reasonably clear what was intended. An analysis of most of the details there foretold would become a tiresome recital of the names of ancient kings and of their fortunes and misfortunes in battle. Here we shall be concerned only with highlights of the prophecy, particularly those that correspond with Daniel's other visions.

The same two world powers that figure so prominently in Daniel 8 appear again in Daniel 11. Persia and Greece are specifically named in both.[13] As the Greek goat attacked and subdued the Persian ram of chapter 7, so in Daniel 11 a king yet to reign in Persia would "stir up all against the kingdom of Greece." This proved to be Xerxes, the Ahasuerus of the Book of Esther, whose forces were roundly defeated by the Greeks at Salamis and Plataea.

"Then a mighty king shall arise, who shall rule with great dominion and do according to his will"—obviously, again, Alexander the Great—"and when he has arisen, his kingdom shall be broken and divided toward the four winds of heaven." This corresponds exactly with the fate of the "conspicuous horn" between the eyes of the he-goat of chapter 8, which "was broken" almost as soon as the latter became "strong," and the role of the "four conspicuous horns" that came up in its place "toward the four winds of heaven."

From this point on, the vision of Daniel 11 focuses on the two principal kingdoms that emerged from Alexander's short-lived empire: the Seleucids, who ruled Syria on the north of Palestine, with parts of Asia Minor and Mesopotamia; and the Ptolemies, who ruled Egypt and, at first, Palestine. Both reigning houses were of Greek descent, and Greek culture prevailed. Daniel calls the successive rulers of these two kingdoms, collectively, the "king of the north" and the "king of the south." Ancient Arabian inscriptions refer to them as "Lord of the North" and "Lord of the South."[14] Instead of "king of the south," the original Greek translation of Daniel, made about 165 B.C., reads "king of Egypt."

## Visions of Daniel 8 and 11 Compared

| The Symbolic Vision of Daniel 8 | The Literal Explanation of Daniel 11 |
| --- | --- |
| 1. A ram specifically identified as representing Media and PERSIA. | 1. PERSIA specified by name. Verse 2. |
| 2. A he-goat specifically identified as representing GREECE. | 2. GREECE specified by name. Verse 2. |
| 3. A conspicuous horn identified as "the first king." Verses 5, 8, 21. | 3. "A mighty king"—Alexander the Great. Verse 3. |
| 4. "FOUR conspicuous HORNS toward the four winds of heaven," identified as "four kingdoms" to emerge from the first king's "nation." Verses 8, 22. | 4. The mighty king's kingdom "broken and divided toward the FOUR WINDS of heaven"—the divisions of Alexander's empire. Verse 4. |

The exact correspondence between the parts of the two visions here considered is so close as to require no further discussion. Persia and Greece thus figure in four of Daniel's visions, those recorded in chapters 2, 7, 8, and 10-12. This conclusively establishes the fact that the four visions are basically parallel in nature and should be studied together. Each provides details not furnished by the others and which are needed to complete the picture. Further points of correspondence will be considered in our next chapter, where the vision of chapter 9 will be found to parallel the others.

Daniel's thumbnail sketch of the great empires of antiquity is, in reality, incidental to his main purpose

—a presentation of the great climactic events of history that precede the inauguration of God's universal, eternal reign of righteousness. The parallel nature of the several visions up to this point is conclusive evidence that the great future tribulation and triumph foretold are likewise the same throughout. To these dramatic events we now turn.

## NOTES

1. Daniel 8:20-24.

2. Daniel 12:10.

3. See, for instance, Jeremiah 25:32.

4. Verses following each statement are found in the chapter indicated at the head of each column.

5. Jeremiah 4:7; 50:17, 44; compare Ezekiel 17:3, 12; Habakkuk 1:8.

6. Daniel 8:20, 21; 11:2, 3.

7. The Greeks called themselves *Hellas*. The classical period of Greek history is known as the Hellenic Age. The term Hellenistic refers to the period between the death of Alexander the Great and the time when Rome became supreme in the eastern Mediterranean, when Greek influence was dominant.

8. Polybius, *Histories* xxix. 21; translated by W. R. Paton, Vol. 6, in *Loeb Classical Library*, pp. 77-79. *Livy* xlv. 9; translated by Alfred C. Schlesinger, Vol. 13, in *Loeb Classical Library*, pp. 271-273.

9. See 2 Samuel 22:3; Psalm 132:17; Jeremiah 48:25; Ezekiel 29:21; Micah 4:13; Zechariah 1:19, 21.

10. Daniel 7:6, 7.

11. See page 50.

12. Note the following: In chapter 8 Daniel expresses concern and perplexity only for what the little horn does. It alone persecutes his people. He shows no interest whatever in the ram, the he-goat, or its four horns, but he "was appalled" by what he saw the little horn do, and as a result "was overcome and lay sick for some days." On the other

hand, in chapter 7 his alarm covers the actions of the fourth beast as well as the little horn, but does not extend to any of the other beasts or horns. Apparently both were associated in the oppression referred to. Daniel 7:11, 12, 26.

A comparison of what is said concerning the little horn in chapter 7 with what is said about its counterpart in chapter 8 shows that the former stresses the tyrant's power, pride, arrogance, shrewdness, and deceptiveness, while the latter emphasizes the destructive acts this attitude leads to. The same fearful destruction attributed exclusively to the little horn in chapter 8 is attributed particularly to the fourth beast in chapter 7, but not to the little horn of that chapter. In chapter 7 the little horn defies God and plots to annihilate His loyal subjects on earth, but it is the fourth beast with its great iron teeth and bronze claws that carries out the evil plot. The two are partners in crime. No such relationship exists between the little horn of chapter 8 and its predecessor, the he-goat. In fact, the he-goat disappears from the vision before the little horn rises, and it is not so much as mentioned again.

The fourth beast and the little horn of chapter 7 continue to exist together to the very close of time, for they are judged and destroyed together when the Ancient of Days sits in judgment. In contrast, the other beasts have long since passed from the stage of action. They were not slain, destroyed, or burned with fire by the decree of the Ancient of Days, but simply lost their dominion to their successors and disappeared in the normal course of historical change. The fourth beast is punished "because of the sound of the great words which the horn was speaking." In chapter 7 the fourth beast and the little horn share responsibility before God for the persecution of the saints, while in chapter 8 the little horn alone stands forth as guilty. Like its counterpart, the leopardlike beast of chapter 7, the he-goat of chapter 8 disappears in the normal course of historical change. Neither is represented as persisting till the close of time.

13. Daniel 8:20, 21; 11:2.
14. Glaser No. 1155.

# Under the Tyrant's Heel

IN AWE and wonder Daniel watched the symbolic beasts come and go across the prophetic stage. Before his astonished gaze the history of coming centuries to the close of time was compressed into a few dramatic moments, something like a time-lapse motion picture of a rosebud bursting into bloom and then withering away, all in a matter of seconds. Who among the leaders of earth would not give a king's ransom to know what the future holds in store? How we all would like to know, for that matter! The fact is that, with the right key to the cryptic visions in which God unveiled the future to Daniel, we can know.

## A Time to Try Men's Souls

More than anything else, Daniel longed for the time when God's eternal, righteous reign would be established on earth, when injustice, oppression, and the inhumanity of man toward his fellowmen would forever be at an end. But the angel who attended Daniel in vision told him that those who love God and purpose to be loyal to Him must expect to pass through a time of the most severe trial, suffering, and persecution before that glorious age of universal and everlasting justice and peace should dawn.

Of everything the angel Gabriel presented to him, it was this fearful prospect that absorbed the prophet's attention and interest. As a matter of fact, two thirds of all he was shown and told in vision had to do with that dark era of adversity, and deliverance from it. These dramatic events stand out as the central theme of the last six chapters of his book. The information given concerning the great empires of antiquity is actually more or less incidental and seems to have been intended primarily to help locate these other events in the stream of time.

Although the angel explained that the era of deep distress was still in the remote future, far beyond his own day, Daniel felt the utmost personal concern about it and kept praying earnestly for further information on the subject. The more complete and detailed picture the angel presented to him, in successive installments, appalled him beyond words. In his prolonged anxiety for more exact information, and especially in his mounting stress of soul upon being shown more of what the future held in store, we have a vivid reflection of the grave nature of the crisis that lay ahead. Let Daniel tell us in his own words how he felt about it.

## Daniel's Anxiety for the Future

Following the first vision, that of chapter 7, he wrote, "My spirit within me was anxious. . . . My thoughts greatly alarmed me, and my color changed; but I kept the matter in my mind." The fearful prospect haunted him day and night. The second vision, recorded in chapter 8, proved to be more, at his ad-

vanced age, than the prophet could well bear, and
again he wrote, "I was appalled by the vision and did
not understand it," and "was overcome and lay sick
for some days." Even after the third vision, which he
recounts in chapter 9, he was still perplexed and later
devoted three weeks to "mourning" over the problem,
to fasting, praying, and humbling himself before God.

Finally, just before the last vision, which is the subject of chapters 10 to 12, Gabriel strengthened the
aged prophet to endure the final installment of the
inspired preview of the fearful ordeal. Daniel relates
that at last he "had understanding of the vision," except for certain minor details which the angel told him
to leave in God's hands "until the time of the end,"
when knowledge concerning these things would increase and when "those who are wise" would "understand" everything.[1]

The prophet's eager anxiety for the success of God's
plan to rescue the human race from the clutches of
Satan, as if this were a matter of supreme concern to
him personally, testifies to his own ardent, soul-con-
suming commitment to God. Little wonder that Gabriel upon his final visit twice reassured Daniel that
he was a "man greatly beloved."[2] How the heart of
God must have thrilled that someone on earth should
be so profoundly concerned about matters that were
uppermost in His own great heart of infinite love!
Would that we, in our day, might feel equal solicitude
for the well-being of the church and the advancement
of the gospel in all the world!

Daniel's absorbing anxiety over the supreme crisis
that lay ahead also suggests that all who purpose in

their hearts to be loyal to God may well give earnest heed, as the prophet did, to the things that were revealed to him. The complicated play of human events is still under divine control, and amid the strife and tumult of earth an unseen hand still guides the affairs of men. The increasingly degenerate state of society and bitter rivalry among the nations alike testify that we are standing today on the threshhold of great and solemn events, that the world is on the verge of a stupendous crisis, that something great and decisive is about to take place. Through the inspired preview of the future revealed to Daniel in the long ago, God speaks imperatively to us in the space age. Here, if they will but listen, sincere seekers for truth will find counsel, guidance, and inspiration to help them stand firm through the climactic events that loom just ahead.

At the time of the end, promised the angel, "those who are wise shall understand."[3] According to the sure word of prophecy, as we shall see, that time has now fully come;[4] and today it is our privilege, by the illumination of the Holy Spirit, to understand these things even more perfectly in some respects, perhaps, than Daniel did. By God's grace, let us purpose to be counted among those whom Heaven will one day acclaim as "wise."

## The Tyrant's Ruthless Attack

In vision the angel repeatedly speaks of God's loyal people as "the saints of the Most High" and "the holy people."[5] They are "holy," or "saints," not in the sense of being sinless, but of being dedicated in heart, mind, and life to God. Also, they are His chosen representatives on earth. By a picturesque metaphor the angel also calls them "the host of heaven" and "the host of the stars." Happy thought! Like the stars of a bright winter sky on a moonless night, God's loyal people were to shine amid the darkness of the long period of persecution and suffering. Then, finally, they will shine forth in His kingdom "like the stars for ever and ever."[6]

As Daniel watched, a great persecuting tyrant "made war with the saints," "prevailed over them," and wore them out. He "cast [them] down to the ground, and trampled upon them" in a determined attempt to "shatter" and "destroy" them. The focal point of his savage attack on the saints was to be their loyalty to God and to His revealed will. In that future time of trouble, affliction, distress, and anguish such as the world had never seen, it appeared that they would "be utterly swept away before him and broken."[7] The Valley Forge of their experience, this ordeal would "refine," "cleanse," and "purify" them.[8]

## An Attempt to Eradicate True Religion

Not content to wage war on men like himself, this arrogant impostor would even presume to attack deity. "He shall even rise up against the Prince of princes," said the angel, that is, against Christ.[9] "He shall exalt himself and magnify himself above every god, and shall speak astonishing things against the God of gods."[10] He would defy God and boast of his own vaunted greatness.

How would this cruel tyrant go about defying God? The angel declared that his heart would "be set against the holy covenant" between God and His loyal people, and that he would "be enraged and take action against" it.[11] In pursuit of this policy he would "think to change the times and the law," that is, the sacred religious observances appointed by God and the divine revelation that has come from God, the Holy Scriptures.[12] He would not actually be able to make such changes, of course, since no human being can alter the divine precepts, but he would endeavor to do so. He would enact religious precepts and requirements of his own and attempt to force men to comply with them instead of with those ordained by God.[13] He would thus effectively "cast down to the ground"[14] the "truth" as set forth in the Holy Scriptures.

Daniel also saw God's sanctuary "overthrown," made "desolate," and given over to this archenemy, who was to "profane" and "destroy" it.[15] The sanctuary, or Temple, in ancient Jerusalem was the hub of Jewish religious life. But that structure was completely destroyed in A.D. 70, and its services permanently discontinued. They have never been resumed. As we shall see, however, the New Testament writers speak of a "sanctuary" in heaven where Christ now ministers as our great High Priest, and specifically declare that it replaced the earthly sanctuary when He died on the cross and rose again.[16] It is evidently to this great heavenly "sanctuary" that the words of the prophet now apply.

In this process of desecration, the angel told Daniel, the tyrant would "take away the continual burnt offering."[17] The "continual burnt offering" of the an-

6

cient sanctuary was presented twice daily, at the prescribed hours of prayer in the early morning and late afternoon. These two daily sacrifices and the ritual associated with them constituted the very heart and center of the ancient sanctuary service. They represented God's continual provision for the salvation of His people, who, by participating in worship at these stated times, reaffirmed their acceptance of salvation and devotion to the true God. To "take away the continual burnt offering" would be to disrupt and terminate the entire Temple service, and thus, in effect, to abolish the worship of the true God.

## A Time of Great Apostasy

But the great impostor would not be content to proscribe true worship, the angel went on to say. He would also prescribe and enforce a false system of his own. Daniel calls this apostate form of worship "the transgression that makes desolate," or "the abomination that makes desolate."[18] The inauguration of this apostate form of worship would make the sanctuary in heaven "desolate," inasmuch as it would deprive men of the merits of Christ's atonement and compel them to accept a counterfeit way of salvation.

Apparently the impostor would succeed in persuading many to "forsake" and to "violate" the holy covenant, that is, to desert the faith of their fathers. The angel called those who do so "men of violence" because they "violate the covenant," and "wicked" men who "do wickedly." They "acknowledge" the usurper, and he, on his part, honors them and rewards them handsomely for collaborating with him.[19]

In other words, the great persecution was to be accompanied by a great apostasy, when many would depart from the truth. But in that dark hour there would also be heroes of the faith, loyal men and women who would "stand firm and take action" to "turn many" who had apostatized, back "to righteousness." Those who thus courageously "stand firm" for the truth are called "wise" because they "understand" the divine purpose as revealed through the prophets, particularly Daniel, and because they remain loyal to God in the face of powerful inducements to disloyalty.[20]

How the persecuting tyrant, whose actual operations are limited to this earth, could possibly desecrate the great sanctuary in heaven above and hinder Christ's ministry there as our great High Priest is the subject of a future chapter.

## Who Is This Fearful Tyrant?

Who is this bold impostor who, in the name of religion, launches the most severe and relentless attack of all time against the true faith and against those who choose to remain loyal to it, come what may? The angel lists a number of clues by which we may identify him beyond the shadow of a doubt. In the first two visions he appears under the strange, cryptic symbol of "a little horn," which the angel interprets to mean a "king" or "kingdom."[21] In literal language, the third and fourth visions call him simply a "prince" or "king."[22]

To us, a horn is a strange symbol by which to represent a king or nation. But to Daniel and his fellow Jews, originally a pastoral people, it was both natural and appropriate that an animal's horns—its weapons of offense and defense—should come to symbolize strength and power, whether personal or national, and eventually nations themselves as instruments of power.[23]

The great tyrant was to appear on the stage of history after the rise and fall of the great empires of antiquity—Babylon, Persia, Greece, and Rome. As a "little horn" in the symbolism of Daniel 7, the tyrant is represented as rising up among the ten horns on the head of the fourth beast, which stand for the fragments into which the Roman Empire split up when it fell.[24] Prophecy thus clearly pinpoints the breakup of ancient Rome as the time when, and western Europe as the locality where, the cruel tyrant presented to Daniel would rise to power.[25]

## A Shrewd and Arrogant Despot

The angel went on to describe the persecuting tyrant as a shrewd and treacherous despot. For one thing, he said that the little horn would have "eyes like the eyes of a man."[26] A man with eyes characterized by the vacant stare of a dumb brute would look dull and stupid. Conversely, an animal, or a horn, with "eyes like the eyes of a man" would have an unusually intelligent or shrewd appearance. It is appropriate that the "eyes" of a symbolic horn representing a king should appear to be human.

The same characteristic is stressed in the further statement that the tyrant "understands riddles," and that he is "cunning," or clever. The angel added that he would "act deceitfully" and "seduce with flattery."[27]

The word translated *riddles* means "ambiguous say-
ings," that is, statements so cleverly phrased as to conceal their true meaning, or that may be interpreted to
mean any one of a number of different things. We
would call it double talk. The word translated *flattery*
means "slipperiness," or "falsehood." The tyrant would
thus be shrewd, subtle, and treacherous. He would
speak and act "deceitfully," pretending to be doing one
thing but actually doing something far different. The
angel told Daniel, further, that the persecuting tyrant
was to be "a contemptible person" with a "bold coun-
tenance." In attitude and conduct he would be haughty,
insolent, and fierce beyond words.[28]

Comparatively "little" to begin with, the tyrant
would eventually become "greater" and "stronger"
than his "fellows," that is, than the nations represented by the other ten horns. In fact, he would grow
"exceedingly great" and would "prosper" in his evil
plot to annihilate God's people. "He shall work his
will," the angel said, and "none shall stand before
him."[29] All who bar his way would be cut down without mercy. The tyrant was thus to dominate the political scene in western Europe following the downfall of
the Roman Empire.

## How Long Under the Oppressor's Heel?

One important question remains: How long would
God permit this despot to "work his will" against true
religion and against His loyal subjects on earth? As
we have seen, the tyrant was to appear on the stage of
history during the breakup of the Roman Empire. According to the eighth and eleventh chapters of Daniel,

the climax of his reign of terror would come "in the latter days," at "the time of the end."[30] In Daniel the term "latter days" refers to the remote or distant future, and "the time of the end" to a relatively brief period immediately preceding the close of the present age. This "time of the end" was to be marked by climactic events destined to prepare the world for the inauguration of God's eternal reign of righteousness. Between the fall of Rome and "the time of the end," then, the tyrant was to appear on the stage of history and carry out his sinister plot against the truth and those who remain loyal to it.

The length of time during which the tyrant would oppress God's people is given cryptically as "a time, two times, and half a time," or three and a half times.[31] It will be recalled that the "seven times" during which Nebuchadnezzar lapsed into a state of insanity proved to be seven years of literal time.[32] Practically all authorities, ancient and modern, thus understand the word here translated "time." The three and a half "times" would then be three and a half years. An equivalent expression in Revelation 12:14, "a time, and times, and half a time," is defined earlier in the same chapter as "one thousand two hundred and sixty days." On the basis of thirty days to the month and twelve months to the year, 1260 days prove to be exactly three and a half years.

In Daniel 8 another time period connected with the era of great persecution is mentioned. There it is stated that after "two thousand and three hundred evenings and mornings," the sanctuary would be "restored to its rightful state."[33] According to Genesis 1:

5, an "evening," or the dark part of the day, and a "morning," or the light part of the day, together constitute a whole "day."[34] On this basis, 2300 "evenings and mornings" would be equivalent to as many days.

One further fact relating to both the 1260 and the 2300 days remains to be mentioned. Bible usage points to the conclusion that, in symbolic prophecy such as we find in Daniel 7 and 8, a "day" of prophetic time stands for a full year of actual time. This day-for-a-year principle in predictive prophecy first appears in Numbers 14:34 and is illustrated again in Ezekiel 4:6. Accordingly, 1260 and 2300 "days" on the prophetic slide rule of time represent as many actual years. The application of these time periods to the events of history is the subject of a future chapter.[35]

## Deliverance and Restoration

But there is a happy ending to the long reign of terror. When it seems that the great tyrant is on the point of triumph, God intervenes in the course of history to deliver His people, to destroy their wily foe, and to inaugurate His own righteous reign on earth.[36] By the verdict of the supreme court of the universe, those who have suffered at the hands of the great persecuting tyrant will eventually be awarded eternal justice.

Except for divine intervention, the tyrant's triumph would apparently be complete and permanent. God wisely permits him to demonstrate his sinister plot to annihilate the saints and to usurp divine authority in the world, beyond any possible alibi. But as the angel explains in Daniel 11:45, when the persecuting tyrant

comes to his ignominious end, there are none to help
him, for none can deliver out of God's hand.

Then "the time came when the saints received the
kingdom," the angel declared finally, adding that
"their kingdom shall be an everlasting kingdom," and
that "all dominions shall serve and obey them."[37]
There is also to be a resurrection of the dead, for
"many of those who sleep in the dust of the earth
shall awake," he says, "to everlasting life." Then
"those who are wise shall shine like the brightness of
the firmament . . . for ever and ever."[38] Under the
supreme pressure of persecution they have been transformed into living diamonds.

The fact that there is to be a general resurrection
and that the angel promised Daniel he would "stand"
in his "allotted place," with those to be raised from
the dead, and thus to enter upon his eternal reward,[39]
imparts to the vision a clearly supernatural overtone.
Any application to historical events that do not climax
in the resurrection and in the inauguration of God's
eternal, righteous reign clearly does not meet the
specifications of the prophecy.

Through these momentous things revealed to Daniel in the long ago God speaks to us today. To their
interpretation and application we now turn.

### NOTES

1. Daniel 12:3, 10.
2. Daniel 10:11, 19.
3. Daniel 12:10.
4. See pages 298, 299.
5. Daniel 7:21, 25; 8:24; 10:14; 12:7.
6. Daniel 12:3.
7. Daniel 11:22.

8. Daniel 11:35.

9. Each of the four visions makes reference to a personage most conservative Bible scholars consider to be the Messiah. Daniel 7:13 speaks of a "son of man," a designation by which Jesus commonly spoke of Himself while here on earth. (Matthew 16:13; 17:9; etc.) This is not the place for an extended technical discussion of the expression, the meaning of which Bible scholars have debated at length. Suffice it to note that ancient Jewish writers as well as Christian scholars have identified this "son of man" as the Messiah.

Daniel 8:11, 25 refers to a "Prince of princes" or "Prince of the host," and chapter 9:25, 26 to "an anointed one, a prince." In chapters 11:22 and 12:1 we find the expressions "prince of the covenant" and "Michael, the great prince." The identical Hebrew expression translated "Prince of the host" in chapter 8:11 is rendered "commander of the army" in Joshua 5:14, 15, where it is used of a celestial visitor who appeared to Joshua, and in numerous other instances.

In Daniel 10:13 the context clearly requires that "Michael, one of the chief princes," be considered a celestial personage, and no mere human being. The same is true in chapter 10:21, where "Michael, your prince" is said to "contend" by the side of Gabriel in behalf of the chosen people. Chapter 12:1 mentions "Michael, the great prince," as one "who has charge of your people," because he comes to deliver them. The role of the "son of man" in chapter 7:13, 14 is very similar. In chapter 7:13, 14 he receives the everlasting kingdom from the "Ancient of Days" and enters into possession of it jointly with the saints.

The interrelationships here noted indicate that one and the same being is mentioned in all four visions. In Daniel 7 and 12 He is clearly a divine being, whereas in chapters 8, 9, and 11 He is also a human being living on earth, inasmuch as the great tyrant-persecutor attacks Him personally. Taken together, these passages identify this Prince as a divine being who becomes incarnate as the leader and defender of His people, who dies but lives again, and who ultimately receives the eternal kingdom from the Ancient of Days—in their behalf. This, of course, is the very picture presented by the New Testament writers with respect to Christ. (John 1:1-3, 14; 1 Corinthians 15:4; Revelation 11:15.) According to Daniel 9:26, the "anointed" prince was to "have nothing" at the time of His death—literally, "and nothingness to him." This may be understood to mean that His death is vicarious, of benefit to others but not to Himself. (See Isaiah 53:4-6.)

The Hebrew expression in Daniel 9:25 rendered "an anointed one, a prince" may also be translated "anointed prince," or possibly "Prince Messiah." Our word *Messiah* is from the Hebrew *mashíach,* which means "anointed." Translated into the Greek of the New Testament, *mashíach* becomes *christos,* the Greek word for "anointed," and, in the New Testament sense, Christ. Thus, the terms *Messiah* and *Christ* both mean "anointed," and the Messiah of the Old Testament is the Christ of the New. In Old Testament times it was the practice to "anoint" both the king and the high priest, the civil and religious leaders of the nation, in order to set them apart for their high offices. (Numbers 35:25; 1 Samuel 9:16; 2 Samuel 2:4.) This ritual anointing was the religious counterpart to the civil coronation service. According to Acts 10:38, "God anointed Jesus of Nazareth with the Holy Spirit and with power" at the commencement of His earthly ministry. It is in this sense that the Messiah is God's "anointed one," or "Messiah"—the one set apart by God to be the Saviour of His people.

The various expressions, "son of man," "Prince of the host," "Prince of princes," "an anointed one, a prince," "prince of the covenant," and "Michael, the great prince," are appropriate designations for the Messiah, and there is no convincing reason for applying them otherwise.

10. Daniel 11:36.
11. Daniel 11:28, 30.
12. Daniel 7:25.
13. See page 162.
14. Daniel 8:12.
15. Daniel 8:11, 13; 9:26; 11:31.
16. See pages 309, 310.

17. Daniel 8:11, 13; 11:31; 12:11.
18. Daniel 8:12, 13; 9:27; 11:31, 38, 39; 12:11.
19. Daniel 11:14, 30, 32; 12:10.
20. Daniel 11:32-35; 12:3.
21. Daniel 7:8, 24; 8:9, 23.
22. Daniel 9:26; 11: 5, 6.
23. See note 9 on page 154.
24. See pages 147, 148.
25. See page 50.
26. Daniel 7:8, 20.
27. Daniel 8:23, 25; 11:23, 32.
28. Daniel 8:23; 11:21, 36, 37.
29. Daniel 7:20; 8:9, 10, 12, 24; 11:5, 15, 16, 28, 36.
30. Daniel 8:17, 19, 26; 10:14; 11:35.
31. Daniel 7:25; 12:7.
32. See page 85.
33. Daniel 8:14.
34. The Hebrew word for *evening* refers to the waning light of the late afternoon and evening, and the word for *morning* means "daybreak, dawn," or the increasing light of the early morning hours. This is the sense in which the terms are used in the creation account in Genesis 1, where it is said of the daily cycle of sunrise and sunset, for instance, that "there was evening and there was morning, one day." According to 1 Chronicles 16:40, a burnt offering was to be offered "continually morning and evening." This suggests that "continual" and "evenings . . . mornings" in Daniel 8:14 are equivalent expressions. The evening and morning services of the sanctuary were the heart and center of its continual, uninterrupted ritual service. Thus understood, "the vision of the evenings and the mornings" in chapter 8:26 is a reference to what Daniel saw concerning the "continual burnt offering" of verses 12-14.
35. See page 304.
36. Daniel 7:9-14, 22, 26; 8:25; 9:27; 12:1, 7.
37. Daniel 7:18, 22, 27; 12:1-3.
38. Daniel 12:2, 3.
39. Daniel 12:2, 13.

# Wanted—A Master Key

HAVE YOU ever experimented with various keys on a ring that had been given you, one of which you had been assured would open a locked door? In a similar way, down through the years, different students of the Book of Daniel have proposed diverse interpretations, or keys, which they have claimed would unlock its mysteries. Three principal, and mutually exclusive, interpretations have been offered.

One applies all the predictions concerning the coming of a great tyrant and a great future period of persecution to an episode in Jewish history that took place more than two thousand years ago. Another theory recognizes a partial fulfillment of Daniel's prophecies in ancient times, but assigns the great tyrant and the time of tribulation to a brief, future period at the close of the age. According to a third explanation, these prophecies have been in process of continuous fulfillment ever since Daniel's day and will reach their climax only when God intervenes to bring human history to a halt and begins His own eternal, righteous reign.

Let us briefly examine these three, in order, in the hope of discovering which one is, after all, the master key, which one conforms to all the specifications made by Daniel and the other inspired Bible writers.

## The Antiochus Theory

Advocates of the first of these three theories identify the persecuting tyrant as Antiochus Epiphanes, a king of the Seleucid Empire who oppressed the Jews from 168 to 165 B.C. The noteworthy resemblance of some incidents during this episode in Jewish history to certain details of Daniel's prophecy gives this interpretation an appearance of plausibility. A generation after the time of Antiochus, the writer of the apocryphal book of 1 Maccabees evidently believed Antiochus to be the villain here foretold, for in recounting what took place he uses the very language of Daniel.[1] Two centuries later the Jewish historian Josephus declared that Antiochus had, indeed, fulfilled these prophecies.[2] A considerable number of modern scholars also hold this view.

Despite the remarkable similarities, however, there are compelling reasons that altogether preclude the possibility of considering Antiochus Epiphanes to be the tyrant prince foretold by Daniel. For one thing, Antiochus reigned about midpoint of the Hellenistic kingdoms that followed Alexander the Great, not "at the latter end of their rule" as Daniel specifies in chapter 8:23.[3] His oppression of the Jews was a temporary affair, and by no stretch of the imagination can it be said that he "prevailed over them, until the Ancient of Days came, and judgment was given for the saints of the Most High, and the time came when the saints received the kingdom," as Daniel explicitly declares in chapter 7:21, 22. It is a simple, historical fact that God did not establish His eternal, righteous reign on earth in the long ago when the Jews were still His chosen people. The reign of Antiochus was in no sense a prelude to the Messianic age, and the resurrection of chapter 12:2 which Daniel declared would take place when the tyrant king should "come to his end," certainly did not follow the expulsion of Antiochus from Judea.

Antiochus never proved to be the imposing personage required by the prophecies of Daniel.[4] Instead of Epiphanes, "the Illustrious"—the title by which he wished to be known—his contemporaries nicknamed him Epimanes, "the madman." Rome thwarted his ambition to annex Egypt, his grandiose plans to build his empire into a second Greece failed utterly, his oppression of the Jews proved to be no more than a momentary success, and a short time later he lost his life trying to plunder a heathen temple of its treasures. "Exceedingly great"—greater than Nebuchadnezzar, Cyrus, or Alexander—as Daniel had predicted? Not Antiochus Epiphanes, by any standard. Furthermore, no events connected with his oppression of the Jews correspond in any way with the time periods specified by Daniel. Thus, despite certain impressive similarities, the attempt to make Antiochus Epiphanes out to be the tyrant prince of Daniel breaks down at every major point.

As if to clinch the matter, two centuries *after* the time of Antiochus Christ categorically declared that the tyrant prince and the great tribulation of Daniel's prophecies were *still* in the future.[5] To accept Antiochus Epiphanes as the historical counterpart of Daniel's persecuting tyrant is thus to reject Christ's own interpretation of Daniel.[6]

Usually those who assign the prophecies of Daniel to the time of Antiochus also claim that the book was not actually written by its pretended author, some five centuries before Christ, but by an unknown Jew nearly four hundred years later, during the oppression under Antiochus. Its purpose, they say, was to inspire hope for deliverance and courage to resist. This interpretation is based on the *a priori* assumption that genuine predictive prophecy is impossible. It is not a conclusion reached after a candid examination of all the facts, but in reality an exegetical escape mechanism contrived to avoid acknowledging the validity of Bible prophecy.

Generally speaking, those who hold this view look upon the Bible as merely another human book, one that expresses no more than the opinions of its various writers. They also deny the deity, supernatural birth, substitutionary death, and literal resurrection of Christ, and His promise to return visibly at the end of the age. For the reasons cited, together with those set forth at some length on pages 121 to 129, we find this explanation wholly out of keeping with an objective examination of the facts.

## The Gap Theory

The view that the great tyrant and the great tribulation foretold by Daniel are yet to come is based on what is known as the "gap theory." According to this theory, Daniel's predictions were fulfilled literally, in

order, up to the moment Christ died on the cross.
Then, so the theory goes, because of the Jews' rejection of Jesus as the Messiah the clock of prophecy
stopped dead still in the midst of the seventieth
"week" of the prophecy of Daniel 9, something like
an interrupted countdown in the launching of a
guided missile or spacecraft.

Presumably, the prophetic countdown will not be
resumed—nor will the prophetic clock start ticking
away the last half of the seventieth "week"—until the
Jews as a nation have once more been restored to their
role as the chosen people, to rule the world for a thousand years. Those who advocate this theory point to
the new State of Israel and the return of some two
million Jews to Palestine as the fulfillment of the Old
Testament promises of the restoration of Israel as a
nation. They consider these developments as preparatory to the reinstatement of the Jews as God's chosen
people.

There are two chief difficulties with this theory. In
the first place, as we shall see, it is only by taking the
promises of restoration completely out of their literary
and historical context that they can be made to apply
to the Jews today. Understood in the sense in which
they were originally intended by the Holy Spirit, the
statements of the inspired writers clearly preclude
such an application. In the second place, nothing in
Daniel or elsewhere in the Bible even remotely hints
of a "gap" in the fulfillment of his prophecy. This
theory is simply a theory, and nothing more. However, in view of the fact that it has come to be rather
widely accepted in recent years, brief consideration

should be given at this point to the role the Bible assigns the Jews as a nation, particularly since the time of Christ's first advent.

## Israel as God's Chosen People

In order to prepare the way for the coming of the Messiah and for the proclamation of the good news of salvation to all men everywhere, God entered into a solemn agreement, or covenant, with the Hebrew people as a nation. They voluntarily accepted Him as their sovereign and became in a special sense *His* people, subjects of His authority. To them He committed a knowledge of His infinite purpose, and with it the sacred trust of being His chosen representatives on earth.

The prophet Isaiah compared Israel to a "vineyard" the Lord had "planted" in the land of Palestine, in the expectation that it would "blossom and put forth shoots, and fill the whole world with fruit." But instead, lamented Isaiah, it yielded only "wild grapes."[7] Again and again God warned His people that the result of continued disobedience would be exile from their homeland.[8] These warnings were fulfilled when Nebuchadnezzar overturned the kingdom of Judah and carried the Jews captive to Babylon.[9] Toward the close of the allotted seventy years of captivity Daniel, in prayer, acknowledged this bitter experience to be the fulfillment of the earlier warnings:

"All Israel has transgressed thy law and turned aside, refusing to obey thy voice. And the curse and oath which are written in the law of Moses the servant of God have been poured out upon us, because we have

sinned against him. He has confirmed his words, which
he spoke against us and against our rulers who ruled
us, by bringing upon us a great calamity."[10]

In the midst of adversity God mercifully granted
His people an opportunity to learn the lessons they
had been unwilling to learn in times of prosperity.[11]
After the seventy years God restored them to their
homeland and renewed His covenant with them. All
that He had promised might yet come to pass if they
would only cooperate with Him.[12] It is important to
note that, taken in their literary and historical context, *all* the Old Testament promises looking forward
to a restoration era in the future were given *with this
return from Babylonian captivity in view.*[13] In answer
to his prayer, the angel Gabriel informed Daniel that
"seventy weeks of years," or 490 years, had been "decreed" for the Jews, "to restore and build Jerusalem,"
"to finish the transgression, to put an end to sin, and to
atone for iniquity, to bring in everlasting righteousness."[14]

## Israel Rejected as the Chosen Nation

Toward the close of the 490 years thus allotted the
Jews in their role as the chosen people, Christ came to
earth and lived as a man among men. But in the supreme tragedy of all time "his own people received
him not."[15] Jesus devoted the last day of His public
ministry, during crucifixion week, to teaching in the
Temple courts at Jerusalem and to answering loaded
questions put to Him by the Jewish leaders. During
the course of His debate with these men Jesus told
them a story in which, like Isaiah, He compared the

Jewish people, in their role as the chosen nation, to a vineyard.[16] The vine was Israel's national symbol, and over the main entrance to the Temple a gold and silver replica with green leaves and large clusters of grapes, a gift of Herod the Great, reared its resplendent branches.[17]

In this story a certain landowner (God) planted a vineyard (the Jewish nation) and let it out to tenants (the Jewish leaders). As the vintage season approached, he sent his servants (the prophets) to receive his share of the fruit (character), but the tenants abused and murdered them. Last of all, every other means having failed, he sent his own son (the Messiah), but the tenants said among themselves, "This is the heir; come, let us kill him and have his inheritance." So "they took him . . . and killed him."

Jesus concluded the story by asking the Jewish leaders, who were already secretly plotting to murder Him, "When therefore the owner of the vineyard comes, what will he do to those tenants?" Inadvertently pronouncing sentence upon themselves, they replied, "He will put those wretches to a miserable death, and let out the vineyard to other tenants who will give him the fruits in their seasons." Jesus immediately drove the lesson of the story home: "Therefore I tell you, the kingdom of God will be taken away from you and given to a nation producing the fruits of it."[16]

Then it was that for the first and last time, Jesus publicly denounced the leaders of the nation. He accused them of refusing to enter the kingdom of heaven themselves, and of bolting and barring it against all who sought to enter. That very day they were, in fact, filling the nation's cup of guilt to the brim. Jesus concluded His withering denunciation with the ominous pronouncement, "O Jerusalem, Jerusalem, killing the prophets and stoning those who are sent to you! How often would I have gathered your children together as a hen gathers her brood under her wings, and you would not! Behold, your house is forsaken and desolate."[18]

That fateful day the leaders of Israel refused God's last solemn appeal to cooperate with His glorious purpose for their nation. The day before, Jesus had claimed the Temple as His own rightful property, calling it "my house"; today as He turned and left the sacred precincts of the Temple forever, He spoke of it as "your house."[19] In effect, and in their official capacity, the leaders had renounced their allegiance to God and repudiated Him, and He in turn reluctantly abandoned the nation to the fate it had chosen. Their rejection of Jesus meant the permanent, irrevocable cancellation of Israel's special standing before God as a nation under the covenant relationship. Set of sun that day marked also the eternal sunset of divine grace. Three days later they declared before Pilate their allegiance to "no king but Caesar."

Within a few years Roman armies laid Jerusalem waste and drove the Jews from their beloved city. Now there was no divine promise of reinstatement, as there had been at the time of the Babylonian exile. Instead, as Moses had warned many centuries before, they were driven from the land God had given them, and scattered "among all peoples, from one end of earth to the other." "You shall surely perish," said Moses, "because you would not obey the voice of the Lord your God."[20] In the words of Jeremiah, the time had finally come for God to "break this people and this city, as one breaks a potter's vessel, so that it can never be mended."[21]

## A Great Turning Point in History

Despite Israel's failure as a nation, however, God's plan for the salvation of the world will ultimately succeed, for God "is the same yesterday and today and for ever"; His word "abides for ever."[22] The plan itself never changes, because God never changes, though the manner in which, and the human instruments through whom, it is eventually carried forward to success do change when those who have been called persistently refuse to cooperate. The Bible record is replete with instances of the reversal of promised blessings and threatened judgments, involving both nations and individuals.[23]

As we have seen, when the Jews rejected Christ as the Messiah and crucified Him on Calvary, they forfeited the privileges and responsibilities that had been theirs under the covenant relationship, permanently and irrevocably. The new "nation" to which God assigned the rights and privileges of the kingdom proved to be the Christian church, which henceforth became God's chosen instrument for the salvation of the world. Though in its basic features God's plan for the world remained unchanged, this transition from ancient, literal Israel to the Christian church, or spiritual Israel, involved also a profound change in the manner in which some aspects of the plan would now have to be worked out in history.

For instance, instead of a literal nation made up of the literal descendants of Abraham and Gentile converts to Judaism, there was now to be an international organization, the church universal, a spiritual "nation" in which people of all nations, including individual Jews, were to compose the new chosen people.[24] Instead of the land of Palestine as the stage where God would concentrate His efforts in behalf of the human race, henceforth the world was to be the scene of action. Instead of literal Jerusalem, the New Jerusalem in heaven above became the focal center of the believer's hope.[25]

Instead of a literal sanctuary located on Mount Moriah, the great sanctuary in heaven above became the place to which all who choose the worship and service of the true God were to come, by faith, to find mercy and "grace to help in time of need."[26] Instead of a human priesthood to mediate between repentant sinners and God, Jesus Christ was to be their great High Priest in the sanctuary above, and all men might now come to Him directly by faith.[27] Instead of animal sacrifices, the infinite sacrifice of Christ on Calvary, once for all, was to provide salvation for all men of all ages.[28] Instead of a system of types and ceremonies, we have a religion of the heart and the life.[29]

## The New "Chosen People"

What God originally purposed to do for the world through Israel of old, the chosen nation of ancient times, He will finally accomplish through His church on earth today. The glorious promises originally made to the Jewish people now belong to the church, and it is God's purpose to accomplish through His church on earth today what He formerly planned to accomplish through Israel.[30]

Paul makes this transition his subject in the ninth to the eleventh chapters of his Epistle to the Romans. Here he affirms that the rejection of the Jews did not mean that the promises of God had failed, for, as he goes on to explain, these promises are to become effective through spiritual Israel. "Those who were not my people I will call 'my people,'" he declares, applying the words of Hosea to the Christian church. In spiritual Israel He now includes both Jews and Gentiles, but as individuals and not as groups.[31]

Peter similarly refers to Gentile Christians as the "chosen" of God: "You are a chosen race," he says, "a holy nation, God's own people." "Once you were no people but now you are God's people." God's choice of the church has the same grand purpose, Peter goes on to say, as His former choice of the Jewish nation— "that you may declare the wonderful deeds of him who called you out of darkness into his marvelous light."[32] Paul declares, furthermore, that Gentile Christians will succeed where the Jews failed.[33] Now, he says, there is no longer any distinction between Jew and Gentile, or as Peter had said even earlier, "God shows no partiality, but in every nation any one who fears him and does what is right is acceptable to him."[34]

Paul stresses the fact that the rejection of literal Israel as God's chosen instrument for the salvation

of the world did not mean that individual Jews can
no longer be saved, for as a Jew he himself has found
salvation by faith in Christ Jesus. But they are to be
saved *as Christians* and not as Jews. True, he says,
the Jewish nation "stumbled" at accepting Christ as
the Messiah foretold by the prophets, but individual
Jews did not therefore forfeit the opportunity for salvation. "By no means!" he exclaims. Literal Jews, the
descendants of Abraham, may still find personal salvation by being grafted into spiritual Israel—by be-
coming Christians and joining the church, in precisely
the same way as Gentiles. Every last Jew can still
find salvation and "will be saved" if he accepts Christ
as the promised Deliverer.[35]

## An Unscriptural Theory

Clearly, then, the Bible itself precludes any interpretation of the prophecies of Daniel that envisions
a future restoration of the Jews as a nation to their
former role as God's chosen people. Such an idea
proves to be merely a man-made theory superimposed
upon the Scriptures. The establishment of the modern
State of Israel and the return of the Jews to Palestine
in our day have no significance whatever as a fulfillment of prophecy. The so-called "gap theory" completely ignores the plain statements of Scripture that
all God's promises and threats of punishment are alike
conditional.[23] Furthermore, its advocates usually hold
to the idea of what they call a "secret rapture," for
which, as we shall see, the Bible provides no support.[36]

Weighed thus by the infallible declarations of Holy
Writ, the "gap theory," like its antithesis the Antio-

chus theory, is found altogether wanting. In the chapter that follows we will consider the third of the three principal interpretations mentioned earlier in this chapter.

## NOTES

1. See chapters 1 to 4 of 1 Maccabees, especially 1:29-54; 2:12-15; 3:29, 58, 59; 4:36-45.

2. Josephus, *Antiquities* x. 11. 7 (Loeb Classical Edition, 266-281); xii. 5. 4 (Loeb, 248-256); xii. 7. 6, 7 (Loeb, 316-326); *Wars* i. 1. 1, 2 (Loeb, 31-35).

3. Antiochus IV (Epiphanes) was the seventh of twenty-three Seleucid kings of Syria, from 312 to 64 B.C. He reigned from 175 to 164/163 B.C.

4. See pages 160-165.

5. Matthew 24:15-20.

6. See the following chapter.

7. Isaiah 27:6; 5:1-7.

8. Deuteronomy 4:9; 8:19; 28:1, 2, 14; Jeremiah 18:7-10; 26:2-6; Zechariah 6:15.

9. For warnings, see Deuteronomy 28:15-68; Ezekiel 12:3-28; 16:37; 21:25-32; Hosea 9:3, 15; Micah 2:10; compare Hosea 2:6-13. For the fulfillment of these warnings, see 2 Chronicles 36:16, 17; Ezekiel 36:18-23.

10. Daniel 9:11, 12.

11. Jeremiah 25:5-7; 29:18, 19; 30:11-14; 46:28; Ezekiel 20:25-38; Micah 4:10-12.

12. Jeremiah 31:10-38; 33:3-26; Ezekiel 36:8-15, 21-38; 43:10, 11; Micah 4:6-8; Zechariah 1:12, 17; 2:12; 6:15; 10:6; compare Isaiah 54:7.

13. Isaiah 14:1-7; 40:2; 61:4-10; Jeremiah 16:14-16; 23:3-8; 25:11; 29:10-13; 30:3-11; 32:37-44; Ezekiel 34:11-15; 37; Amos 9:10-15; Micah 2:12; etc.; compare Jeremiah 32:7-27.

14. Daniel 9:24, 25; compare Jeremiah 12:14-17.

15. Isaiah 53; John 1:11.

16. Matthew 21:33-46.

17. Isaiah 5:7; Josephus, *Antiquities* xv. 11. 3.

18. Matthew 23:13, 32-37.

19. Matthew 21:13; compare 23:38.

20. Deuteronomy 8:19, 20; 28:58-68.

21. Jeremiah 12:14-17; 19:11; also see Deuteronomy 8:19, 20.

22. Hebrews 13:8; 1 Peter 1:25.

23. Jeremiah 18:6-10; Matthew 21:40-43; 22:2-10; Luke 14:24. For the reversal of threatened judgment, see Jonah 3:3-10; compare 2 Kings 20:1-6. For the reversal of promised blessing, see Exodus 6:2-8; compare Numbers 14:26-35.

24. Matthew 21:43; 28:19, 20; Acts 1:8; 10:34, 35; Galatians 3:28, 29; 1 Peter 2:9, 10.

25. Galatians 4:25, 26; Hebrews 12:22; Revelation 3:12; 21:2, 10.

26. Hebrews 4:14-16; 8:1, 2; 9:11.

27. Hebrews 2:17; 3:1; 4:14, 15; 7:12-24; 10:19-22.

28. Hebrews 7:26, 27; 9:25, 26; 10:9-14.

29. Hebrews 9:1-14.

30. Galatians 3:26-29.

31. Hosea 2:23; Romans 9:6, 24-26.

32. 1 Peter 2:9, 10; compare 1:2.

33. Romans 9:30, 31; 10:12, 13.

34. Acts 10:34, 35; Romans 10:12; Galatians 3:28.

35. Romans 9:3, 6, 31-33; 10:1; 11:1, 2, 11, 12, 15, 25, 26.

36. See pages 351-353.

# Christ Provides the Master Key

T HE ANGEL Gabriel concluded the fourth and last vision accorded Daniel with the remark that further information about the future must remain "shut up and sealed until the time of the end," when "knowledge" about such matters would "increase." The conversation that followed this remark makes evident which aspects of the prophecy, in particular, were still not clear to Daniel, and yet on which the angel declined to give further information.

Daniel asked, "*How long* shall it be till the end of these wonders?" that is, until "the shattering . . . of the holy people" in the great future "time of trouble, such as never has been," should come to an end, and when "Michael, the great prince" should arise to deliver His people. Gabriel answered by repeating the cryptic language of the prophecy, that "it would be for a time, two times, and half a time."[1]

Daniel says that he "heard" distinctly what the angel said, but still "did not understand." Accordingly he asked a second time, "O my lord, what shall be the *issue* [the climax, or final end] of these things?" In other words, How will all this finally work out? The

angel had already told him that the vision just concluded dealt with what was to befall his people "in
the latter days."[2] Significantly, the word *issue* in Daniel 12:8 is translated from the same Hebrew word as
*latter* in chapter 10:14. Daniel's second request was
thus for further information about the great climactic
events foretold for "the latter days." In reply to this
question Gabriel simply reiterated what he had already
said: "Go your way, Daniel, for the words are shut up
and sealed until the time of the end." Evidently, exact
information as to just *when* and *how* the predicted
tribulation and triumph would take place could not
be revealed in Daniel's time.

Had the Jews proved faithful to their sacred trust
and accepted the Messiah when He came, all the
glorious promises made to Israel of old could have
been fulfilled to them as the chosen people, and the
transfer of the covenant privileges and responsibilities
to the Christian church would never have been necessary. We have noted the fact that these promises were
all conditional upon their corporate response as a nation.[3] Only when their decision in the matter had become final and irrevocable one way or the other, at
the coming of the Messiah, could a definitive answer
be given to Daniel's two questions. Until then, the
precise time and the actual manner in which the predictions would be fulfilled in history must remain
"shut up and sealed."

This is not to suggest that God did not know what
the future held in store, but only to point out that as
long as His covenant with Israel was in effect, it
would have been inconsistent for Him categorically to

predict their ultimate failure and rejection, and thereby precipitate that very result.

## A Noteworthy Coincidence

As we have seen, the great issue of Israel's role in the divine plan was decided for time and eternity when the Jewish nation rejected and crucified Christ.[4] When the transfer of the covenant promises and responsibilities to the Christian church thus became an inevitable, historical fact, then more complete information as to just when and how Daniel's prophecies were to meet their fulfillment could be given. It is worthy of note that on the very day the Jewish leaders officially rejected Jesus Christ as the Messiah, He directed His disciples' attention to the Book of Daniel and told them specifically that *now* those who read the prophecy *could* begin to understand more perfectly what had been "shut up and sealed." Then He went on to explain when and how the prophecy was to be fulfilled, with the Christian church as heir to the covenant privileges and responsibilities.[5]

Christ's explanation of the prophecies of Daniel has appropriately been called the "historical interpretation," in view of the fact that He envisioned a continuous fulfillment down through history to the close of time. His comments on the subject definitely exclude both of the theories considered in the preceding chapter. He assigned the great persecuting tyrant, perpetrator of "the desolating sacrilege spoken of by the prophet Daniel" and the resulting "great tribulation," to the *future*. This rules out Antiochus Epiphanes, who lived more than a century and a half earlier.[6]

As we have already seen, a careful examination makes evident that Christ's remarks on this occasion likewise preclude the introduction of any so-called "gap" in the fulfillment of Daniel's prophecy.[7] This theory, it will be remembered, inserts a blank period of some two thousand years in the fulfillment of the prophecy, between the death of Christ on the cross and the great era of persecution. It ignores, and goes far beyond, the interpretation that Christ here gives, and the later, inspired comments of the New Testament writers as well. In so doing it ventures into the shadowy realm of speculation where the Scriptures are silent and where the phantoms of personal opinion beguile the unwary.

Even yet, however, Christ did not see fit to reveal everything about the future. "I have yet many things to say to you," He told the disciples, "but you cannot bear them now."[8] They would have been dismayed beyond words had He explained that two thousand years were to elapse between the destruction of Jerusalem, of which He now spoke, and His promised return. They expected that all things foretold by the prophets would be fulfilled in their own generation. He revealed as much as they were ready to understand and then assured them, "When the Spirit of truth comes, he will guide you into all the truth."[8] Nevertheless, Christ's interpretation of the prophecies of Daniel provides us with the master key for unlocking the mysteries that Gabriel told Daniel were "shut up and sealed."

In this chapter we will consider Christ's interpretation of Daniel's prophecy, and in the chapter that follows, the inspired comments of the apostles, who were instructed by Christ and later by the Holy Spirit on the subject.

## Christ Unveils the Future

As Jesus withdrew from the Temple for the last time, never again to enter its portals or to teach in public, He retired with His disciples to the Mount of Olives, directly across the narrow Kidron Valley from Jerusalem. There, as the declining light of the sun bathed the marble walls and gilded the dome of the Temple in its fading rays, and as the shades of night drew on, He unveiled the future to them. He explained how things would work out now that the Jewish leaders had made their irrevocable decision to reject Him as the promised Messiah.

On their way out of the Temple area the disciples remarked about the magnificent sanctuary, the courts, the colonnades, the porticoes, and the other buildings that made the great Temple complex the pride and joy of the nation. Jesus replied with the dire prediction, "You see all these, do you not? Truly, I say to you, there will not be left here one stone upon another, that will not be thrown down." Brooding over this ominous prospect as they made their way together to the Mount of Olives, ten or fifteen minutes' walk distant, they asked upon arrival, "Tell us, when will this be, and what will be the sign of your coming and of the close of the age?"[9]

This question makes evident that the disciples associated together in their minds three climactic events already foretold by Daniel: (1) the destruction of

Jerusalem and the Temple, (2) Jesus' promised second coming, as "Son of man," to deliver His people, and (3) "the close of the age," or "time of the end."[10] What they wanted to know was "when" all this would be, and by what "sign" they could recognize the approach of these events.[11] These were the very points on which Daniel had sought further information, but which the angel told him were "shut up and sealed until the time of the end." Jesus' answer to this question, recorded in Matthew 24:3 to 25:30, is His key to the interpretation of Daniel's prophecy.

## When "the End" Would Come

Jesus told the disciples that "the end" would come when the "gospel of the kingdom"—the good news about the establishment of the eternal, righteous "kingdom" foretold by Daniel and more recently proclaimed by Christ Himself—should be "preached throughout the whole world . . . to all nations."[12] The Jewish nation having failed, He now commissioned the disciples with the same task that had formerly been entrusted to Israel.[13] "Go therefore and make disciples of all nations," He said, "teaching them to observe all that I have commanded you."[14]

Jesus did not see fit to inform the disciples that, under the new arrangement involving the transfer of the covenant privileges and responsibilities to them as leaders of the future Christian church, the destruction of Jerusalem would not be followed almost immediately by His second coming and the end of the world, as they supposed. He simply said, "When you see the desolating sacrilege spoken of by the prophet

Daniel, standing in the holy place (let the reader understand), then let those who are in Judea flee to the mountains." Or, as Luke reports it, "When you see Jerusalem surrounded by armies, then know that its desolation has come near."[15] This came to pass with the destruction of Jerusalem by the Romans in A.D. 70. But it is evident that even more was involved, for John, who heard Jesus on this occasion and who wrote the Book of Revelation many years *after* the fall of Jerusalem, assigned the great apostasy and persecution foretold by Daniel and Christ to a time still future.[16]

It is important to note that, in His reply, Jesus *did not* directly associate the fate of Jerusalem with His second coming and the end of the world. Time would be required for the gospel to go to all the world. It is significant, however, that He here confirms the reliability of Daniel's great prophecy, assigns its fulfillment to the future, and bases His own preview of future events on it.

As if to confirm beyond a doubt that Christ intended the disciples to understand His remarks on this occasion as His interpretation of Daniel, He mentions the prophet by name, tells them that they are to understand what he wrote, and then proceeds to explain it. In doing so He uses the very words by which Daniel refers to the great future apostasy and persecution, though this is not apparent in the English translation. In the Greek of Matthew 24:15, for instance, the expression translated "desolating sacrilege" is identical with the Greek (Septuagint) translation of Daniel 12:11, which is rendered directly from the Hebrew into English as "abomination that makes desolate."

7

And after the desolation of Jerusalem? "There will be great tribulation, such as has not been from the beginning of the world until now, no, and never will be."[17] The Greek word here used for "tribulation" is identical with the Greek (Septuagint) translation of Daniel 12:1, which is rendered directly from the Hebrew into English as "a time of *trouble,* such as never has been since there was a nation till that time." As we have seen, this time of trouble, or tribulation, is the great focal point of Daniel's prophecies.[18] Not only will there be tribulation, said Jesus, but "false Christs and false prophets will arise"[19]—a counterfeit gospel and an apostate form of Christianity.

## Two Great Signs

After the destruction of Jerusalem, after the great apostasy, after the great persecution—then what? Christ now introduces an important fact that Daniel did not mention, and presents it as *the* major sign of His coming and of the close of the age. This sign is to be given *after* the great apostasy and the great tribulation, but *before* His coming and the end of the world. "Then"—after this sign—said Jesus, "all the tribes of the earth . . . will see the Son of man coming on the clouds of heaven with power and great glory." And what is the sign? "Immediately after the tribulation of those days the sun will be darkened, and the moon will not give its light, and the stars will fall from heaven."[20]

This prediction, confirmed by its fulfillment in history, stands as Christ's own clue to the answer to Daniel's unresolved question about "how long . . . [it would] be till the end of these wonders." The fact that these astronomical phenomena were to come "immediately after the tribulation of those days"—or even more exactly, "in those days, after that tribulation," as Mark has it—thus provides the approximate terminal point for the time of trouble here envisioned.[21] Speaking of the same phenomena, John later wrote, "The sun became black as sackcloth, the full moon became like blood, and the stars of the sky fell to the earth as the fig tree sheds its winter fruit when shaken by a gale."[22] Does history record any events that might properly be described thus? Let us see.

## The Great Dark Day

On May 19, 1780, there occurred a phenomenon so unusual that it has gone down in history as "*the* Dark Day," and fifty-three years later, on November 13, 1833, another, commonly spoken of as "*the* falling of the stars." These two events are unique in all recorded history. Numerous eyewitness accounts of these phenomena have come down to us, some of them by competent observers such as astronomers and other scientifically trained people. Concerning the Dark Day of May 19, 1780, a Harvard professor wrote:

"The *degree* to which the darkness arose, was different in different places. . . . People were unable to read common print—determine the time of day by their clocks or watches—dine—or manage their domestic business, without the light of candles. In some places, the darkness was so great, that persons could not see to read common print in the open air, for several hours together: but I believe this was not generally the case.

The *extent* of this darkness was very remarkable. . . .
With regard to its *duration,* it continued in this place
at least fourteen hours: but it is probable this was not
exactly the same in different parts of the country."[23]

Another observer, describing the darkness of the
night following the Dark Day, wrote:

"The darkness of the following evening was probably as gross as ever has been observed since the Almighty fiat gave birth to light. . . . If every luminous
body in the universe had been shrouded in impenetra-
ble shades, or struck out of existence, the darkness
could not have been more complete. A sheet of white
paper held within a few inches of the eyes was equally
invisible with the blackest velvet."[24]

One eyewitness told about creatures of the wild
acting as they ordinarily do only at nightfall. Another
related that farmers were obliged to leave their sowing
and other work in the field, for want of light. *The
Boston Gazette and the Country Journal* for May 29,
1780, commented that "there was the appearance of
midnight at noonday." This could not have been an
eclipse of the sun, in view of the fact that the moon
had fulled the day before and two weeks would have
to pass before the earth, the moon, and the sun would
be in line for such an eclipse. Furthermore, the sun remains in total eclipse for only a few minutes at most,
and the darkness is never so intense as that which
lasted for several hours on May 19, 1780.

On that remarkable day the Connecticut Legislature
was in session. The lower house adjourned because it
was unable to transact business, but an impassioned
appeal by Abraham Davenport kept the upper house

in session. According to Timothy Dwight, one-time president of Yale University, "a very general opinion prevailed, that the day of judgment was at hand. . . . A proposal to adjourn the Council [upper house] was under consideration. When the opinion of Colonel [Abraham] Davenport was asked, he answered, 'I am against an adjournment. The day of judgment is either approaching or it is not. If it is not, there is no cause for an adjournment: if it is, I choose to be found doing my duty. I wish therefore that candles may be brought.' "[25]

Commemorating this incident in the Connecticut Legislature, the poet John Greenleaf Whittier wrote:

"Meanwhile in the old State House, dim as ghosts,
 Sat the lawgivers of Connecticut,
 Trembling beneath their legislative robes.
 'It is the Lord's Great Day! Let us adjourn,'
 Some said; and then, as if with one accord,
 All eyes were turned to Abraham Davenport.
 He rose, slow cleaving with his steady voice
 The intolerable hush. 'This well may be
 The Day of Judgment which the world awaits;
 But be it so or not, I only know
 My present duty, and my Lord's command
 To occupy till He come. So at the post
 Where He hath set me in His providence,
 I choose, for one, to meet Him face to face,—
 No faithless servant frightened from my task,
 But ready when the Lord of harvest calls;
 And therefore, with all reverence, I would say,
 Let God do His work, we will see to ours.
 Bring in the candles.' "[26]

The fact that the thoughts of even intelligent and informed people were turned to God's great day of judgment does not prove that the darkness was supernatural, but it does reflect the solemn impression the phenomenon made on those who witnessed it. Actually, whether it was due to natural or to supernatural causes is beside the point. The important fact is not always the means God may deem appropriate to use, but the fact that He uses it at a particular time and in a way designed to accomplish a certain result. The Dark Day so impressed those who witnessed it that their thoughts inevitably turned to the prophecies of Scripture which foretold the day of divine judgment, of which these signs were ordained to be Heaven's harbinger.

The darkness was unique in its intensity, in its extent, in its duration, and in its effects. No other such obscuration of the light of the sun has ever been recorded, before or since. Yet, seventeen centuries before, the Saviour had foretold such a day and predicted that it would occur at a particular time in history— toward the close of an era of great apostasy and persecution, and not indefinitely long before His return to earth. The event precisely fulfills the prediction.

## The Falling of the Stars

Fifty-three years after the Dark Day of May 19, 1780, the other great sign foretold by Christ appeared in the heavens. Professor Denison Olmsted, who was teaching astronomy at Yale University when the stars fell in 1833, wrote the first scientific paper on the subject. He described the phenomenon as follows:

"The morning of November 13th, 1833, was rendered memorable by an exhibition of the phenomenon called SHOOTING STARS, which was probably more extensive and magnificent than any similar one hitherto recorded. . . . Probably no celestial phenomenon has ever occurred in this country, since its first settlement, which was viewed with so much admiration and delight by one class of spectators, or with so much astonishment and fear by another class."[27]

That this evaluation of the unique character of that event still holds good is evident from an article by W. J. Fisher in *The Telescope,* October, 1934, entitled, "The Ancient Leonids," in which he refers to it as "the most magnificent meteor shower on record." In an article entitled "The Falling of the Stars" in the same journal, May-June, 1940, Peter M. Millman describes it as "one of the most spectacular natural displays that the night sky has produced" and adds that "more than a billion shooting stars appeared over the United States and Canada alone."

This shower of falling stars is now known to have occurred when the earth, in its orbit about the sun, crossed the path of a swarm of periodic meteors known as the Leonids, so named from their radiant point in the constellation Leo. Other meteoric showers occur from time to time. But since men began to record such events, none have occurred that remotely compare in intensity and brilliance with that of November 13, 1833. Again, as with the Dark Day of May 19, 1780, the significant fact is not the means used, but the timing and the effect on men's minds. This phenomenon likewise was unique in all the annals of astronomy.

Henry Dana Ward, an Episcopal minister and another eyewitness, wrote:

"We felt in our hearts, that it was a sign of the last days. For, truly, 'the stars of heaven fell *unto the earth,* even as a fig tree casteth her untimely figs, when it is shaken by a mighty wind.' . . . This language of the prophet has always been received as metaphorical. . . . [It] was literally fulfilled in the phenomenon of yesterday, so as no man before yesterday had conceived to be possible that it should be fulfilled."[28]

Frederick Douglass, a Presbyterian clergyman, commented: "I witnessed this gorgeous spectacle, and was awe-struck. . . . I was not without the suggestion, at the moment, that it might be the harbinger of the coming of the Son of man; and in my then state of mind I was prepared to hail Him as my friend and deliverer. I had read that the 'stars shall fall from heaven,' and they were now falling."[29]

Here are two events, each in its own way altogether unique in all recorded history. They occurred relatively close together, within the span of one lifetime. Both meet every specification of prophecy, even to the order in which they were to occur. Furthermore, as we shall see, another great event foretold by inspired writers of both the Old and the New Testaments occurred at approximately the midpoint between these two signs. It would be difficult to imagine a more accurate or appropriate fulfillment of prophecy than that afforded by the impressive celestial phenomena of 1780 and 1833.

Christ's prediction of these great signs in the heavens and its literal fulfillment are our key to when in the stream of time the great apostasy and the great tribulation were to take place, and when Jesus' coming would be "near, at the very gates." In other words, the great era of apostasy and persecution would take place *after* the destruction of Jerusalem in A.D. 70, but *before* the appearance of these signs in 1780 and 1833.

## The End of the Age

How long after the signs in the heavens had appeared would Christ come? "Of that day and hour," said Jesus, "no one knows." For this reason He admonished all who eagerly look for His appearing: "Watch therefore, for you do not know on what day your Lord is coming. . . . Be ready; for the Son of man is coming at an hour you do not expect." "When you see all these things"—when the great apostasy, the great tribulation, and the signs in the heavens have all come to pass—"know that he is near, at the very gates."[30]

Jesus next gave three illustrations of the importance of being alert and ready for His return.[31] The first of these parables was a warning against taking the attitude "My master is delayed," the second an admonition to "watch therefore, for you know neither the day nor the hour," and the third, to make use of the waiting time by the diligent employment of one's talents in the Master's service. In these three parables Jesus warned the disciples that His coming would be *delayed* beyond their expectation, that things would work out *differently* from what they expected, and that there was *work* for them to do in preparation for His return.

According to Matthew 24:30, everyone on earth

will see Jesus when He comes the second time—"for as the lightning comes from the east and shines as far as the west, so will be the coming of the Son of man."[32] Christ here speaks of Himself as "the Son of man," the very expression used in Daniel 7:13 of the divine being who appears before the Ancient of Days to receive the everlasting kingdom.[33] When He returns "in his glory, and all the angels with him, then he will sit on his glorious throne." "He will send out his angels . . . and they will gather his elect," and He will say to them, "Come, O blessed of my Father, inherit the kingdom prepared for you."[34]

We turn next to the writings of the apostles, particularly Paul and John, for the additional light that was later revealed to them on the experiences through which the church was to pass ere Christ should return again to this earth in power and glory.

## NOTES

1. Daniel 12:5, 7, 13; see also verses 1, 4.

2. Daniel 10:14.

3. See page 181.

4. See pages 178-181.

5. Matthew 24:15. Christ's explanation is recorded at length in Matthew 24, 25; Mark 13; Luke 21.

6. Matthew 24:15, 21.

7. See pages 175-185.

8. John 16:12, 13.

9. Matthew 24:1-3.

10. Daniel 9:26, 27; compare Matthew 24:1-3 and Luke 21:20. Daniel 7:13, 14; 12:11; compare Matthew 24:27, 30, 31; 25:31. Daniel 11:40; 12:1; compare Matthew 24:3.

11. Mark 13:4.

12. Daniel 7:14, 18, 22, 27; Matthew 4:17; 24:14; 28: 19, 20.

13. See page 177.

14. Matthew 28:19, 20.

15. Matthew 24:15-20; Luke 21:20.

16. As set forth in the following chapter.

17. Matthew 24:21.

18. See Daniel 7:21, 25; 8:10, 13, 24, 25; 9:26; 11:32-35; 12:1.

19. Matthew 24:4, 5, 23-27.

20. Matthew 24:29.

21. Matthew 24:29; Mark 13:24.

22. Revelation 6:12, 13.

23. Samuel Williams, "An Account of a Very Uncommon Darkness in the States of New-England, May 19, 1780," in *Memoirs of the American Academy of Arts and Sciences,* Vol. 1 (published in 1785), pp. 234, 235. (Emphasis his.)

24. Samuel Tenney, in *Collections of the Massachusetts Historical Society,* Vol. 1 (1792), pp. 95, 97, 98.

25. Timothy Dwight, quoted in *Connecticut Historical Collections,* p. 403.

26. John Greenleaf Whittier, "Abraham Davenport," in his *Complete Poetical Works* (Cambridge ed., Boston: Houghton, 1894), p. 260.

27. Denison Olmsted, "Observations on the Meteors of November 13th, 1833," in *The American Journal of Science and the Arts* for 1834. (Emphasis his.)

28. Henry Dana Ward, in *The New York Journal of Commerce,* November 14, 1833.

29. Frederick Douglass, *Life and Times of Frederick Douglass,* p. 117.

30. Matthew 24:33, 36-44.

31. Matthew 24:45 to 25:30.

32. Matthew 24:27.

33. See also Matthew 25:31; compare chapter 16:27, 28.

34. Matthew 25:31; 24:31; 25:34.

# Prophecy's Most-Wanted Criminal

O N THAT far-off evening of which we have already spoken Christ warned His disciples that impostors arising in His name would "lead many astray," and that "false prophets" would appear and "deceive many."[1] A quarter of a century later the Apostle Paul declared that, following his death, men would "arise . . . speaking perverse things, to draw away the disciples after them."[2] Writing to the church in Thessalonica, he repeated Christ's warning, "Let no one deceive you," and explained that "the day of the Lord" would not come until after the appearance of a great apostate he calls variously "the man of lawlessness," "the mystery of lawlessness," and "the son of perdition," and after what he refers to as "the rebellion."

Borrowing, in some instances, the very words with which Daniel described the great tyrant, Paul explained that this "lawless one" would oppose God and exalt himself "against every so-called god or object of worship, so that he takes his seat in the temple of God, proclaiming himself to be God." "The coming of the lawless one," he continued, "by the activity of Satan

204

will be with all power and with pretended signs and wonders, and with all wicked deception." This great apostate, he warned, would camouflage his activities so successfully that only those who love God's revealed truth with all their hearts could expect to be safe from his deceptions.[3] Beyond a doubt, Paul here describes the same great impostor against whom both Christ and the prophet Daniel warned.

In the Book of Revelation, last book of the Bible, the Apostle John presents the future experiences of the church at some length. The picture is basically the same as that given by Daniel, Christ, and Paul, but John goes into considerably more detail and provides the information necessary to complete the picture. Let us now consider what John wrote on the subject.

## Satan's Inveterate Hatred of Christ

In the twelfth chapter of Revelation the apostle briefly traces Satan's attempts to destroy the church down through the long centuries of the Christian era. With the sky for a stage, the symbolic characters in this drama of the ages enter one by one, acting out their respective roles. First to appear was a noble, virtuous woman clothed, as it were, in resplendent sunlight, wearing a crown set with twelve stars and standing on the moon. "She was with child," John relates in the symbolic language of the prophecy, "and she cried out in her pangs of birth, in anguish for delivery."

Then "a great red dragon, with seven heads and ten horns, and seven diadems upon his heads" came into view. As he marched menacingly across the sky, "his tail swept down a third of the stars of heaven, and cast them to the earth." He halted "before the woman who was about to bear a child," intending to "devour her child when she brought it forth." Finally her time came and "she brought forth a male child," John continues, but instead of being devoured by the great red dragon the child "was caught up to God and to his throne."

New Testament writers often refer to the church as Christ's bride, and in the figurative language of the Bible a virtuous woman represents the true church, and an immoral woman an apostate church.[4] John here pictures the true church in all ages as a corporate institution and its individual members as "her offspring, . . . who keep the commandments of God and bear testimony to Jesus."[5] The sun may well represent the glorious light of the gospel; the moon, its light reflected in the rites and ceremonies of Old Testament times; and the twelve stars in the woman's crown, the twelve apostles.[6]

In this figurative scene the child who "was caught up to God and to his throne" is Christ. Again and again New Testament writers speak of the risen Christ, upon His ascension to heaven, as being "seated at the right hand of the throne of the Majesty in heaven."[7] Furthermore, this child was destined "to rule all the nations with a rod of iron," a role John and other Bible writers assign exclusively to Christ. In Revelation 19:11-16 a being identified as "King of kings and Lord of lords" and "The Word of God" is said to "smite the nations" and "rule them with a rod of iron."[8] The title *Word of God* is one John consistently reserves for Christ.[9] Accordingly, the scene of Revelation 12:1-3 represents the church of Old Testament times eagerly expecting the coming of the promised Messiah.

As the prophet explains in verse 9, the dragon represents the devil, or Satan, in his role as "the deceiver of the whole world" and as "the accuser" and persecutor of God's people. "Your adversary the devil," wrote Peter, "prowls around like a roaring lion, seeking some one to devour."[10] The dragon's attempt to devour the child represents Satan's unsuccessful efforts to destroy Christ at His birth, during His ministry, and at the cross.

## An Agelong Conflict

The fact that the dragon does not at first attack the woman, but awaits the birth of her Son, implies that he already knows and hates the unborn child. Verses 6 through 9 explain this prior acquaintance and hatred: "War arose in heaven," John says, with "Michael and his angels fighting against the dragon." As we have seen, Michael, Captain of the heavenly host, is none other than Christ, the Son of God.[11] This cosmic contest in the remote past, before the dawn of history, began when Lucifer, who became Satan, jealously swore to himself, "I will ascend to heaven; above the stars of God I will set my throne on high; . . . I will make myself like the Most High."[12] It was his rash intention to usurp divine authority, to subvert the loyalty of intelligent beings, to secure their allegiance to himself, and to drive the Creator Himself from His own universe.

When Lucifer raised the banner of revolt, war broke out in heaven, but he was defeated and expelled, together with all who deliberately chose his leadership. "The dragon and his angels fought," says John, "but they were defeated" and cast out of heaven. Peter and Jude also allude to this great conflict.[13]

In infinite wisdom and patience God did not at once destroy the archrebel, but afforded him an opportunity to demonstrate his principles and policies, lest created beings look upon God as arbitrary and vindictive, and serve Him from fear. When the demonstration was complete, all could make an intelligent choice, and on this basis the question of divine justice and authority would be settled forever.

Then, in times primeval, the moral virus of sin found its way to our planet, and by man's own choice Satan became what Christ later called "the ruler of this world."[14] In the ultimate analysis, human history is the story of Satan's maneuvers to infect all mankind with this fatal virus, and thus to consolidate his authority over the entire human race. But it is also the story of God's counterplan to stamp out the virus and to save those who accept His prescribed cure for it, to live on forever in a perfect world.[15] Of course, all who refuse the remedy prescribed by the great Physician of men's souls will eventually perish along with the virus, when God mercifully eradicates it forever. To the inspired writers of the Bible this world is the stage on which the agelong conflict between good and evil, between Christ and Satan, the dragon, is being slowly but inexorably fought out to a certain and definitive conclusion.

The dragon evidently recognizes that the child about to be born to the woman is the very one who had defeated him in ages past, and he now seeks to avenge that defeat. The symbolic scene of Revelation 12 is reminiscent of the time in Eden when "the serpent" tempted "the woman," of the inveterate hatred that arose between them, and of the promise that the woman's "seed," or offspring, would eventually crush the serpent.[16]

## Victory at the Cross

It was on the cross that Christ won the decisive victory over Satan.[17] Looking forward to the crucifixion, the Saviour declared, "Now shall the ruler of this world be cast out," and again, "I saw Satan fall like lightning from heaven."[18] Of this cosmic event the Apostle John wrote, in the symbolism of Revelation 12, "The great dragon was thrown down, that ancient serpent, who is called the Devil and Satan, the deceiver of the whole world—he was thrown down to the earth, and his angels were thrown down with him."

At the cross Satan's true character was fully revealed before the universe, and he and his angels were permanently expelled from heaven.[19] Then John heard a triumphant voice from the realms of glory proclaiming, "Now the salvation and the power and the kingdom of our God and the authority of his Christ have come, for the accuser of our brethren has been thrown down." In other words, it was at the cross that "salvation" became an accomplished, historical fact, that God's "power" and "kingdom" were made secure, and that Christ received "all authority in heaven and on earth."[20] It was by "the blood of the Lamb" shed on Calvary that the inhabitants of heaven "conquered" Satan. Well might they "rejoice."

## Satan's Hatred of the Church

The same voice from heaven next warns the inhabitants of earth that "the devil has come down to you in great wrath, because he knows that his time is short." At this juncture "the woman fled into the wilderness, where she has a place prepared by God, in which to be nourished for one thousand two hundred and sixty days." God provides her with "the two wings of the great eagle that she might fly from the serpent into the wilderness, to the place where she is to be nourished for a time, and times, and half a time." An eagle in flight from a dragon would have a decided advantage over it. Old Testament writers often make eagles' wings a figure for divine protection.[21] The three and a half prophetic "times" of Revelation 12: 14 are equivalent to the 1260 "days" of verse 6, and in the symbolism of prophecy both represent 1260 years of literal time.[22] This is identically the same period of time Daniel assigns to the career of the persecuting tyrant and to his "shattering of the power of the holy people."[23]

A "wilderness" is an uninhabited region where life is fraught with hardship, privation, and danger. Food, shelter, and possibly even water would be difficult to obtain, and there would be danger from wild animals and perhaps marauding outlaws. At the same time, the wilderness would provide refuge from enemies.

In ancient times the Hebrew people wandered for forty years in the wilderness on their way from Egypt to the land of Canaan. The prophet Elijah twice took refuge in the wilderness from enemies bent on his life. Christ met the devil in a personal encounter in the wilderness.[24] Accordingly, the figurative "wilderness" of Revelation 12 represents a situation fraught with hardship and danger for God's people, but also protection from enemies who are bent on destroying them.

In bloodthirsty pursuit, "the serpent poured water like a river out of his mouth after the woman, to sweep her away with the flood." In the Old Testament flood waters are a common figure for great suffering and destruction, particularly when caused by invading armies.[25] In view of the fact that John elsewhere explains his use of "waters," as a symbol for "peoples and multitudes and nations," reference in Revelation 12 is evidently to armed attacks on the church.[26] This is the same era of severe persecution of which Daniel repeatedly spoke and to which Christ referred as the "great tribulation." A religious war of extermination is here foretold.

"The earth came to the help of the woman," John continues, and "opened its mouth and swallowed the river which the dragon had poured from his mouth." Since "waters" are a prophetic symbol for "peoples and multitudes and nations,"[26] "the earth"—standing in contrast with the "waters"—may indicate sparsely populated, wilderness areas. This might be either mountainous areas remote from civilization or large, unpopulated regions of earth. On the other hand, "the earth" may simply designate regions to which the church could flee for refuge. Thus there is respite from persecution, and the wily dragon is once more frustrated in his murderous design.

In chapter 12 the dragon is defeated three times. First, Michael vanquished him in heaven. Then he was prevented from destroying the "male child," Christ. Finally, "the woman" was providentially delivered from "the river which the dragon had poured from his mouth" in an endeavor to destroy her. Little wonder that the dragon, frustrated these three times, "was angry with the woman, and went off to make war on the rest of her offspring." This final attempt, however, is the subject of a future chapter.[27]

## A Clever Camouflage

But the picture is not yet complete. Daniel saw a lion, a bear, a leopard, and a nondescript ten-horned monster come up in succession from the sea. In Revelation 13 John relates that he saw another "beast rising out of the sea, with ten horns and seven heads, with ten diadems upon its horns and a blasphemous name upon its heads." This new beast closely resembles the seven-headed, ten-horned, seven-crowned dragon of chapter 12, but the two are not identical. It is a composite creature that resembles a leopard. But it has a bear's paws and a lion's mouth—in both instances the predatory features of the animal mentioned. It thus combines selected features of the same four beasts Daniel saw emerge from the sea.

But why is it necessary to introduce still another beast into the prophetic menagerie? John says that "the dragon gave his power and his throne and great authority" to the leopardlike beast. Apparently the dragon appoints this new beast to act as his secret agent on earth. He works through an accomplice, and by this clever camouflage hopes to accomplish that which he has been unable to do in person. It is through the leopard beast, then, that the dragon goes about making war on the church. Satan does not appear in person on the stage of history, but like a puppet player he is always backstage manipulating affairs through men and organizations that submit to his principles and his leadership.

There is still another side to the leopard beast's character and career. It not only persecutes God's people, but utters "haughty and blasphemous words . . . against God, blaspheming his name and his dwelling" and "those who dwell in heaven." Furthermore, "all who dwell on earth will worship it," John says, "every one whose name has not been written . . . in the book of life of the Lamb that was slain." Bewitched, they ask, "Who is like the beast, and who can fight against it?" In reality, John explains, they are worshiping Satan, who had given his authority to the beast.

Like its counterpart in the Book of Daniel, this beast defies God, demands recognition of its religious authority, and persecutes all who refuse to comply with its will. Also like its counterpart in Daniel, it is eminently successful. Except for those who choose to be loyal to God, it eventually wins at least the nominal allegiance of the whole world.

As a final mark of identity, John says, "Let him who has understanding reckon the number of the beast, for it is a human number, its number is six hundred and sixty-six." We will deal thoroughly with the interpretation of this puzzling, cryptic number in a later chapter.

The seven heads of the scarlet beast of chapter 17, which closely resembles the leopardlike beast of chapter 13, are specifically declared to represent seven "kings," or major political powers, through which the dragon persecutes God's people.[28] It is therefore reasonable to conclude that the same is true of the seven heads of the leopard beast of chapter 13. John does not explain whether the seven heads represent seven particular nations, or whether the number seven is here used in an all-inclusive sense, as so often elsewhere in the book, and thus symbolizes all such persecuting kingdoms. Nor does it matter. Under any circumstances, the seven heads stand for major world powers through which Satan has persecuted God's people since the dawn of history. In the Book of Daniel the ten horns, as we have seen, represent the less important nations, but neither Daniel nor John explains whether ten particular nations are represented, or whether the number ten is also used in a more general, inclusive sense.

The dragon of chapter 12 pursued the woman for a period of 1260 prophetic "days," or literal years, seeking to destroy her. The beast of chapter 13 "was allowed to exercise authority for forty-two months," and "to make war on the saints and to conquer them" during that period of time. As we have seen, forty-two thirty-day months are equivalent to 1260 prophetic "days," or literal years.[22] Here, the dragon and the beast—Satan and his accomplice on earth—are both represented as making war on God's people during the same period of time as Daniel allotted to the persecuting tyrant of his prophecy.

What brings the leopard beast's criminal career to a halt? As John watched, he observed that "one of its heads seemed to have a mortal wound." In verses 12 and 14 of the same chapter the beast itself is said to have been wounded. In view of the fact that Revelation 13 is concerned with the beast's actions during the 1260 prophetic "days," or years, it is reasonable to conclude that the "mortal wound" here referred to was inflicted at the close of that period of time. During its 1260 years of life it had taken God's people captive and slain them with the sword. Now it suffers the same fate.

## The Great Harlot

The seventeenth chapter of Revelation presents the religious aspect of the persecutor's character and conduct under still another symbol, that of a "great harlot who is seated upon many waters." As we have seen, an immoral woman is the usual prophetic symbol for an apostate church.[29] Accordingly, this great persecuting power is a religious as well as a political organization. "The waters . . . where the harlot is seated," the angel told John, represent "peoples and multitudes and nations and tongues."[26] The harlot's name, which John saw written on her forehead, is "Babylon the great."[30] She is said to be the "mother of harlots and of earth's abominations." She is a harlot herself, and she has daughters who are harlots. Since this harlot stands for a church, her daughters must represent other apostate churches.

The angel "carried me away in the Spirit into a wilderness," John relates, "and I saw a woman sitting on a scarlet beast which was full of blasphemous names, and it had seven heads and ten horns." Evidently this is the same beast as the leopard of chapter 13, and the same wilderness as in chapter 12, where the dragon (and later the beast) persecute the virtuous woman of that chapter.

This harlot has "committed fornication" with "the kings of the earth." Since the harlot represents an apostate religious organization, and the "kings" or "kingdoms" of the earth are political organizations, an unholy alliance between the two would be a union of church and state. In verse 18 the angel tells John, "The woman that you saw is the great city which has dominion over the kings of the earth." In other words, this church dominates world politics. What is her objective in doing so?

In the first place she compels "the dwellers on earth" to "become drunk" with "the wine of . . . [her] fornication," that is, to accept her false teachings. Here as in chapter 13:8 "the dwellers on earth whose names have not been written in the book of life from the foundation of the world" stand in awe before the beast, and submit to it. In the second place, she herself is "drunk with the blood of the saints and the blood of the martyrs of Jesus." In other words, she is bent on murdering her rival, the virtuous woman of chapter 12. An apostate church enters into an unholy alliance with the political powers of earth for the purpose of compelling the people of earth to submit to her authority, and of destroying all who choose instead to remain loyal to God.

## Why God Has Revealed These Things

Why did God reveal this bleak picture of the future? "Here," says John, "is a call for the endurance [and faith] of the saints."[31] The information given was revealed to strengthen our faith and to give us courage to endure. Were we to encounter the devil's fearful onslaughts unexpectedly, we might be tempted to doubt that God is still in charge of affairs and that He will eventually bring the reign of evil to an end. We would be in danger of relinquishing our faith and abandoning all hope.

Now that we have finished examining the fearful portrait of this criminal power on display in the rogue's gallery of prophecy, let us go out onto the highway of history in search of the culprit. Our concern is not so much over his past crimes as over those the inspired writers of the Bible warn us he is bent on committing in the future. A review of his past record, in history, will prepare us to recognize his clever devices and to cope more effectively with them. Otherwise we are in grave danger of joining his long list of hapless victims.

### NOTES

1. Matthew 24:4, 5, 11, 23, 24.
2. Acts 20:29, 30.
3. 2 Thessalonians 2:1-12.
4. See Isaiah 54:5, 6; Jeremiah 3:20; Ezekiel 23:2-4; 2

Corinthians 11:2; Ephesians 5:25-32; Revelation 17:1-3; etc.

5. Revelation 12:17.

6. John 8:12 (compare Malachi 4:2); Colossians 2:16, 17; Hebrews 8:5; Matthew 19:28 (compare Daniel 12:3).

7. Hebrews 8:1 (compare Ephesians 1:20-22); Hebrews 1:3; 10:12; Revelation 3:21; etc.

8. Compare also Psalm 2:7-9; Hebrews 5:5; 2 Peter 1:17.

9. See John 1:1, 14; 1 John 1:1-3.

10. 1 Peter 5:8.

11. See note 9, page 169.

12. Isaiah 14:13, 14; Revelation 12:7-9.

13. 2 Peter 2:4; Jude 6.

14. Genesis 3:1-19; John 12:31; 14:30.

15. John 3:16; 2 Corinthians 4:4.

16. See Genesis 3:1-6, 15.

17. Colossians 2:14, 15.

18. Luke 10:18; John 12:31, 32.

19. See page 131.

20. Revelation 12:10-12; compare Matthew 28:18.

21. See Exodus 19:4; Deuteronomy 32:11.

22. See pages 166, 167, 210.

23. Daniel 7:25; 12:7.

24. Numbers 14:33; 1 Kings 17:1-7; 19:4-9; Matthew 4:1, 2.

25. See Psalms 32:6; 69:2; Isaiah 8:8; 28:2, 15; 43:2; Jeremiah 47:2; Nahum 1:8; Daniel 11:22.

26. Revelation 17:15.

27. See Revelation 12:4, 5, 7, 8, 15-17.

28. Revelation 17:9, 10.

29. See page 206.

30. See page 290.

31. Revelation 14:12.

# History's Greatest Hoax

W E HAVE now surveyed, at some length, the surprisingly complete and vivid prophetic picture of the experience of the church down through the centuries. In this chapter and the next it is our purpose to discover how the scenes thus foretold have been and are still being acted out on the stage of history. We shall then be able to determine our own position more accurately in the great trajectory of time and to prepare intelligently for the momentous events that lie just ahead. First of all, however, let us summarize rather briefly the information presented in the preceding four chapters.

## A Brief Synopsis of the Prophecies[1]

The great villain of the prophecies of Daniel, Christ, Paul, and John was to arise in western Europe during the decline and fall of the ancient Roman Empire, and as it did so to eliminate three troublesome competitors. Relatively insignificant at the outset, it would become superlatively great and achieve almost unbelievable success. In reality, it would be an accomplice of Satan cleverly disguised as a representative of Christ —history's greatest hoax. In a supreme endeavor to gain complete control of the human race, Satan would invest it with his own power and authority and make it his agent on earth. It was to be a religiopolitical organization, an integral union of church and state, and was to dominate the religion and politics of western Europe after the fall of Rome.

This sinister power would impose its authority over the peoples and nations of the civilized world, and except for stalwart heroes of faith who determined to be loyal to God, even at the cost of life itself if need be, all would submit to its will. Many would be led astray by supernatural signs and wonders to which it would point as supposed evidence of its claims. It would be shrewd, arrogant, treacherous, and cruel in the pursuit of its objectives.

This religiopolitical organization would come into being as the result of a great apostasy within the Christian church and would usurp the prerogatives and authority of Christ over the church. It would defy God and, for practical purposes, deify itself. Its course of action would constitute rebellion against the Most High. It would arrogate to itself the right to alter, or even abolish, the divine precepts and sacred observances and would substitute its own authority for that of the Holy Scriptures. It would suppress the knowledge and practice of the way of salvation in Christ as set forth in the Bible and require, instead, compliance with its own counterfeit teachings and system of salvation. Its secret identification number was to be 666.

In its attempt to control the world this apostate power would wage a determined and ruthless war of extermination against all who chose to remain loyal to God. The result would be a long era of unprecedented suffering and hardship. God's faithful people would be driven into hiding, but He would watch over them and provide for their needs. Many Christians would lay down their lives, but through it all God promised to preserve His church on earth intact. He would not permit the light of truth to go out completely.

Among those who remained faithful would be men wise in the truth as it is revealed in the Scriptures. They would succeed in turning many back to a knowledge of God and the Holy Scriptures, and a genuine reformation would result.

This apostate, persecuting power would dominate the political and religious scene in western Europe for approximately 1260 years, at the close of which it was destined to suffer what would at first appear to be a mortal wound. Christ foretold two great signs in the heavens, the darkening of the sun and the falling of the stars, to mark the close of its period of supremacy, and the imminence of His return and the end of the world. But it would recover from its mortal wound, regain its former power, and flourish until Christ destroys it at His second coming and inaugurates His own eternal, righteous reign on earth.

## History Confirms Prophecy

Does the history of the past two thousand years record any developments that correspond with those foretold by Christ and the inspired writers of the Bible? Let us see.

Ominous forces were already silently at work within the church, even before the death of the apostles. The pure gospel gradually became diluted with error and human tradition, piety and zeal waned, and standards of personal conduct were relaxed. The presence of the Holy Spirit, the invisible bond of unity that originally bound Christians everywhere together in one great fellowship, was lost, and an authoritarian spirit gradually took its place. Worship became formal, and ritual replaced the simple preaching of the Word. Popularity and personal influence came to determine the appointment of leaders, who began to assume increasing authority within the local churches and then to extend their control over neighboring churches.

A trend toward ecclesiastical autocracy gradually concentrated power in the hands of a single official, the bishop, to whom every church member was personally subject and through submission to whom alone he was supposed to have access to salvation. Instead of serving the church, those who were greatest in it became princes over the household of God and ruled it with an increasingly heavy hand. Thus developed the concept of a priestly hierarchy that interposed itself between the individual Christian and his Lord. In time, this system cut men off almost completely from direct access to their heavenly Father and bound them in chains of ignorant submission to these apostate leaders.

## How Rome Attained Supremacy

To begin with, the church at Rome was much like any other, and its leaders exercised no authority beyond the local membership. As one of the earliest churches founded in the West, however, it enjoyed a position of honor and respect even before the death of the apostles. Irenaeus, who died about A.D. 200 and who was one of the so-called Fathers of the early church, seems to have been first to give expression to the idea that all other churches should, of necessity, agree with the church at Rome in matters of faith and doctrine. Cyprian, who lived half a century later and who is usually considered the founder of the Roman hierarchy, put forth the claim that Peter had founded the church at Rome, that the bishop of Rome should therefore be honored above other bishops, and that his opinions and decisions should always prevail.[2]

It was no accident that the leaders of the church at Rome eventually gained both religious supremacy and a dominant voice in politics throughout the western lands of the Roman Empire. As the imperial capital and metropolis of the civilized world, Rome was the natural location for the headquarters of a world church. Furthermore, the church there was the only one in the West that claimed apostolic origin, a fact which was supposed to accord it a sort of seniority, dignity, and authority.

When Emperor Constantine was nominally converted to Christianity early in the fourth century A.D. and became a member of the church at Rome, he established the Roman form of Christianity as the official religion of the empire. His personal relationship to the bishop of Rome almost inevitably invested the latter with prestige and authority other bishops could not hope to claim. With one important exception, all the later Roman emperors were at least nominally Christian.

Constantine initiated the policy of making the church, which was by this time strongly established in most parts of the empire, an instrument of imperial policy to assist him in his endeavor to reunify it and consolidate his control over it. By this time the empire had been tottering precariously on the brink of chaos for half a century or more. Constantine's removal of the imperial capital to Constantinople in A.D. 330 left the bishop of Rome comparatively free of imperial control, and thereafter the emperor rather consistently supported his claims as against those of his fellow bishops. This situation also left a sort of political vacuum in which the bishop of Rome, henceforth the most important personage in the West, became the emperor's unofficial ally and gradually came to perform certain civil functions.

During the early centuries the church at Rome successfully resisted various heretical movements, and contending factions elsewhere often appealed to the bishop of Rome to arbitrate their differences. While major theological controversies rocked the church in the East, the bishop of Rome was free to devote himself to more practical matters and to extend his authority. In this way Rome won a reputation for orthodoxy, and with it, by tacit consent, a unique position of influence as custodian of the faith.

Repeatedly the bishop of Rome persuaded invading barbarian chieftains to spare the city from assault and plunder. Amid increasingly chaotic conditions, especially after A.D. 476, when the last emperor was deposed, he provided the city with the essential functions of civil government. From the seventh century onward

Mohammedan invasions greatly weakened the church in the East and eliminated his chief rivals—the bishops of Alexandria, Antioch, and Constantinople—from the contest for supremacy.

In contrast, most of the barbarian invaders of the West professed to accept the Roman form of Christianity. With the nominal conversion of Clovis, king of the Franks, in A.D. 496 the bishop of Rome gained a strong ally to champion his interests and to convert other barbarian tribes. For more than twelve centuries the sword of France, so-called "eldest son" of the papacy, became an effective instrument for spreading and maintaining papal authority.

When Constantine gave Christianity official status, he also linked the interests of the church with those of the state for the first time and, in effect, subordinated the church to the state. Generally speaking, from that time forward the emperor of Rome and the bishop of Rome cooperated closely to advance their mutual interests. One result of this companionate marriage of church and state was that the ecclesiastical administration of the papacy, which now began to develop rapidly, was patterned after Constantine's reorganized political administration of the Roman Empire. That hierarchical system remains essentially unchanged today.

## The Bishop of Rome Becomes the Pope

The first Roman bishop to claim jurisdiction over the entire Christian world, though unable actually to exercise that power, was Pope Innocent I, who died in A.D. 417. A few years later Saint Augustine, who is known as the founder of medieval theology, wrote a treatise entitled *The City of God,* in which he spelled out what has been ever since the Catholic ideal of world organization and unity—a universal church in control of a universal state. This work provided the theoretical basis for the medieval papacy.

Pope Leo I, who died in 461 and who became one of three popes to be known as "the Great," was first to succeed in applying these principles effectively as a part of papal policy. He procured an edict from the emperor declaring that papal decisions have the force of law, and ruled as both a temporal and spiritual prince. Later papal claims to temporal power were based largely on his reign as a precedent and on certain forged documents, or "pious frauds." Among these were the Pseudo-Isidorian Decretals, especially the so-called Donation of Constantine.[3] Throughout the Middle Ages these fraudulent documents bolstered the authority of the pope.

As we have seen, most of the barbarian invaders of the West accepted the Roman form of Christianity. Three, however—the Heruli, the Vandals, and the Ostrogoths—had accepted Arianism, another heretical form of Christianity, and were bitterly opposed to the teachings and claims of the papal hierarchy. For instance, Genseric, leader of the Vandals, announced his determination to crush out Roman Catholic Christianity altogether and to replace it with Arianism. A little later he sacked and burned the city of Rome. Attacks on the city of Rome and the occupation of central Italy by Arian powers prevented the pope from exercising his full authority.

In A.D. 533 Emperor Justinian issued an edict officially declaring the bishop of Rome supreme over the churches of both East and West. But this decree could not become effective until Belisarius, his military commander, defeated the Vandals and, in A.D. 538, drove the last of these Arian powers, the Ostrogoths, from Rome. From that time onward effective opposition ceased, and the papacy was free to exercise the prerogatives it had long claimed. This trend became fully evident during the pontificate of Gregory I (the Great), who died in 604 and who is recognized as the first great medieval prelate of the Church.

In A.D. 756 the Frankish king Pepin responded to a frantic plea from the pope for assistance against the barbarian Lombards, who were already entrenched in northern Italy and were menacing Rome and central Italy. Pepin completely subdued the Lombards and presented the pope with the territory he took from them. This gift, which is commonly known as the Donation of Pepin, gave birth to the Papal States and marks the formal beginning of the temporal rule of the pope.[4]

From the eighth to the eleventh centuries papal power was at low ebb, as one ineffective pontiff succeeded another. The next great pope, and one of the greatest of them all, was Gregory VII, who died in 1085. Claiming that the pope is entitled to the homage of all princes and that he alone may depose kings and emperors, Gregory elevated the papacy to a position of power and prestige it had never known before. A little more than a century later, with the pontificate of Innocent III, who died in 1216, the papacy reached the zenith of its power and for another century or so basked in the high noon of its medieval glory.

## Gradual Decline of the Papacy

When Pope Boniface VIII, who died in 1303, attempted to exercise the authority and power of his predecessors, he found that times had changed. Kings and princes were beginning to ignore papal demands with impunity. The waning power of the papacy became fully evident a few years later, during the so-called Babylonian captivity of the church (1309-1377), when the French forcibly removed the seat of the papacy from Rome to Avignon in France. Only a year after the return to Rome, the Great Western Schism (1378-1417) greatly weakened the prestige and influence of the papacy, spiritually as well as temporally. During this time two and sometimes three rival popes were solemnly vilifying and excommunicating one another, each claiming to be the lawful successor to Saint Peter.

Long before Reformation times numerous voices were raised within the Church in protest against its arrogant claims and its many abuses of both secular and spiritual power.[5] The Renaissance (the rebirth of learning in Western Europe), the age of discovery, burgeoning commerce, the growth of strong national states, the birth of modern science, the invention of printing, the age of enlightenment, and various other factors—all contributed to the gradual loss of papal power which, like its growth, was a long and involved process that went on for nearly five centuries, from about A.D. 1300 to 1800. Not least among these other

factors was widespread corruption among the very
highest of the prelates of the church. This was especially true of the popes of the Renaissance, who neglected its spiritual affairs and ruled almost altogether
as secular princes. By the time of Martin Luther and
the Reformation much had already been done to un-
dermine Rome's authority in the councils of Europe
and in the hearts of men.

The great Protestant Reformation, which is usually
thought of as beginning in 1517, completely destroyed the Church in large areas of northern Europe
and in many of the new colonial regions of the world.
Wars of religion ravaged the continent for generations. Finally, the French Revolution outlawed the
Church in France, which had been the first nation officially to espouse its cause and which had for more
than twelve centuries been its foremost champion. In
France papal principles and policies had been thoroughly tested, more fully than in any other country.
As French historians themselves candidly admit, the
Revolution was, fundamentally, a revolt against the
Church.[6]

In 1798 the French government determined to exterminate the papacy, as the inveterate enemy of freedom and progress. With this in view it directed
Napoleon, then campaigning in Italy, to take the pope
prisoner. Napoleon in turn trusted this mission to his
general Berthier, who transported the pope to France,
where he died in exile.[7] Ironically, it was at the hands
of France, its "eldest son" and chief sword-bearer
throughout the 1260 years, that the papacy sustained
its mortal wound. This episode came as the climax to

a long series of stunning blows to the prestige and power of the papacy over a period of centuries.

Throughout the nineteenth century the papacy remained shorn of its former power. Whereas heretofore its voice had been paramount in the councils of Europe, it now spoke in scarcely a whisper. Knowledgeable people of the day believed that *rigor mortis* had set in and that the final chapter in the long story of papal power was, at long last, about to be written.

In 1870, when the Papal States became a part of the united kingdom of Italy, the temporal power the papacy had formally exercised for well over a thousand years came to an end. With this turn of events Pope Pius IX voluntarily assumed the role of what he called "prisoner of the Vatican," and for practical purposes the papacy was prostrate. This state of affairs continued until the temporal power of the pope was restored in 1929, by a treaty with Mussolini which established the tiny state of Vatican City.

## A Record of Arrogant Intolerance

Throughout the history of western civilization the Church of Rome has distinguished herself by a spirit of arrogant intolerance toward all who honor the authority of the Bible above her own. She has made it her first business to obliterate all dissent and to crush all who do not submit to her will. In the twelfth and thirteenth centuries the pope mounted massive crusades against the Albigenses of southern France and all but exterminated them. Other notorious examples of this policy were the measures taken in England against the followers of John Wycliffe, a war to the death against the Hussites of Bohemia, the Inquisition in Spain under Torquemada, the reign of blood in the Netherlands under the Duke of Alva, repeated attempts to exterminate the Waldenses, and the martyrdom of the Huguenots in France, especially the Saint Bartholomew's Day Massacre. A long list of other mass attacks on Protestants, all carried out in the name of religion, indict the papacy as a ruthless persecutor.

It is a simple fact of history that the Church of Rome has been responsible for the torture and death of more Christians than all the pagan powers of earth. The early persecutions staged by the Roman emperors Decius and Diocletian pale into insignificance when compared with the bloody deeds perpetrated by the so-called "Holy Office" of the Church of Rome. Papal persecution has not been an occasional, temperamental outburst, but is the result of a fixed policy based on dogmatic necessity that obliges Rome to eradicate dissent whenever and wherever possible, by whatever means promises to be most effective.

Only in certain lands where the Church of Rome is fully in control and which are comparatively remote from the gaze of the civilized world, however, are oppressive measures approved today. Persecution slumbers, not because Rome has had a change of heart, but because, at the moment, the spirit of religious freedom in the world makes that method inopportune and inexpedient. The Church would lose more than it could expect to gain. It is true that some Roman Catholic leaders now speak in favor of religious liberty, according to their definition of the term, but the official policy on persecution has never changed.

The "wilderness" into which John saw the church flee for safety during the 1260 years of papal supremacy represents such places of refuge as the fastnesses of the Alps and the Protestant lands of northern Europe. Many others migrated to the New World. There was evidence, also, of a divine hand guiding the course of history in a way to advance the cause of the Reformation. Consider, for instance, the long reign of Emperor Charles V, which spanned the early decades of the Reformation and which he dedicated to the obliteration of the Protestant "heresy." Again and again he poised his army for the attack, but each time was diverted from his purpose—by the Turks, by the king of France, and by his own quarrels with the pope.

These are the simple facts of history. It is evident from this brief sketch that, as with most historical developments, the rise and decline of the papacy were both gradual processes that covered many centuries. By 538 the papacy was completely formed and functioning unhindered in all essential aspects. By 1798, exactly 1260 years later, it had lost practically all its accumulated authority and power and survived only as a shadow of its former self. This 1260-year period spans its time of supremacy. In a later chapter we will follow the fortunes of the papacy since 1798 and trace its future role as pictured in Bible prophecy.

## Positive Points of Identification

The striking similarity between the prophetic blueprint and the facts of history conclusively identifies the papacy as the power foretold. What other person or organization could even begin to meet the specifications of prophecy? Let us briefly summarize the main points of correspondence:

The great persecuting power of prophecy was to be a successor to the Roman Empire. As we have seen, the papacy took over and maintained exclusive control of Rome, capital of the Roman Empire, for more than a thousand years. The western part of the Roman Empire, its heartland, became the private parish of the bishops of Rome, politically as well as spiritually. The name Rome, which formerly applied to the ancient empire, became the identifying part of the name— Roman Catholic Church. The language of the Roman Empire, Latin, became and remains today the official language of the Catholic Church. The hierarchical administration of the papacy was originally patterned after, and remains essentially to this day, that of the Roman Empire as reorganized by Emperor Constantine. The name, capital, territory, language, administration, and legal status of the Church of Rome were thus a direct heritage from the realm of the Caesars. Out of the ruins of the Roman Empire rose the Roman Church, and in a sense the empire lived on, reincarnate, in the Church. It would be difficult to imagine a more exact correspondence between the specifications of Bible prophecy and their historical fulfillment.

The persecutor was to be relatively insignificant to begin with, but to meet with phenomenal success and eventually to dominate western Europe. The Church of Rome eventually did, in fact, act as overlord of the nations of western Europe, to the point of appointing and deposing kings, for centuries. Its period of supremacy was to be 1260 years. As we have seen, the papacy was fully formed by A.D. 538 and maintained its political dominance until approximately 1798.

The papacy is the only institution in the world today that has existed continuously since ancient times. It was fully established long before Mohammed was born and while the Arabs were still worshiping idols at Mecca, when the Anglo-Saxons set foot on the shores of Britain, and when the French migrated to France. It has witnessed the birth of every government now in existence. Babylon endured for less than a century, Persia for a little more than two centuries, the Greek kingdom for less than two, and the Roman Empire for five or six centuries. But the papacy has maintained continuity of administration for more than sixteen centuries—a feat never equaled by any other nation in history. It was to remain dominant politically until the great signs foretold by Christ should appear in the heavens, when it would be the recipient of a mortal wound.

The persecutor was to wage relentless war on those who chose to remain loyal to the pure teachings of the Bible. The papacy claims absolute sovereignty over the souls of all men, including those who have never submitted to its authority. As we have seen, these claims have been ruthlessly put into effect upon countless occasions over many centuries.

In every significant particular thus far considered, the Church of Rome has precisely fulfilled the specifications marked out by the Bible writers for the great apostate power that was to oppress and persecute God's people during the long interval between the first and second advents of our Lord.

The points considered in this chapter have been chiefly historical and political in nature. In our next chapter we will consider the fulfillment of the religious and theological specifications of prophecy.

## NOTES

1. For details see pages 156-171, 187-218.

2. For verification and further information on the points of early church history referred to in this discussion, see any standard church history.

3. About A.D. 1440 Lorenzo Valla, a Roman Catholic scholar, proved the so-called Donation of Constantine to be a forgery. For centuries this document and the Pseudo-Isidorian Decretals have been universally recognized as deliberate, if "pious," frauds. Nevertheless, the Church of Rome relied on them throughout the Middle Ages as documentary proof of the supremacy of the pope.

4. The Papal States occupied a large area of central and northern Italy, with boundaries that varied from time to time, from A.D. 756 to 1870. The pope ruled over them as a sovereign prince.

5. Such as Joachim of Fiore, Marsilius of Padua, Michael of Cesena, William of Ockham, John Wycliffe, Lorenzo Valla, John Huss, Jerome of Prague, and Savonarola.

6. Alexis de Tocqueville, *The Old Regime and the Revolution,* translated by John Bonner (New York: Harper and Brothers, 1856), pp. 18, 19, 248; A. Aulard, *Christianity and the French Revolution,* translated by Lady Frazer (Boston: Little, Brown, and Company, 1927), pp. 13, 14, 50, 89, 100, 123, 137, etc.

7. On the 13th of the month Pluviose of the Year V (1797) the Directory, the French revolutionary government, declared that the Roman religion would always be "the irreconcilable enemy of the Republic," and directed Napoleon, who was then campaigning in Italy, "to destroy, if possible, the centre of unity of the Roman Church." (A. Aulard, *Christianity and the French Revolution,* p. 151.)

# A Man Impersonates God

WHAT A MAN believes about God and about himself; about his duty in this life toward God, his fellowmen, and the problems of life; and about his future destiny—this determines his basic attitude toward life, his conduct, and his character. But how can a man be certain of the truth regarding these great central problems of existence, duty, and destiny? There is no laboratory, workshop, proving ground, or museum where he can go and observe a full demonstration of the principles involved, and on this basis arrive at his own conclusions about right attitudes and conduct in all the situations and relationships of life. For this reason the scientific method of arriving at truth, by reasoning from observed evidence, cannot provide him with the answer to these questions. Furthermore, his own brief span of life and his limited experience and perspective leave him, at best, not much better off than a mosquito contemplating the vast universe.

Some may suggest that philosophy can provide the answers, that man is able to reason his way through these problems. But on matters such as these philosophy is a blind and crippled guide, simply because the human mind cannot escape the gravitational pull of its own preconceived opinions, biases, and a penchant for jumping at conclusions from a jerry-built platform of insufficient evidence.

There is only one other way by which a man can attain to truth, and that is by supernatural revelation. It is the very essence of the teachings of Christ, and thus of the Christian religion, that the Scriptures alone provide reliable answers to these vital questions. The Bible is the great bureau of standards on such matters, and its word alone is final. Christ declared, "The words that I have spoken to you are spirit and life," and again, "If you continue in my word, you are truly my disciples, and you will know the truth, and the truth will make you free."[1]

Christ is the author of all truth, and the devil the author of all error. During the course of His personal encounter with the devil in the wilderness, Christ insisted that "man shall not live by bread alone, but by every word that proceeds from the mouth of God."[2] When it comes to the great central facts of man's existence, it is of little consequence what a man may think or what scientists and philosophers may say on the subject. The only thing that really counts is what God has said and placed on record in the Scriptures.

## Tradition Versus Scripture

On one occasion the religious leaders of the day accosted Christ with the question as to why He did not require His disciples to "live according to the tradition of the elders." Now, religious tradition is simply the cumulative body of religious opinions, beliefs, practices, and customs that have been handed down from generation to generation. Tradition is accumulated *human* wisdom. To this question Christ replied, "In vain do they worship me, teaching as [divinely revealed] doctrines the precepts of men. . . . You have a fine way of rejecting the commandment of God," He said, "in order to keep your tradition."[3] Again and again when asked about points of religious belief Christ referred His questioners to the Scriptures. "What is written in the law [the Scriptures]? How do you read?" He would ask in reply.[4]

Paul wrote to Timothy that "the sacred writings . . . are able to instruct you for salvation through faith in Christ Jesus." "All scripture," he said, "is inspired by God and profitable for teaching, for reproof, for correction, and for training in righteousness, that the man of God may be complete, equipped for every good work."[5]

Joining the discussion, Peter declared, "We did not follow cleverly devised myths when we made known to you the power and coming of our Lord Jesus Christ, but we were eyewitnesses of his majesty." Then he hastened on to explain that the Christian has something even more convincing than eyewitness testimony —"the prophetic word." "You will do well to pay attention to this as to a lamp shining in a dark place," he declared, "until the day dawns and the morning star rises in your hearts." And why so? Because what the prophets wrote was not "a matter of . . . [their] own interpretation [opinion]." In fact, "no prophecy ever came by the impulse of man, but men moved by the Holy Spirit spoke from God."[6] Yes, the Bible came from God, and it alone can lead men to God. It is a unique and authoritative revelation about God and His will for man. This is the unanimous and invariable teaching of Christ and the apostles on this important subject.[7]

## The Master Delusion

The inspired writers of the Bible picture our planet as the great cosmic battleground on which the agelong conflict between Christ and Satan, good and evil, truth and error, is being fought out to a certain and definitive conclusion. As we have said, the devil is the author of all falsehood and error. Christ branded him "a liar and the father of lies."[8] The Apostle Paul warned that "Satan disguises himself as an angel of light,"[9] and that as Christians "we are not contending against flesh and blood, but against the principalities, against the powers, against the world rulers of this present darkness, against the spiritual hosts of wickedness."[10] From the beginning Satan's policy has been one of camouflage and deception; in fact, it was through deception that he became "the ruler of this world" in the first place.[11] If Satan were to appear in his true character, no one would buy his bill of goods.

Christ and the apostles predicted that the agelong contest between truth and error would become increasingly sharp and bitter during the interval between His first and second advents. Paul foretold a great "rebellion" within the church in which a "man of lawlessness" he characterized as "the mystery of iniquity" (King James Version) would appear, an impostor "who opposes and exalts himself against every so-called god or object of worship" and who "takes his seat in the temple of God, proclaiming himself to be God." As we have seen, that is precisely what Satan aspired to do in heaven before his expulsion. Paul goes on to say that the coming of this impostor was to be "with all power and with pretended signs and wonders, and with all wicked deception."[12]

But is it credible, as we found in the preceding chapter, that an organization posing as the true church and whose head claims to be Christ's vicegerent, or officially designated representative, should in fact have become Satan's master instrument in an attempt to thwart God's purposes on earth? A bold and clever scheme, indeed! Yet, if "Satan disguises himself as an angel of light," Paul wrote, "it is not strange if his servants also disguise themselves as servants of righteousness."[13] The papal system is so clever a counterfeit that even its best informed proponents honestly and sincerely believe it to be God's true church, and its teachings to be God's own truth.

Surely, with his aeons of experience, the master deceiver himself would not be content to perpetrate a clumsy counterfeit. We would expect his camouflage to be so nearly perfect as to be beyond detection, except by those who know for themselves what Christ and the inspired writers of the Bible actually taught, and who test everything by that standard. The more closely counterfeit money resembles the genuine, the greater is its power to deceive. In fact, Paul said, only those who know the truth and who have dedicated their hearts and lives to it will be secure against this master delusion. Sooner or later the man who deliberately clings to error in the face of known truth will actually come to "believe what is false."[14] Our only protection against error is to cherish truth with all our hearts.

## The Great Apostasy

As we have seen, Christ warned that "false Christs and false prophets" would arise and seek "to lead astray, if possible, even the elect." "Many," He said, "will come in my name, saying, 'I am the Christ,' and they will lead many astray."[15] Accordingly, He warned His disciples to "take heed that no one leads *you* astray." Paul similarly cautioned believers at Ephesus to "be alert" in view of the fact that "fierce wolves will come in among you, not sparing the flock," and that "from among your own selves will arise men speaking perverse things, to draw away the disciples after them."[16] A few years later Peter likewise warned that "there will be false teachers among you, who will secretly bring in destructive heresies."[17]

Paul explained that this "mystery of iniquity" was already secretly at work in his day. For a time, he said —during the lifetime of the apostles and their immediate successors as it proved to be—God's Holy Spirit would hinder or restrain it. But when God removed His restraining hand and permitted this sinister power to develop freely, there would be a great "rebellion," or apostasy from the truth.[18] As we have seen, history points to the papacy as the fulfillment of this and other Bible prophecies.

Now, the papacy is an integral union of church and state. It is a political as well as a religious institution, and the chief function of its political power is to enforce its supposed religious authority. Down through the centuries it has seldom hesitated to employ this often tremendous political power in a determined endeavor to force its religious teachings on others and to eradicate all dissent therefrom—by persuasion if possible, but failing that, by exterminating, or at least silencing, all who do not submit to its assumed authority. In greater or lesser degree this is true even today in all Catholic lands.

In this chapter we are to consider certain key papal dogmas in the light of what the Scriptures teach on these subjects. It would be both foolhardy and unchristian to make charges as grave as these without offering objective evidence in proof. In each instance, therefore, we will cite authoritative statements by recognized Catholic writers and compare these with the Bible. We shall see, also, that the Catholic Church frankly admits that many of its most important teachings cannot be substantiated from the Bible alone. It acknowledges that these teachings rest primarily, and in some instances solely, on the authority of the church.

## With Malice Toward None and Charity for All

As we investigate this question, let us bear in mind that when Catholic writers use the word *church,* they refer primarily to the papal hierarchy—the pope, the cardinals, the archbishops, and the bishops—and not to the lay members as a body. Strictly speaking, individual Catholics belong *to* "the Church," as subjects; they are not a part *of* it in the Protestant sense, and have no voice in its councils. We shall use the term *church* in the Catholic, not the Protestant, sense.

Let it be clearly understood that our remarks have nothing whatever to do with the hundreds of millions of adherents of that communion around the world, but only with the organization itself, as a system. Countless numbers of Catholics are entirely sincere in their beliefs and devout in their observance of religion as they understand it. But sincerity alone will not save a man. God holds us individually accountable for every ray of truth that shines into our hearts.

Even those who administer the system, and most particularly those in positions of lesser responsibility and authority, are not to be censured as evil geniuses, but befriended and helped as innocent victims of a clever system devised by "the ruler of this world." The remarks that follow have nothing to do with any individual Catholic, from the pope on down the line to his humblest parishioner, or with the membership of the Church collectively as a body. The spirit of Christ leaves no room for prejudice or bigotry of any kind or in any degree. The comments and conclusions set forth in this book are offered in the spirit of Christ, as a warning against delusion and not as a malicious attack.

## Usurping the Dignity and Prerogatives of God

Has the papacy indeed spoken "astonishing things" against God and thought to alter "the times and the law" ordained by God, as Daniel predicted? The official literature of the Church of Rome is replete with exhibits of papal claims that would be blasphemous even for angels to make. The following typical examples, by a doctor of canon law and a consultant at the Holy Office in Rome, are from a large encyclopedic work called *Prompta Bibliotheca:*

"The Pope is of so great dignity and so exalted that he is not a mere man, but as it were God, and the vicar of God. . . .

"The Pope is crowned with a triple crown, as king of heaven and of earth and of the lower regions. Moreover the superiority and the power of the Roman Pontiff by no means pertain only to heavenly things, to earthly things, and to things under the earth, but are even over angels, than whom he is greater. So that if it were possible that the angels might err in the faith, or might think contrary to the faith, they could be judged and excommunicated by the Pope. For he is of so great dignity and power that he forms one and the same tribunal with Christ.

"The Pope is as it were God on earth, sole sovereign of the faithful of Christ, chief of kings, having plenitude of power, to whom has been intrusted by the omnipotent God direction not only of the earthly but also of the heavenly kingdom. . . .

"The Pope is of so great authority and power that he can modify, explain, or interpret even divine laws. . . .

"The Pope can modify divine law, since his power is not of man but of God, and he acts as vicegerent of God upon earth with most ample power of binding and loosing his sheep.

"Whatever the Lord God himself, and the Redeemer, is said to do, that his vicar does, provided that he does nothing contrary to the faith."[19]

Addressing the pope at the Fifth Lateran Council, Archbishop Christopher Marcellus declared, "Thou art the shepherd, thou art the physician, thou art the director, thou art the husbandman; finally, thou art another God on earth."[20]

Augustinus Triumphus, a notable Catholic theologian, wrote, "The Pope alone is said to be the vicar of God; wherefore only what is bound or loosed by him is held to be bound and loosed by God Himself. Therefore the decision of the Pope and the decision of God constitute one decision, just as the opinion of the Pope and of his assistant are the same."[21]

Pope Leo XIII declared, "The supreme teacher in the Church is the Roman Pontiff. Union of minds, therefore, requires, together with a perfect accord in the one faith, complete submission and obedience of will to the Church and to the Roman Pontiff, as to God Himself." And again: "We [the popes] hold upon this earth the place of God Almighty."[22]

These claims to equality with God, to universal jurisdiction even over the inhabitants of heaven, and to the right to make changes in God's revealed will are strangely reminiscent of Lucifer's boast, "I will make myself like the Most High," of Daniel's persecuting tyrant, who was to "speak astonishing things against the God of gods," and of John's apostate villain who would utter "haughty and blasphemous words" against God.[23]

The pope's claim to absolute jurisdiction over all Christendom, to absolute infallibility when, in his official capacity as head of the Church, he defines doctrine and morals, and to the right to determine who shall be saved and who shall be consigned to hellfire are other prerogatives that belong to God alone. Could any claims a mere man might make be more "astonishing," to use Daniel's word for it? For that matter, what more *could* a man claim? When Christ declared Himself to be the Son of God, the Jewish leaders accused Him of blasphemy and proceeded to stone Him because, being only a man, as they pretended to believe, He had made Himself out to be God. Another time they sought to kill Him, saying that He "called God his Father, making himself equal with God."[24]

What kind of God would thus, in effect, abdicate His divine prerogatives to men whom history has again and again demonstrated to be erring mortals like the rest of us? What attitude would we take toward a President of the United States, for instance, who delegated his office to someone who had no legal right to it and who proceeded to act as a despot? Or, what would we think of a person who usurped the official prerogatives and full power and authority of the President, and set out to enforce these claims on pain of death? If held mentally responsible, such a person would be declared guilty of high treason. By its own testimony the papacy has qualified fully for the role assigned it by Daniel, Paul, and John. No other person or power in all history even remotely measures up to the prophetic specifications.

## A Positive Mark of Identification

One of the pope's official titles is *Vicarius Filii Dei,* which means "Vicar of the Son of God." This is a very common title for the pope, one that occurs throughout

Catholic literature. It designates him as Christ's officially delegated representative and spokesman on earth. The Latin word *vicarius* means "deputy" or "substitute," that is, a person appointed to substitute for someone else and to act in his name and with his full authority. That the title *Vicarius Filii Dei* reflects the pope's claim to the dignity and prerogatives of deity makes it especially significant.

In answer to the query, "What are the letters supposed to be in the pope's crown, and what do they signify, if anything?" the national Catholic journal *Our Sunday Visitor,* April 18, 1915, replied, "The letters inscribed in the Pope's mitre are these: *Vicarius Filii Dei,* which is the Latin for Vicar of the Son of God. Catholics hold that the Church which is a visible society must have a visible head." According to the *Catholic Encyclopedia,* the pope wears this mitre for liturgical functions. On August 3, 1941, the same journal denied that this title appears on the pope's *tiara,* which is not worn for liturgical functions. Whether the inscription appears on the mitre and not on the tiara, however, is beside the point. This name is acknowledged to be one of the official titles of the pope.

As if to avoid any error or uncertainty in recognizing the great future apostate, persecuting power, John revealed a secret identification mark, or "number," which he calls "the number of its name." That number is "six hundred and sixty-six."[25] In ancient times, before Arabic numerals came into use, certain letters of the alphabet did double duty as numerals. This was true among the Hebrews, the Greeks, the Romans, and other peoples of antiquity. We are all more or less familiar with the Latin letter-numerals—which until recent years appeared on clock and watch faces—the letter "I" standing for 1, "II" for 2, "V" for 5, "X" for 10, etc. Anciently it was a common practice for a man to add up the letters in his name that had a numerical value and take their sum as his secret code "number." The numerical value of *Vicarius Filii Dei* follows:

| | | | | | |
|---|---|---|---|---|---|
| V | = | 5 | F | = | 0 |
| I | = | 1 | I | = | 1 |
| C | = | 100 | L | = | 50 |
| A | = | 0 | I | = | 1 |
| R | = | 0 | I | = | 1 |
| I | = | 1 | | | |
| U | = | 5 | D | = | 500 |
| S | = | 0 | E | = | 0 |
| | | | I | = | 1 |

$$666$$

An attempt is sometimes made to blunt the force of this application of John's prophecy by pointing out that other names can also be made to "add up" to 666. This may well be, but it should be remembered that the number 666 is only one of a number of identifying marks given by John, and is significant only when considered in connection with them.

## Papal Authority Supersedes the Word of God

Let us ask next what claim the Church of Rome makes concerning its supposed authority to modify, amplify, or even to nullify God's revealed will as set forth in the Holy Scriptures—"to change the times and the law." First of all, the church claims that the Bible is a Roman Catholic work, that it is God's Word only by virtue of the fact that she vouches for its authenticity as such, and that she alone has the right to interpret and explain it. On this basis the Church, and not the Bible, becomes the norm of belief and the Christian's ultimate authority in faith and morals.

Formerly the Church of Rome prohibited unauthorized persons from reading the Bible or even owning a copy of it. Today she encourages its reading, but hastens to make clear that her own authority and teachings supersede those of the Bible. She still demands blind obedience to her interpretation of it. Note the following statements by Catholic writers:

"How doth man obtain a clear knowledge of the institute of salvation, proffered in Christ Jesus? The Protestant says, by searching Holy Writ, which is infallible: the Catholic, on the other hand, replies, by the Church, in which alone man arrives at the true understanding of Holy Writ."[26]

"Since the truths contained in Scripture and those handed down by Tradition both come from God, Scripture and Tradition [the accumulated teachings of the Church] are of equal value as sources of faith. Both deserve the same reverence and respect. . . .

"Scripture and Tradition are called the *remote rule of faith,* because the Catholic does not base his faith *directly* on these sources. The *proximate rule of faith* is for him the One, Holy, Catholic, and Apostolic Church, which alone has received from God the authority to interpret infallibly the doctrines He has revealed, whether these be contained in Scripture or in Tradition."[27]

"Like two sacred rivers flowing from Paradise, the Bible and divine Tradition contain the Word of God, the precious gems of revealed truths.

"Though these two divine streams are in themselves, on account of their divine origin, of equal sacredness, and are both full of revealed truths, still, of the two, TRADITION is to us more clear and safe."[28]

"It is only the infallible teaching of the Church that secures us against error as to the truths contained in Tradition as well as in Holy Scripture. The voice of the Church is the voice of God."[29]

## Exactly What the Bible Foretold

Papal claims to the dignity and prerogatives of Deity constitute an exact duplicate of the specifications given by Daniel, Christ, Paul, and John. Daniel predicted that the great tyrant would "rise up against the Prince of princes [Christ]," that he would "exalt himself and magnify himself above every god" and "speak astonishing things against the God of gods," and that he would "think to change the times [appointed religious observances commanded by God] and the law [the will of God as revealed in the Scriptures]."[30]

Jesus warned against "false Christs," or impostors, who would come in His name claiming to be Christ. Paul foretold a mysterious power that would take "his seat in the temple of God, proclaiming himself to be God." He called this power "the mystery of lawlessness," which would characterize it as refusing to be subject to the revealed will of God and would be a law to itself.[31] John said that it would utter "haughty and blasphemous words . . . against God, blaspheming his name."[32]

The claims of the papacy to divine dignity and authority tally exactly with the specifications of prophecy. It would be difficult to imagine a more precise fulfillment. To our knowledge no other responsible organization has ever made such claims.

In the chapter that follows we will examine a few of the more important changes the papacy has made in the teachings of Scripture.

### NOTES

1. John 6:63; 8:31, 32.
2. Matthew 4:4.
3. Mark 7:5-9.
4. Luke 10:26; see also Luke 24:25-27, 44; John 5:39.
5. 2 Timothy 3:15-17.
6. 2 Peter 1:16, 19-21.
7. For example, see references listed in notes 4 to 6.
8. John 8:44.
9. 2 Corinthians 11:14.
10. Ephesians 6:12.
11. Genesis 3:1-19; compare 2:16, 17.
12. 2 Thessalonians 2:3-10.
13. 2 Corinthians 11:14, 15.
14. 2 Thessalonians 2:11.
15. Matthew 24:4, 5, 24; see page 194.
16. Acts 20:29-31.
17. 2 Peter 2:1.
18. 2 Thessalonians 2:7, 8, 3.
19. Lucius Ferraris, article entitled "The Pope," in *Prompta Bibliotheca,* Vol. VI, pp. 25-29, *passim.*
20. Christopher Marcellus, in Mansi SC, Vol. 32, col. 761. Latin.

21. Augustinus Triumphus, *Summa de Potestate Ecclesiastica,* folio 61 v. Latin.

22. Encyclicals entitled "On the Chief Duties of Christians as Citizens," and "The Reunion of Christendom."

23. Isaiah 14:12-14; Daniel 11:36, 37; Revelation 13: 5, 6.

24. John 5:18; 10:33.

25. Revelation 13:18.

26. John Adam Moehler, *Symbolism,* p. 277.

27. John Laux, *A Course in Religion for Catholic High Schools and Academies,* Part 1, pp. 50, 51. (Emphasis his.)

28. Joseph Faà di Bruno, *Catholic Belief,* revised by Louis A. Lambert, p. 45.

29. Francis J. Butler, *Holy Family Series of Catholic Catechisms,* p. 63.

30. Daniel 7:25; 8:25; 11:36.

31. 2 Thessalonians 2:4, 7.

32. Revelation 13:5, 6.

# Clever Counterfeits

IN THE preceding chapter we took note of papal claims to dignity and authority that the Scriptures ascribe to God alone. In this chapter we shall examine certain major instances in which the papacy has exercised its alleged authority in an attempt "to change the times and the law"—religious observances appointed by God and the sacred revelation that has come from God.

Has the papacy indeed countermanded certain divine precepts, substituting requirements of its own, and replaced essential truths of the gospel with its own man-made ordinances as a way of salvation? Let us now note a few major instances of the liberties the Church of Rome has taken with the plain teachings of Holy Writ. Again we will cite authoritative statements by recognized Catholic authors as evidence.

## Tampering With the Decalogue

Let us take the fourth precept of the Decalogue as an example. The fourth commandment designates the seventh day of the week, Saturday, as the day when those who honor and serve the true God are to rest and worship. God calls the seventh-day Sabbath "my holy day," and Jesus claims it, in a special sense, as His day.[1] It may come as a surprise to some that the Bible nowhere designates Sunday as a holy day or commands its observance, nor does it record even one instance of Christians observing it as a holy day or attaching particular religious significance to it. A careful reading of the three or four New Testament passages sometimes carelessly cited to this effect reveals that the writers actually made no such claim for Sunday, either stated or implied.[2] By no logical process of reasoning can one or two isolated instances of believers meeting together on the first day of the week be construed as evidence that they attached special significance to it. Many churches today conduct a midweek prayer meeting every Wednesday night, but pastor and parishioners alike would be shocked if anyone seriously interpreted this custom as implying that they considered Wednesday more sacred than the other days of the week.

The Church of Rome boldly claims that the change of the Sabbath from Saturday to Sunday was made solely by her authority, and points to the almost universal observance of that day by Protestants as tacit assent on their part of her authority to revoke explicit Bible requirements and to substitute religious observances not required by the Scriptures. A catechism for converts to Catholicism explains the matter thus:

"Q. *Which is the Sabbath day?*

"A. Saturday is the Sabbath day.

"Q. *Why do we observe Sunday instead of Saturday?*

"A. We observe Sunday instead of Saturday because the Catholic Church transferred the solemnity from Saturday to Sunday."[3]

Another catechism frankly acknowledges the lack of Scriptural authority for the change:

"Q. *Have you any other way of proving that the Church has power to institute festivals of precept?*

"A. Had she not such power, she could not have done that in which all modern religionists agree with her;—she could not have substituted the observance of Sunday the first day of the week, for the observance of Saturday the seventh day, a change for which there is no Scriptural authority."[4]

A third Catholic writer emphasizes the futility of trying to base Sunday sacredness on a supposed divine command apart from the authority of the Church:

"Some theologians have held that God likewise directly determined the Sunday as the day of worship in the New Law, that He Himself has explicitly substituted the Sunday for the Sabbath. But this theory is now entirely abandoned. It is now commonly held that God simply gave His Church the power to set aside whatever day or days, she would deem suitable as Holy Days. The Church chose Sunday, the first day of the week, and in the course of time added other days, as holy days."[5]

Another Catholic authority chides Protestants for implicitly acknowledging the authority of the Catholic Church above that of the Scriptures on the matter of a weekly rest day but rejecting its authority on other matters:

"The Catholic Church for over one thousand years before the existence of a Protestant, by virtue of her Divine mission, changed the day from Saturday to Sunday. . . .

"But the Protestant says: How can I receive the teachings of an apostate Church? How, we ask, have you managed to receive her teaching all your life, *in direct opposition* to your recognized teacher, the Bible, on the Sabbath question? . . .

"The Christian Sabbath is therefore *to this day* the acknowledged offspring of the Catholic Church, as Spouse of the Holy Ghost, without a word of remonstrance from the Protestant world."[6]

Two other Catholic writers pose the question thus:

"Q. How do you prove that the Church has power to command Feasts and Holy-days?

"A. By this very act of changing the Sabbath into the Sunday, which is admitted by Protestants, and therefore they contradict themselves by keeping Sunday so strictly, and breaking most other Feasts commanded by the same Church."[7]

"It was the Catholic Church which, by the authority of JESUS CHRIST, has transferred this rest to the Sunday in remembrance of the resurrection of our Lord. Thus the observance of Sunday by the Protestants is an homage they pay, in spite of themselves, to the authority of the [Catholic] Church."[8]

## How the Change Came About

Throughout New Testament times Christians universally observed the seventh day of the week as the Sabbath.[9] The transition from Saturday to Sunday was a gradual process that began after all the apostles had died and after the last book of the New Testament had been written. It took three centuries or more to complete the process. No documentary record of how

Christians first began to observe Sunday has been preserved, but it is known that the very first references to this practice in Christian literature date from about fifteen years after the disastrous Jewish revolt against the Roman Empire in A.D. 132-135. The Christian observance of Sunday is first mentioned in the post-Biblical *Epistle of Barnabas* and in Justin Martyr's *First Apology,* both written about A.D. 150.[10]

Prior to the Jewish revolt the Roman Empire recognized Judaism as a legal religion and permitted Christianity as a Jewish sect. But after the revolt the Romans banned the practice of Judaism and subjected the Jews to severe persecution. Whereas formerly it had been a distinct advantage to Christians to be thought of by the Romans as Jews, it now became a grave, and often fatal, liability. In the new situation Christians naturally sought by every means possible to make clear to the Romans that they were not Jews, and that their religion was not Jewish. This explains, in part, why early Christian writers speak of the observance of the seventh-day Sabbath as "Judaizing." The fact that no references to Sunday as a sacred day occur prior to the Jewish revolt, but begin to appear almost immediately thereafter, points to that period as the time when Christians began to attach Sabbath sacredness to the first day of the week, a practice never followed by the Jews. The first authentic reference to Sunday as the "Lord's day" is from Clement of Alexandria, toward the close of the second century after Christ.[11]

The observance of Sunday, however, did not immediately replace that of the Sabbath, and several

9

centuries passed before the practice was generally accepted. About A.D. 400 Chrysostom observed, "There are many among us now, who . . . keep the sabbaths in the same manner" as the Jews.[12] In fact, as late as A.D. 440 the Christian historian Socrates wrote that "although almost all churches throughout the world celebrate the sacred mysteries on the Sabbath of every week, yet the Christians of Alexandria and at Rome, on account of some ancient tradition, have ceased to do this."[13] About the same time Sozomen wrote that "the people of Constantinople, and almost everywhere, assemble together on the Sabbath, as well as on the first day of the week, which custom is never observed at Rome or at Alexandria."[14]

For centuries Christians continued to observe both days, but by about A.D. 325 Sunday had achieved definite official preference over the Sabbath. Eusebius, foremost church historian of the period, wrote, "All things whatsoever it was duty to do on the Sabbath, these we have transferred to the Lord's day, as being more authoritative and more highly regarded and first in rank, and more honorable than the Jewish Sabbath."[15]

The first official action of the Catholic Church expressing preference for Sunday was taken at the Council of Laodicea later in the century. This Council decreed that "Christians shall not Judaize and be idle on Saturday but shall work on that day; but the Lord's day they shall especially honor, and, as being Christians, shall, if possible, do no work on that day. If, however, they are found Judaizing, they shall be shut out from Christ."[16]

Writers of the fourth and fifth centuries repeatedly warn their fellow Christians against Sabbath observance as being "Jewish," as if that were enough reason for condemning the practice. Apparently they forgot that Christ was a Jew and that the writers of the New Testament, with the possible exception of Luke, were also "Jewish." In point of time, the increasing importance attached to Sunday in the early centuries, at the expense of the Sabbath, closely parallels Rome's gradual rise to power. In fact, the Church of Rome candidly admits making the change and boasts of it as prime evidence of her authority to alter divine precepts on record in the Bible.

## A Denial of Salvation by Faith in Christ

As we have seen, the angel Gabriel told Daniel that the great apostate power would cast the truth down to the ground, that his heart would be "set against the holy covenant," and that he would "take action against" it. The "holy covenant," of course, was the working arrangement between God and Israel by which He accepted them as His chosen people, and they acknowledged Him to be their God. It was the basis of salvation in Old Testament times. In Christian times "the holy covenant" is the gospel promise of salvation by faith in Jesus Christ.[17]

Daniel warned also that the great apostate would "profane" and "desolate" the sanctuary. John said that it would blaspheme, or speak disparagingly of, God's "dwelling," the sanctuary He ordered Israel to build in order that He might "dwell in their midst."[18] Daniel also foretold that this daring impostor would "take away the continual burnt offering."[19] In Old Testament times the sanctuary, and later the Temple in Jerusalem, was the place God designated where the people were to assemble to worship Him and where the sacred rites and ceremonies connected with atonement for sin were conducted.

The "continual burnt offering," it will be remembered, was God's continual provision for the salvation of His people, who by participating in worship each time it was offered, morning and evening, reaffirmed their acceptance of salvation and their devotion to God. To "take away the continual burnt offering" would be to disrupt the entire Temple service and to deprive people of the benefits of the atonement. In Christian times, as we have seen, reference would be to the heavenly sanctuary where Christ ministers as our great High Priest. Instead of the "continual burnt offering," the great apostate was to set up "the abomination that makes desolate"—an apostate form of worship.[20]

Has the papacy taken action against the means of salvation ordained by Christ and explained by the inspired writers of the New Testament? Has it profaned, or treated with irreverence and contempt, the heavenly sanctuary where, as the New Testament writers declare, Christ is now ministering the merits of His vicarious sacrifice on Calvary? Has it deprived God's people on earth of the benefits of Christ's great sacrifice, thereby in effect and for practical purposes making the sanctuary in heaven above desolate? Has it interfered in any way with God's continual provision for the salvation of His people? Has it set up a substitute system of salvation of its own, contrary to that set forth in the Bible? Let us see.

## The Way of Salvation As Taught in the New Testament

The change of the Sabbath from Saturday to Sunday is but one of numerous deliberate alterations the Church of Rome has made in the plain teachings of the Scriptures. There are equally amazing differences between the teachings of the inspired Bible writers and those of the Church with respect to Christ's infinite sacrifice on Calvary, His continuing ministry in heaven in our behalf, and the means by which we become recipients of divine grace. In fact, the two systems are mutually exclusive.

First, let us inquire what the Scriptures teach on these matters which are the very basis of the Christian faith. It is written that Christ "appeared *once for all* at the end of the age to put away sin by the sacrifice of himself," that He offered "*for all time a single sacrifice* for sins," and that by this "*single offering* he has *perfected for all time* those who are sanctified." There is no need for Him "to offer himself repeatedly," "to suffer repeatedly," or "to offer sacrifices daily," because "he did this *once for all* when he offered up himself."[21] These repeated, emphatic declarations concerning the absolute sufficiency, for all time, of the sacrifice on Calvary preclude the need for, or validity of, any further sacrifice to atone for sins.

Continuing, we read that when Christ had thus "made purification for sins," "he entered once for all" into "heaven itself" in order "to appear in the presence of God on our behalf," "taking . . . his own blood" and "thus securing an eternal redemption." The purpose of Christ's ministry "at the right hand of God," where He "intercedes for us" since His ascension, is "to give repentance to Israel and forgiveness of sins." In God's own Son we thus have "a great high priest" who serves as "a minister in the sanctuary" in heaven above. "In every respect" He was "tempted as we are, yet without sinning," and for this reason He is able "to sympathize with our weaknesses." He is therefore our *"advocate with the Father,"* the *"one mediator* between God and men,"* and "is *able* for all time *to save* those who draw near to God through him, since *he always lives to make intercession"* for us. Inasmuch, therefore, as "we have a great high priest over the house of God," He invites us to "draw near with a true heart in full assurance of faith" "to the throne of grace, that we may receive mercy and find grace to help in time of need."[22]

The Scriptures thus clearly teach that since Christ ascended to heaven forty days after His resurrection from the grave He has been ministering in the presence of God, in the great sanctuary in heaven above. As our great High Priest and only Mediator He intercedes for us and forgives our sins, thus applying to us individually the infinite merits of His once-for-all sacrifice on Calvary.

## Salvation As Taught by Catholic Writers

It is amazing beyond words to find that standard Roman Catholic works on theology unanimously contradict every one of these fundamental facts of salvation as taught by the Bible writers. The conclusion is inevitable that Roman theologians are either grossly ignorant of the teachings of Scripture, or that they have deliberately chosen to ignore these teachings and substitute their own ersatz means of salvation instead.

According to Catholic theology, Christ's sacrifice on Calvary was not sufficient to atone for sins, but must be repeated many thousands of times every day around the world in what they call "the sacrifice of the Mass." They teach that the bread of the Eucharist, when consecrated, becomes in reality the very body of our Lord, that the presence of this bread upon the altar constitutes a true sacrifice without which that on Calvary is inadequate to atone for sins, and that this bread is to be worshiped as if it were Christ in person. In fact, they claim that it *is* Christ.

As a substitute for the perfect priesthood of Christ they have ordained a human priesthood. They deny men the privilege of confessing their sins directly to Christ, and require instead that all sins be confessed to the priests they have ordained. Instead of Christ, our *one* intercessor and mediator, they substitute the Virgin Mary and the saints. Note the following statements from standard Catholic works:

"The priest daily offers a great sacrifice; and the victim which he immolates is the Lamb of God, bearing the sins of the world."[23]

"The Sacrifice of the Mass is and ought to be considered one and the same Sacrifice as that of the cross, for the victim is one and the same, namely, Christ our Lord."[24]

"So far as the practical effects produced upon the soul are concerned, the Holy Mass has in some sense

the advantage over Calvary; for, given the same dispositions, it is more profitable for us to assist day by
day at the Sacrifice of the Mass than it would have
been to have been present once upon Calvary. And,
the reason is this. In the Mass Jesus Christ dispenses
and applies to the soul, according to its dispositions,
that which was won, but not dispensed, on the Cross.
On the Cross we were redeemed; but on the Altar 'the
work of our redemption is carried out.' "[25]

"In obedience to the words of his priests—Hoc Est
Corpus Meum ["This is my body"]—God himself
descends on the altar, . . . he comes wherever they call
him, and as often as they call him, and places himself
in their hands, even though they should be his enemies. And after having come, he remains, entirely at
their disposal; they move him as they please, from
one place to another; they may, if they wish, shut him
up in the tabernacle, or expose him on the altar, or
carry him outside the church; they may, if they choose,
eat his flesh, and give him for the food of others. . . .
Thus the priest may, in a certain manner, be called
the creator of his Creator, since by saying the words of
consecration, he creates, as it were, Jesus in the sacra-
ment, by giving him a sacramental existence, and produces him as a victim to be offered to the eternal
Father."[26]

"If any one saith, that in the mass a true and proper
sacrifice is not offered to God; or, that to be offered is
nothing else but that Christ is given us to eat: let him
be anathema. . . .

"If any one saith, that the sacrifice of the mass is
only a sacrifice of praise and of thanksgiving; or, that

it is a bare commemoration of the sacrifice consummated on the cross, but not a propitiatory sacrifice [that is, a sacrifice by which sins are remitted] . . . let him be anathema."[27]

In contrast with the plain Bible teaching that sins are to be confessed to God alone, the Church of Rome teaches that the sinner is to confess his sins to a priest, and that "the priest . . . remits sins as God."[28] "The priest holds the place of the Saviour himself, when, by saying 'Ego te absolvo,' he absolves from sin. . . . What only God can do by his omnipotence, the priest can also do by saying 'Ego te absolvo a peccatis tuis' ["I absolve you from your sins."]."[29]

## Adoration of the Virgin Mary

The Church of Rome attributes to the Virgin Mary honor hardly distinguishable from that which belongs to Christ alone. All Christians honor her as the mother of our Lord; the Church of Rome, on the other hand, has all but deified her. In 1854 Pope Pius IX declared the dogma of the so-called "immaculate conception" of Mary—meaning that, from the moment of conception in her mother's womb, Mary was and ever remained a sinless being, even as Christ was sinless.

By his bull proclaiming the so-called assumption of the Virgin Mary, Pope Pius XII in 1950 declared, also solely on his own authority, that she had ascended to heaven bodily, even as Christ ascended. Catholics are taught to venerate her as the "Mother of God," and to address their most ardent prayers to her "because her intercession is most powerful."[30] Catholic theologians are urging that she be declared "co-re-

demptrix," or co-redeemer, with Christ. Far more
Catholic churches, schools, and hospitals are dedicated
to Mary, and prayers offered to her, than to Christ.
The Church of Rome has appointed her as patron
saint of the United States and dedicated the United
States to her special protection.

Many other unscriptural teachings and practices
might be mentioned, such as the doctrine of purgatory,
prayers for those supposed to be suffering torment
there, the canonization and veneration of saints, the
rosary, penance, indulgences, the seven so-called sacra-
ments, and a host of others. Sufficient evidence has
been cited to demonstrate that the Church of Rome
has wandered far indeed from the pure gospel originally proclaimed by Christ and the apostles. This
wholesale departure from their teachings has properly
been called "the great apostasy."

## A Clever Counterfeit

Thus in many ways the Church of Rome has substituted its own authority for, and contrary to, the revealed Word of God.[31] By blinding men to the truth
it has effectively nullified Christ's sacrifice on Calvary
and His exclusive role as our mediator and intercessor.
Although devout Catholics are altogether sincere in
believing and practicing what their church teaches,
and in their unintentional ignorance of the Scriptures
are doubtless accepted by God, the fact remains that
the entire system of salvation taught and practiced by
the Church of Rome completely contradicts the teachings of the Bible about salvation by faith in Christ. At
the same time, the counterfeit so closely resembles the

true that countless millions, ignorant of the Scriptures themselves, blindly accept it as genuine.

In a very real way the papacy fulfills the predictions of Daniel, Paul, and John concerning a great spiritual despotism that would essay to rule men's minds and souls as well as their bodies. By depreciating Christ's sacrifice and priestly ministry, and then substituting another system of its own devising, the Church of Rome has, in effect, profaned the sanctuary in heaven above of which the inspired writer of the Book of Hebrews speaks, and blasphemes God's "dwelling" as John foretold. She has so effectively deprived millions of people of a knowledge of these fundamental Bible truths and of the benefit of their saving power, that for them the plan devised in heaven has, for practical purposes, ceased to exist. In a very real way the Church of Rome has taken away our Lord's "continual burnt offering." It has erased His sacrifice on the cross and His continuing ministry in heaven above from the minds and lives of men, and set up its own unscriptural system, "the abomination that makes desolate."[32]

What more clever deception could "the prince of this world" have devised than a system that would actually serve to conceal truth, under the guise of stoutly defending it? A wolf in sheep's clothing would be infinitely more dangerous than one in its own garb. In the Battle of the Bulge late in World War II the German army deceived and confused the Allies by sending Germans in Allied uniform to infiltrate the Allied lines, in order to prepare the way for a German breakthrough. The enemy of men's souls could have contrived no more clever device than a

Christian church professing to be God's exclusive representative on earth and adhering to many of the outward forms of Christianity, but at the same time subtly subverting the truth proclaimed by Christ.

The warning of the angel of prophecy to John with respect to the Book of Revelation applies with equal force to the rest of Scripture: "If any one takes away from the words of the book of this prophecy, God will take away his share in the tree of life and in the holy city," and "if any one adds to them, God will add to him the plagues described in this book."[33]

### NOTES

1. Exodus 20:8-11; Isaiah 58:13; Mark 2:27, 28.

2. John 20:19, 26; Acts 20:7; 1 Corinthians 16:2; Revelation 1:10.

3. Peter Geiermann, *The Convert's Catechism of Catholic Doctrine,* 1957 edition, p. 50.

4. Stephen Keenan, *A Doctrinal Catechism,* third American edition, p. 174.

5. Vincent J. Kelly, *Forbidden Sunday and Feast-Day Occupations,* p. 2.

6. *The Christian Sabbath,* pp. 29-31, a pamphlet consisting mostly of four editorials that appeared in *The Catholic Mirror,* official newspaper of the Archdiocese of Baltimore. (Emphasis his.)

7. Daniel Ferris, *Manual of Christian Doctrine; or, Catholic Belief and Practice,* p. 67.

8. Louis Gaston de Ségur, *Plain Talk About the Protestantism of To-day,* p. 225.

9. Luke 4:16; Acts 13:14, 42; 16:13; 17:1, 2; 18:4, 11.

10. *Epistle of Barnabas* (A. Cleveland Coxe ed.), ch. 15; Justin Martyr, *First Apology,* ch. 67.

11. Clement of Alexandria, *Miscellanies,* v. 14.

12. Chrysostom, *Commentary on Galatians* 1. 7.

13. Socrates, *Ecclesiastical History,* v. 22.

14. Sozomen, *Ecclesiastical History,* vii. 19.

15. Eusebius, *Commentary on Psalm (91) 92.*

16. Canon 29 of the Council of Laodicea, in Charles Joseph Hefele, *A History of the Christian Councils* (translated and edited by H. N. Oxenham), Vol. 2, p. 316.

17. John 3:16; Romans 1:16; 1 Corinthians 11:25.

18. Daniel 8:11, 13; 9:26; 11:31; Revelation 13:6; compare Exodus 25:8, 9.

19. Daniel 8:11-13; 11:31; 12:11.

20. Daniel 8:12, 13; 9:27; 11:31; 12:11.

21. Hebrews 7:27; 9:25, 26; 10:12, 14.

22. Acts 5:31; Romans 8:34; 1 Timothy 2:5; Hebrews 1:3; 4:14-16; 7:25; 8:1, 2; 9:12, 24; 10:21, 22; 1 John 2:1.

23. A Nampon, *Catholic Doctrine as Defined by the Council of Trent,* p. 543.

24. *Catechism of the Council of Trent for Parish Priests,* translated by John A. McHugh and Charles J. Callan, pp. 258, 259.

25. Herbert Vaughan, *The People's Manual—The Holy Sacrifice of the Mass,* pp. 42, 43.

26. Alphonsus de Liguori, *Dignity and Duties of the Priest; or, Selva,* pp. 26, 27, 32.

27. Canons I and III of Session XXII of the Council of Trent, in Philip Schaff, *The Creeds of Christendom,* Vol. 2, pp. 184, 185.

28. A Nampon, *Catholic Doctrine as Defined by the Council of Trent,* p. 543.

29. Alphonsus de Liguori, *Dignity and Duties of the Priest; or, Selva,* p. 34.

30. W. Faerber, *Catechism for the Catholic Parochial Schools of the United States,* p. 39.

31. See 2 Timothy 3:15, 16. Paul here declares that the Holy Scriptures "are able to instruct" a person "for salvation through faith in Christ Jesus" and able to make him "complete, equipped for every good work." According to the Church of Rome, the Scriptures are inadequate for this.

32. Daniel 8:12, 13; 11:31; 12:11; see page 162.

33. Revelation 22:19, 18.

# The Coming Crisis

IN HIS historic "House Divided" speech a short time before the Civil War Abraham Lincoln said, "If we could first know where we are, and whither we are tending, we could better judge what to do, and how to do it." The fulfilled prophecies of God's Word tell us "where we are" in the great stream of time, and those that relate to the future provide us with advance information about "whither we are tending." With one eye on the rearview mirror of fulfilled prophecy and the other fixed intently on the prophetic radar screen of future events, we can chart a safe course to our desired destination, through the momentous events that lie just ahead. The prophecies of Scripture thus far considered apply in large measure to past events; we now turn to those that have to do primarily with the future.

The last eleven chapters of the Book of Revelation, last book of the Bible, set forth a connected prophetic narrative of the supreme crisis that is soon to confront the world, and of the transition from the present age to the eternal kingdom of our Lord and Saviour, Jesus Christ. Here the tense, climactic stages of the agelong struggle between good and evil are clearly presented. According to the sure word of prophecy, the forces of evil in this world are preparing for and will soon put forth a supreme effort to consolidate their control over the world. For those who choose to remain loyal to God, come what may, the result will be persecution of unprecedented fury. But these chapters also tell of Heaven's last solemn warning against the deceptions of Satan, and present a most urgent appeal to all men everywhere to accept salvation in Christ and to stand for the right though the heavens fall.

## The Mortal Wound Healed

Let us begin with what John speaks of as the healing of the "mortal wound," which we have found was inflicted on the papacy in 1798. One of the leopard beast's heads, John relates, "seemed to have a mortal wound, but its mortal wound was healed." Of necessity, the healing of the wound would take place this side of 1798. Two years after Pius VI had been taken prisoner, a new pope, Pius VII, was elected. The papacy was thus reestablished, though with only a shadow of its former power.

The actual restoration of papal power first became apparent during the pontifical reign of Leo XIII (1878-1903), who provided the Catholic Church with unusually effective leadership. World War I and the decade that followed added momentum to the process of convalescence, until in 1929 the temporal power of the papacy was completely restored, in form and in fact, by a treaty between Mussolini and Pope Pius XI. This treaty recognized Vatican City, a diminutive "nation" a little less than 109 acres in area, as a sovereign state.

The pontificate of Pope Pius XII (1939-1958), which spanned World War II and the first fourteen years of the "cold war," saw the political influence of the papacy in world affairs, and its spiritual and moral influence upon men's minds, grow at an almost incredible pace. Today this influence is again worldwide, though less obvious perhaps than in former centuries, and is increasing steadily. As a reigning prince the pope exchanges formal diplomatic missions with forty-seven countries, including all the major nations of the world except the United States and the Soviet Union. According to the latest reports available, forty-five nations have a Roman Catholic as their head of state.

Of the time when the process of healing will be complete John wrote, "The whole earth followed the beast with wonder." Obviously, that day has not yet come, but current trends indicate that the time is not far distant when this phase of the prophecy will meet its counterpart in historical fact. There is, for instance, a growing "dialogue," as it is being called, between Protestant and Catholic clergymen in which they discuss their differences together in a cordial atmosphere. There are, as well, an increasing number of friendly contacts at the summit and all the way down into the ecclesiastical foothills. Protestant and Catholic scholars are studying the Bible together. In fact, as various competent observers, both Protestant and Catholic, have noted, the whole climate of relations between the two major branches of Christendom has become warm and cordial as never before in history. This new ecclesiastical climate is leading many religious leaders on both sides to predict the eventual return of all "separated brethren"—non-Roman Catholic Christians—to Rome. Each year, from January 18 to 25, Catholics and many Protestants unite in a week of prayer for the reunion of all Christians.

The Second Vatican Council, which opened in Rome on October 11, 1962, may well go down in history as "the Council of Reunion," despite the presence of a variety of other important matters on the agenda. It is common knowledge that the long-range aim of the Council was to bring all Christian churches back to the fold of Catholicism and submission to the pope. In summoning the Council, Pope John XXIII spoke of it as "a gentle invitation" to non-Catholic Christians "to seek and find the unity" of the faith by returning to Rome.

Among several preparatory bodies set up to advise the Council was the Secretariat for Promoting Christian Unity. One of its announced aims was to provide a channel for contacts with non-Catholic Christian bodies, with a view to improved relations and eventual reunion. The Secretariat also issued formal invitations to other churches which indicated willingness to send unofficial delegates to the Council as observers. Some twoscore Protestant and Eastern Orthodox clergymen attended on this basis.

The death of one pope, the election of another, the appointment of cardinals, a papal proclamation on almost any subject—all make front-page news around the world. The papacy expects the world to listen respectfully and attentively when it speaks—and the world obligingly listens and follows the beast "with wonder," as John said it would.

The "wound" is by no means completely healed, but current trends indicate that the time is not far distant when it will be. When that time comes, the world will witness a restoration of papal authority and power that will, for practical purposes, be a carbon copy of what it was in past centuries.

## The United States in Prophecy

In Revelation 13:11-18 John makes an amazing disclosure of the future role of the United States of America in connection with the restoration of papal power. This inspired preview of the future is of the most vital interest and concern to all today who purpose resolutely in their hearts to remain loyal to God, come what may.

Here John relates that he "saw another beast which rose out of the earth" about the time the leopard beast received its seemingly mortal wound. "It had two horns like a lamb," he says, but "it spoke like a dragon." As we have seen, a beast in Bible prophecy represents a nation. Like the beasts of Daniel 7, the first beast of Revelation 13 came up "out of the sea." We have also found that the waters of the sea are a common prophetic symbol representing people and nations.[1] A beast-nation rising from the waters of the sea would thus signify a new nation taking over the administration of a thickly populated region by conquest, and a nation coming up "out of the earth," one rising to power in a previously unpopulated, or at least sparsely settled, area.

Another distinguishing characteristic of the second beast of Revelation 13 is that it has "two horns like a lamb," thus making the label "lamblike beast" appropriate. This is the only descriptive feature mentioned. As we have seen, a horn in Bible prophecy represents power, or a nation as an instrument of power.[2] The other beasts of prophecy thus far considered have generally been beasts of prey—a lion, a bear, a leopard, and the nondescript beasts of Daniel and Revelation. But here is one that resembles a lamb. Its power, as symbolized by its horns, lies in certain lamblike traits, not in brute strength as with other beasts. The fact that eventually "it spoke like a dragon," exercised "all the authority of the first beast," and made "the earth and its inhabitants worship the first beast" indicates that this ostensibly lamblike beast nevertheless exerts tremendous power.

According to the specifications given in Revelation 13:11-17, then, the lamblike beast represents a nation that (1) was rising to power about the time the leopardlike beast received its seemingly mortal wound in 1798; (2) grew to nationhood in a sparsely populated region; (3) differs from the other nations of prophecy in the nature of its power; and (4) eventually becomes a world power. What nation meets these primary specifications? We know of but one eligible candidate—the United States of America, which declared its independence twenty-two years before the leopardlike beast received its deadly wound, which grew to nationhood in the New World, whose strength as a nation is rooted in the fundamental principles of democracy and the separation of church and state, and which has grown to be a world power. We doubt that any other nation could possibly qualify.

The lamblike horns appropriately represent the two distinctive features of the American system of government—full civil and religious freedom, which are possible only in a democracy where church and state are truly separate. At the time this nation was founded, such an arrangement was unique. The concept that church and state should remain completely separate characterizes the United States, especially in its formative years, as a Protestant nation. The notable absence of crowns on this beast implies, further, that the power it represents would be a republic.

As if in response to the specifications of prophecy, the Declaration of Independence affirmed it to be the purpose of the founding fathers of this nation that the government of the United States should be "of the people, by the people, and for the people." In Article VI of the Federal Constitution they declared that "no religious test shall ever be required as a qualification to any office or public trust under the United States," and in the First Amendment to the Constitution, that "Congress shall make no law respecting an establishment of religion, or prohibiting the free exercise thereof." These civil and religious safeguards, written into the law of the land, have stood for nearly two centuries as a guarantee against the political and religious tyranny that so long prevailed in most of Europe.

But why should the United States find a niche in Bible prophecy? Simply because nations are introduced into prophecy when they affect the work and destiny of God's people on earth in a major way. It must be that the United States, traditional land of liberty, has an important role of some kind to play in the great future crisis. Eventually, says John, it will speak "like a dragon," or with the peremptory authority a dragon might presumably display.

## The United States and Papal Policy

The lamblike beast, said John, "exercises all the authority of the first beast *in its presence"*—that is, while the first beast is still in existence, and with its consent. There was a time in history when "the first beast" dominated the world scene, but it received a seemingly mortal wound. And what does the lamblike beast do with its dragonlike authority? It "makes the earth and its inhabitants worship the first beast, whose mortal wound was healed." Prophecy here foretells a time when the United States will become the chief agent of papal policy and will resort to papal methods in order to implement that policy.

The United States already provides the Church of Rome with more foreign missionaries than any other country and more financial support than the rest of the world combined. In fact though not in name, the United States has already fallen heir to the role of "eldest son" of the papacy—in numerical and financial strength, and in making papal policy effective in international politics. Catholic membership in the United States is more than twice what it was at the beginning of World War II, and since its close enrollment in parochial schools has more than doubled.

Catholic spokesmen are already beginning to talk of the time, within another generation or so, when Catholics will constitute a majority in the United States, and suggesting that it will then be possible to implement Catholic social and political policies that are not now acceptable to the American public generally. As a vocal, determined, and fairly cohesive minority constituting only 24 per cent of the electorate, they are already often able to determine public policy.

For the United States to exercise "all the authority of the first beast," it will have to repudiate its two basic principles of civil and religious liberty. To suggest that this nation will one day become an autocracy and effect a union of church and state is repugnant to red-blooded Americans and may seem, at first, to border on the irrational. But that is what God's Word assures us is to be. At least one of the founding fathers of this nation, Thomas Jefferson, the great champion of personal liberty, warned against just such a turn of events: "The spirit of the times may alter, will alter. Our rulers will become corrupt, our people careless. A single zealot may commence persecution, and better men be his victims."[3]

The change of policy here envisioned will doubtless come about almost imperceptibly, and more or less innocently. It is a fact, however, that current trends in national affairs are already tending to circumscribe religious liberty and to breach the wall separating church and state. For this reason all who cherish liberty must be vigilant against every effort to restrict religious freedom, however plausible the reasons given for such a course of action appear to be.

Take, for instance, the relentless and successful efforts of the papal hierarchy in the United States, over more than a decade, to block Federal aid to public schools unless parochial schools are included. If and when the federal government allocates public funds to schools whose only reason for a separate existence is the inculcation of a sectarian philosophy of life, the government will, to that extent, become an agent of the Church of Rome. The determined attempts of the bishops to bend public policy toward their own ends, now increasingly evident in many areas of public life, is a fair index to the growing power of the Church of Rome in this country.

Intermittently, efforts are being put forth to arrange for an exchange of ambassadors between the United States and Vatican City. It is also being urged that certain candidates for public office should be Roman Catholics, and in some parts of the country, for that matter, only a Catholic can be elected to public office!

## An Ominous Portent of Things to Come

An even more ominous portent of the shape of things to come is the fact that for the first time in history Catholics are uniting with Protestants in a concerted endeavor to force a strict observance of Sunday by law. This active cooperation is being manifested in scores of states and local communities. Take, for instance, the circumstances under which the Massachusetts legislature enacted a stringent new Sunday law in the late spring of 1962. By a vote of twenty-one to fourteen the state senate voted to exempt merchants from the provisions of the law if they remain closed on a day other than Sunday because of religious convictions. Three days later *The Pilot,* official newspaper of the Archdiocese of Boston, launched a fierce editorial attack on senators who voted for the exemption, and listed their names.

Catholics attending mass the following day, Sunday, were urged to read the editorial and to pressure their senators into reversing the vote. On Monday, only five days after the original vote, the senate reversed itself by a vote of thirty-one to eight, which means that approximately half the senators changed their vote as a direct result of the pressure to which they were thus subjected. This abrupt about-face was due to the fact that Massachusetts is 51.8 per cent Catholic. It also stands as a warning of what the United States, or any country for that matter, can expect when the Roman hierarchy controls the ballot box by virtue of a Catholic majority.

The relatively new argument that Sunday laws have lost their religious character and are now strictly health and welfare legislation ignores the unalterable historical fact that the Sunday is a religious institution and that its observance is an act of "homage" Protestants "pay, in spite of themselves, to the authority of the [Catholic] Church," as one Catholic writer has shrewdly observed.[4] It also ignores the obvious fact that pressure for Sunday laws is primarily religious in character, as the experience in Massachusetts indicates. But if one religious observance can be enforced by law, there is no reason why any or all other observances might not also be so enforced.

The lamblike beast, says John, "makes the earth and its inhabitants worship the first beast." Here is an exercise of civil authority to enforce compliance with some requirement, in the observance of which men would acknowledge the authority of the first beast in matters of religion. In other words, this is a specific prediction that, eventually, the United States will enact legislation that gives certain papal dogmas the force of law and, as we shall see, enforce them by penalty of death.

The nature of this enactment is implied in Revelation 14:9-12, where "the saints," who refuse to comply with that law, are characterized as "those who keep the commandments of God," including of course the fourth command of the Decalogue that appoints Saturday, the seventh day of the week, as the weekly day of rest and religious observance for all men in all ages. As we have seen, Daniel predicted that the Church of Rome would "think to change the times and the law" of God, and Rome frankly admits to having transferred the sanctity of the Sabbath command from Saturday, the seventh day of the week, to Sunday, the first day of the week—a change for which there is no Scriptural authority.[5] Inasmuch as John characterizes those who remain loyal to God during the great final crisis as people who keep God's commandments, it is evident that those who still adhere to the papal Sabbath, when that time comes, thereby demonstrate an attitude of disloyalty to God.

The prophecy thus envisions a time when the United States will enact a national Sunday law. The fact that nearly every state in the union, and many local governmental units as well, already have such legislation on their statute books, and further, that unprecedented efforts are currently being put forth to enforce recognition of Sunday as a day of rest, by law, on state and local levels, clearly foreshadows such legislation on the national level as the next logical step. Strangely, the climate of public opinion now seems to be rapidly shifting in favor of such laws.

A national Sunday law would be but the first step in a process which, in the end, would logically give full legal status to all other laws of the Church, as is true in many Catholic lands today. As efforts are put forth to give Sunday sacredness the force of law, and to secure public funds to support church-operated schools, hospitals, and other enterprises, Protestants should not forget that in some lands today the whole cost of erecting churches and parochial schools, of operating these schools and other institutions, and the salaries of the clergy are all paid from the public treasury. Protestants should weigh carefully the ultimate aim of Catholicism—a complete union of church and state, the latter subservient to the former—before acceding to the first step in that direction.

## The "Image" and "Mark" of the Beast

Finally, says John, the United States will decree the making of "an image for the beast" and "give breath to the image of the beast so that the image of the beast should even speak." It will also "cause those who will not worship the image of the beast to be slain." Obviously, an image of the beast would resemble the beast and have its characteristics. Note that this image is a living entity that speaks with the same authority as does the beast. In view of the fact that America is basically a Protestant country, the image to the beast would be a united Protestant church that collaborates with the national government—in other words, an effective union of church and state, which is the fundamental characteristic of the Church of Rome. This becomes possible as the result of "great signs" the lamblike beast performs and by which "it deceives those who dwell on earth" into making this "image for the beast."[6]

To enforce cooperation with this policy, and particularly observance of the national Sunday law, the United States will one day compel all "to be marked on the right hand or the forehead, so that no one can buy or sell unless he has the mark, that is, the name of the beast or the number of its name." In other words, the law will be enforced by economic sanctions, on pain of death. As we have seen, the Church of Rome points to the Sunday as a mark of her authority, and the observance of Sunday as an act of "homage" Protestants "pay, in spite of themselves, to the authority of the Church."[4]

When the observance of Sunday is enforced by a national Sunday law, and when, realizing that compliance involves violation of the fourth command of the Decalogue, a man yields his conscience to the law, he will thereby be accepting what John calls "the mark . . . of the beast." To receive the mark in the forehead would imply assent of the mind, and in the hand, cooperation based on expediency. It is evident that *no one now has this mark.* To observe Sunday out of a sincere but mistaken conviction that God wills it does not constitute reception of the mark.

It is noteworthy that the lamblike beast causes men to "worship"—or cooperate with—*either* the first,

leopardlike beast, the papacy, or the image to the
beast set up in the United States, the Protestant union
of church and state. Prophecy here seems to provide
for Catholicism and Protestantism to exist side by side
in the United States, apparently cooperating together
and with the civil power.

## Preparing for the Crisis

Such is the crisis that now looms ominously before
us—a time when the laws of men are brought into
sharp and relentless conflict with the law and revealed
will of God, a time when church and state will unite
to coerce the conscience, a time when all will have to
make the supreme choice between obedience to human
authority and divine authority, with death as the legal
alternative to compliance. Evil will appear to be on
the point of triumph when God intervenes to deliver
His people. That will be a time to try men's souls, a
time when only those who purpose to be true to God
at the cost of life itself, if need be, will be able to resist the tremendous forces exerted to shake their faith.
Only those who prepare for that time of crisis now, by
making Christ the center and circumference of their
lives, will be able to stand firm in that day.

NOTES

1. Revelation 17:15.
2. See page 48, and note 9 on page 154.
3. *The Writings of Thomas Jefferson,* Vol. 8, p. 402.
4. Louis Gaston de Ségur, *Plain Talk About the Protestantism of To-day,* p. 225.
5. See pages 254-256.
6. Revelation 13:12, 13.

# *Last Countdown*

G OD HAS NOT left the world to drift blindly into that fearful future crisis when an attempt will be made to compel all men everywhere to worship the beast and its image and to accept its mark, with death as the declared alternative. The threefold message recorded in Revelation 14:6-12 warns specifically against the Satanic program foretold in chapter 13, and sets forth God's last great appeal to the world. Of the fact that this is, indeed, the last call of divine grace there can be no doubt, for immediately following its proclamation John saw Christ descending from heaven to reap earth's harvest.[1]

In the great final testing time that lies ahead Satan will attempt to brainwash the whole world into accepting his leadership and will rally the vast majority of the human race behind his program. Circumstances will seem to make further individual resistance appear futile, and it will not be easy to stand alone. But God has provided sufficient information concerning the future course of events and the issues involved in the crisis, to enable us to prepare intelligently for it. To all who choose to remain true to Him in that fateful hour He has promised a special gift of divine grace and fortitude, and eventual victory.

Seen in this perspective, the threefold message of Revelation 14:6-12 deserves our closest scrutiny. Here John relates that he saw three angels "flying in mid-heaven," where they can readily be seen and heard, one following another in rapid succession, and each in turn voicing his own distinctive part of the appeal. How could a universal message for men in the space age—with its sputniks, spaceships, and communications satellites—have been pictured more appropriately? In the symbolism of the Book of Revelation these angels represent the church completing the gospel commission originally entrusted to it by Christ.[2] In the divine economy of the plan of salvation, Heaven's messages to men are always proclaimed by His loyal representatives on earth.

## The First Angel

The first of the three angels addresses his message in a loud voice "to those who dwell on earth, to every nation and tribe and tongue and people." It is universal in its application, and it is given in such a manner as to command worldwide attention. It is for all men everywhere.

This angel, says John, has the "eternal gospel" to proclaim. What is the "eternal gospel"? The word *gospel* means "good news." The gospel is the good news that "God so loved the world," lost as it was in sin, "that he gave his only Son" to be our Saviour, and that "while we were yet sinners Christ died for us." It is the good news that "God was in Christ reconciling the world to himself," and that "while we were enemies we were reconciled to God by the death of his

Son." It is the good news that although "the wages of sin is death," nevertheless "the free gift of God is eternal life in Christ Jesus our Lord," and that "whoever believes in him should not perish but have eternal life."[3]

But that is not all. The everlasting gospel is also the good news that Christ "rose again" from the grave, that He "ascended to the Father," and that He "always lives to make intercession" for us. Finally, it includes the good news that Jesus "will appear a second time, . . . to save those who are eagerly waiting for him,"[4] and to inaugurate His own eternal, righteous reign.

In short, the everlasting gospel is the same good news of God's infinite concern for man declared by the prophets and apostles of old.[5] It stands in sharp contrast with the adulterated gospel of the Church of Rome, with such perverted modern philosophies as liberal theology, theistic evolution, existentialism, and neoorthodoxy, and with everything else that deviates from the plain teachings of God's Word. The three-fold message of Revelation 14 does not present a new or different gospel, but reaffirms all facets of the "eternal gospel." At the same time, it is Heaven's final appeal to the human race, a solemn proclamation that the end of all things is at hand.

## The First Angel's Message

In tones to which no one can plead deaf this angel proclaims, "Fear God and give him glory, for the hour of his judgment has come; and worship him who made heaven and earth, the sea and the fountains of water." This solemn proclamation summons men to "fear," or reverence, God, to give Him "glory," or honor, and to "worship" Him. How appropriate this appeal is for an age when even professed Christians—to say nothing of atheists, infidels, and agnostics—have in large measure forgotten God or relegated Him to a backseat in their lives. Furthermore, in a day when most Christians have accepted the theory of evolution and moved the first chapters of the Book of Genesis over to the fiction shelf of their opinions and beliefs, God summons them to reverence, honor, and worship Him as the Creator of all things.

But there is also a new note to this message—God's great final judgment hour has struck! The certainty of a great final day of judgment that brings this age to a close and ushers in God's eternal kingdom was stressed by the Bible writers generally. Paul, for instance, declared that God "has fixed a day on which he will judge the world." He wrote to the Christians at Rome about "that day when, according to my gospel, God judges the secrets of men," and to those at Corinth, "We must all appear before the judgment seat of Christ, so that each one may receive good or evil, according to what he has done in the body."[6]

The word *judgment* in Revelation 14:7 evidently refers to the entire process by which God brings the reign of sin to a halt and inaugurates His own eternal reign of righteousness. As we shall see, this process includes the arraignment of all men of all ages, first in absentia and later in person, before the bar of divine justice. It includes, also, an investigation of the life record of each, a verdict of acquittal or conviction, and the award of eternal life or eternal death.[7]

Daniel vividly describes one aspect of the awesome scene in which the world is summoned to the bar of divine justice. Christ later depicted the same event in figurative language, and the Apostle John more literally.[8] In the judgment each person's character is measured by the standard of God's holy "law"—all His revealed will—and by his own personal acceptance or rejection of the saving, transforming grace of Christ.[9] When the fateful verdict in each case has been given, Christ will return to earth to welcome the saints to their eternal reward and to consign those who persistently spurn His mercy to the fires of the last day.[10]

## The Second Angel's Message

Following close behind the first angel comes the second, proclaiming the second part of the threefold message: "Fallen, fallen is Babylon the great, she who made all nations drink of the wine of her impure passion."[11] What is Babylon and what is meant by its "fall"?

Our first clue is to be found in the cryptic language of the seventeenth chapter of Revelation, where, in the symbolism of prophecy, John represents "Babylon the great" as a profligate harlot "seated upon many waters"—or ruling despotically over the peoples of earth.[12] "The kings of the earth have committed fornication" with her, and the peoples of earth "have become drunk" with "the wine" of her "fornication." As we have seen, an unchaste woman is a common prophetic symbol for an apostate religious organization.[13] John saw this disreputable woman riding a scarlet beast that represents civil government—a graphic picture of a union of church and state, with the church in control. In other words, "Babylon the great" is an apostate church that has entered into an illicit alliance with the "kings," or nations, of earth. Such was the situation during the 1260 years of papal supremacy and will be again during the great final crisis.[14]

On the harlot's forehead, indicative of character, appears her cryptic title, "Babylon the great." Obviously this cannot refer to the ancient city of Babylon, which already lay in ruins when John wrote, but must stand for some counterpart to which the same name can appropriately be applied. Throughout ancient times Jerusalem and Babylon stand as the two great focal points in the conflict between good and evil. Soon after the dawn of history Babylon began to defy God and oppose His will on earth, and became the chief agent of Satan's master plan to control the human race. It was the traditional foe of God's chosen people, the Hebrews,[15] who suffered more cruelly at the hands of the Babylonians than from any other foreign tyrant except possibly the Romans.

In A.D. 70 Roman armies destroyed Jerusalem, as the Babylonians had done in 586 B.C., and in A.D. 135 they banished all Jews from the city. Remembering the Babylonian exile, the Jews began to use "Babylon" as a code name for Rome, as the literature of the period makes evident.[16] Christian writers of the first two centuries also adopted this terminology.[17] In 1 Peter 5:13 "Babylon" is a pseudonym for Rome.

Thus throughout history Babylon—the literal city and later, figuratively, Rome, first the empire and then the church—has been the archfoe of God's truth and

His people. The name "Babylon the great" stands for all heterodox, apostate religious organizations that have fallen away from the "eternal gospel" from antiquity down to the close of time, but, as used in the Revelation, particularly the papacy and the great apostate religious merger that, together, precipitate the great future crisis.[18] The "wine" of Babylon represents her heretical teachings. John saw the people of earth "drunk" with these false doctrines and Babylon herself "drunk with the blood of the saints and the blood of the martyrs of Jesus," who refuse to accept her errors and to submit to her authority.

Finally, what is meant by Babylon's "fall"? The answer is simple—a fall from the pure teachings and life of apostolic times. The Apostle Paul wrote that there was to be a great "falling away" from the truth after his day, and the early Christian centuries testify that just such a falling away did take place.[19] He also warned that "in the last days" men would arise "holding the form of religion but denying the power of it."[20] As in the early centuries the Church of Rome departed from the teachings of the apostles, so in our time there is a decisive trend in Protestantism away from the great truths of the Reformation and the "eternal gospel" as set forth by the Bible writers.

Modern "Babylon" includes all in our day who reject the authority of the Bible as their norm of faith and conduct, yet call themselves by the name of Christ. In large measure, philosophical speculation and ecclesiastical tradition have been substituted for the teachings of God's Word, and worldliness has replaced primitive purity of life and conduct.[21] There has been a "falling away" ever since apostolic times. Soon that process will be complete, and then it can be said that "Babylon" has completely fallen.

The first angel's message is thus a call to worship God according to the "eternal gospel," and the second, a warning against all substitute gospels.

## The Third Angel's Message

Following in rapid succession came the last of the three angels, proclaiming in a loud voice: "If any one worships the beast and its image, and receives a mark on his forehead or on his hand, he also shall drink the wine of God's wrath, poured unmixed into the cup of his anger, and he shall be tormented with fire and brimstone in the presence of the holy angels and in the presence of the Lamb. And the smoke of their torment goes up for ever and ever; and they have no rest, day or night, these worshipers of the beast and its image, and whoever receives the mark of its name."[22] Whereas the first angel summons men to worship the God of heaven and the second cautions against all substitute forms of worship, the third sounds a special alarm against worshiping the beast and its image— *the* great apostasy of the last days.[23]

This angel pronounces the most solemn and fearful warning to be found in all Scripture. It is a warning that those who yield their faith and submit to human authority in the last great crisis of earth will thereby worship the beast and its image, and when they choose to reverence the counterfeit Sabbath in the full knowledge that it is not God's appointed day of rest and worship, they will then receive the "mark" of the

beast. Whereas in Revelation 13 death is threatened
as the alternative to the worship of the beast and its
image, the fourteenth chapter warns that all who comply with that demand will automatically incur *God's*
death sentence.

This dilemma will confront every living soul with
a personal test and will precipitate the great final crisis
between those who choose to be loyal to Christ and
those who yield their allegiance to Satan. Christ coun-
seled His disciples, under such circumstances, not to
"fear those who kill the body but cannot kill the soul,"
but rather to "fear him who can destroy both body
and soul in hell."[24] Soon, the whole world will be
united against God and against His faithful "remnant," and there will be no place to hide except under
the shadow of the Almighty.[25]

All other warnings of divine judgment recorded in
the Scriptures are tempered with infinite mercy and
long-suffering. That of the third angel is not. It is
final. There will never be another chance. This time,
divine retribution will be "poured unmixed into the
cup of . . . [God's] anger." Men who choose to drink
the wine of Babylon will one day have to drink the
wine of God's wrath, which commences with the
seven last plagues and ends in the lake of fire.[26] The
nature of this judgment is the subject of a later chapter.

## The Significance of the
## Seventh-day Sabbath

In the last great crisis every man will have to choose
between obeying the law of God and obeying man-
made laws that conflict with it. This contest will even-

tually come to a focus in a universal demand to honor Sunday, a day for which there is no sanction in the Word of God, instead of the seventh-day Sabbath.[27]

As we have seen, God claims the seventh day of the week as His. He calls it "my holy day," and summons all who choose to be loyal to Him to "call the sabbath a delight" and to "honor it, not going . . . [their] own ways, or seeking . . . [their] own pleasure, or talking idly" during its sacred hours.[28] Christ declared Himself to be "lord" of the Sabbath day, and said that it had been made for man's benefit.[29] Furthermore, the Sabbath is "a sign" between God and His people, an evidence that Christ's redeeming grace has sanctified them.[30] Walking on earth as a man among men, the Saviour set an example for all men by observing the seventh day of the week as the Sabbath, and instructed His disciples to pray that they would not be tempted to desecrate it, even under extreme personal danger, in years to come.[31]

More is involved in the fourth command of the decalogue than most people realize. In the first place, the same God who directed men to keep the Sabbath day holy also specified the seventh day of the week as the Sabbath. The *Sabbath*ness and the *seventh*ness of the day are inseparable. "The Lord blessed the sabbath day and hallowed it," and commanded men to "remember" it and to "keep it holy" *because* in six days He "made heaven and earth, the sea, and all that is in them, and rested the seventh day."[32]

The Bible writers commonly distinguish the true God from all false gods by identifying Him as the Creator.[33] Alone among the ten, the fourth command of the Decalogue identifies the true God as Creator of all things, and its observance is thus a tacit recognition of His creatorship. Accordingly, recognition of the seventh-day Sabbath implies recognition of and allegiance to the true God as opposed to all false gods. Those who receive the seal of the living God will therefore honor His appointed day of rest. They will "remember the sabbath day, to keep it holy," and their observance of it will be a manifest token of their loyalty to God in the great hour of crisis that lies just ahead.

## God's Evacuation Orders

For emphasis, and in a slightly different setting, John repeats the threefold message in Revelation 18: 1-5, stressing particularly God's call to His people to leave Babylon. The warning of the second angel is sounded again, "Fallen, fallen is Babylon the great!" and Babylon in her fearful, fallen, apostate condition is figuratively described as "a dwelling place of demons, a haunt of every foul spirit, a haunt of every foul and hateful bird." Then John heard another voice from heaven saying, "Come out of her, my people, lest you take part in her sins, lest you share in her plagues; for her sins are heaped high as heaven, and God has remembered her iniquities." It will be fatal to ignore this evacuation summons, just as it was that of the long ago to come out of Sodom and Gomorrah.

The three angels of Revelation 14 thus call men today to reverence, honor, and worship God as the Creator of all things; to return to the everlasting gospel proclaimed by the prophets and apostles of old;

to withdraw from any and every religious organization
that has fallen from the pure teachings of the gospel;
to recognize that the hour of God's judgment has
come; and to order their lives in harmony with these
sublime facts.

Today Christ is seeking intelligent, honesthearted
men and women to enlist in His last legion of faithful
ones, and to take part in giving His last great message
of mercy to the world. No higher privilege, no greater
opportunity, has been accorded men in any generation.

Who will respond, "Here am I! Send me"?[34]

### NOTES

1. Revelation 14:14-20.

2. Matthew 28:19, 20.

3. John 3:16; Romans 5:8, 10; 6:23; 2 Corinthians
5:19.

4. John 14:1-3; 20:17; 1 Thessalonians 4:14; Hebrews
7:25; 9:28.

5. John 3:16; Hebrews 4:2.

6. Acts 17:31; 24:25; Romans 2:16; 2 Corinthians 5:10.

7. Matthew 16:27; Romans 2:3-11; 2 Corinthians 5:10;
Revelation 22:11, 12; compare Matthew 22:13; see the
following chapter.

8. Daniel 7:9-14, 26, 27; Matthew 25:31-46; Revelation
20:11-15.

9. Ecclesiastes 12:13, 14; Matthew 12:36; John 3:18-21;
Romans 2:3-11; 2 Corinthians 5:10; Galatians 6:7, 8;
James 2:10-12.

10. Matthew 16:27; 2 Peter 3:7-13; Revelation 20:15;
22:13; see pages 357, 362.

11. Revelation 14:8.

12. See Revelation 17:15 (compare Isaiah 47:5, 7, 8);
Ezekiel 23:17.

13. See page 206.

14. See pages 220, 224, 225, 227.

15. See Genesis 11:4-9; see note 1, page 34.

16. Sibylline Oracles, Book V, in R. H. Charles, *The Apocrypha and Pseudepigrapha of the Old Testament,* Vol. 2, p. 400; the apocryphal book of 2 Baruch 11:1, in *op. cit.,* p. 486; the Jewish *Midrash Rabbah* on Canticles 1:6.

17. *Against Marcion* iii. 13; *Answer to the Jews* 9; Irenaeus, *Against Heresies* v. 26. 1; "Apostolic Succession," *The Catholic Encyclopedia,* Vol. 1, p. 641.

18. See pages 282-284.

19. 2 Thessalonians 2:3 (King James Version); see pages 204, 205, 221, 222, 241, 242.

20. 2 Timothy 3:1, 5.

21. See pages 287, 288.

22. Revelation 14:9-11.

23. See pages 282-284.

24. Matthew 10:28.

25. See Psalm 91.

26. Revelation 16; 20:7-15.

27. See pages 281-284.

28. Isaiah 58:13.

29. Mark 2:27, 28.

30. Ezekiel 20:12, 20.

31. Matthew 24:20; Luke 4:16.

32. Exodus 20:8-11.

33. Psalm 96:5; Jeremiah 10:11.

34. Isaiah 6:8.

# The Hour of God's Judgment

IN THE TENTH chapter of Revelation John records one of the most dramatic scenes of all Bible prophecy. Here he tells of seeing, in vision, a mighty angel come down from heaven with "a little scroll" *open* in his hand. This angel solemnly declared that now "there should be no more delay" in the fulfillment of all that God had "announced to his servants the prophets," including Daniel of course.

As we have seen, Daniel was told to "shut up" and "seal" his prophecy "until the time of the end," when "many" would "run to and fro" in an earnest endeavor to understand it and when "knowledge" of its import would "increase."[1] It will be remembered that "the time of the end" began with the close of the 1260 years of papal supremacy in 1798, and that this was to be the time when God would set in operation a series of events designed to prepare the world for the transition from this age to the next.[2] In other words, "the time of the end" is that last crucial period of earth's history during which the great cosmic countdown for launching God's eternal, righteous reign on earth goes relentlessly forward, the time when He be-

gins to take the controls of history ever more securely
into His own hands.

Accordingly, the fateful announcement that now
"there should be no more delay" heralds the arrival of
"the time of the end" foretold by Daniel. It is thus a
solemn fact that the time has come, in our generation,
when there is to be "no more delay" in the complete
fulfillment of all that God "announced to his servants
the prophets," and most particularly to Daniel and
John, whose messages focus on these climactic events
of earth's history.

The year 1798, then, ushered in the time when the
Book of Daniel was to be unsealed, or understood, inasmuch as the events therein described would be "at
hand." In view of the fact that, prior to the time of
John, what God had "announced to his servants the
prophets" concerning the great climactic events of
history had been recorded chiefly in the Book of Daniel, we conclude that the "little scroll" John saw open
in the angel's hand is that very book, which the angel
told Daniel was to be understood at the very time the
mighty angel of Revelation 10 appears on the scene.
It was no longer to be "shut up and sealed," but
"open" for men to understand. This identification of
the "little scroll" John saw in the angel's hand with
the Book of Daniel is all the more certain in view of
the fact that no other book of the Bible was ever "shut
up and sealed."

In this figurative vision John takes the role of God's
people at the time of the end. Directed by a voice
from heaven to "take the scroll which is open in the
hand of the angel," he went and asked for it. The

angel gave it to him and said, "Take it and eat; it will
be bitter to your stomach, but sweet as honey in your
mouth." Doing as he was bidden, the prophet relates
that it was "sweet as honey" in his mouth but that it
became "bitter" in his stomach. A strange episode, to
be sure, but a symbolic one of course. To "eat" the
Book of Daniel means to understand it.[3] The meaning
of this strange episode we shall consider in a moment.
After John had eaten the scroll, he was told, "You
must again prophesy."[4] There was still a great work
to be done by God's people, in "the time of the end."
When this task has been completed, a voice from
heaven will announce that "the kingdom of the world
has become the kingdom of our Lord and of his
Christ," and that "he shall reign for ever and ever."[5]

What was John to prophesy? The message to be
given is mentioned in the opening verses of the eleventh chapter, where John, still in the role of God's
people at the time of the end, "was given a measuring
rod like a staff," and told, "Rise and measure the temple of God and the altar and those who worship there."
It was to be a message concerning Christ as our great
High Priest ministering in the sanctuary in heaven
above, and concerning God's people on earth, "who
worship there" by faith.[6] As we shall see, the message
in Revelation 11 about the sanctuary in heaven is
closely related to that of chapter 14 announcing the
arrival of the great hour of God's judgment.

Daniel explicitly locates the great final judgment
*after* the close of the 1260 years.[7] Accordingly, the
announcement that the hour of God's judgment "has
come" could not be proclaimed until after 1798. As

the fateful year 1798 approached, and increasingly thereafter, devout Bible students of all denominations, in both Europe and the United States, turned to a study of the prophecies of Daniel and the Revelation as never before in history, as the angel of Revelation 10 had predicted.

## The Advent Message

Foremost among the hundreds of ministers who began to proclaim the message that the time of the end had come and that the climactic events of history were, even now, beginning to unfold, was William Miller, a Baptist layman of New York State ordained to the gospel ministry. A diligent student of the Scriptures, particularly the prophecies, he soon became the leading exponent of Christ's imminent advent. The preaching of this message came to be known as the great Second Advent Movement. Scores of thousands heard and heeded the warning that the return of Christ and the hour of God's judgment were imminent, and a great revival followed.

As these hundreds of ministers of all denominations, in the Old World and the New, studied the prophecies, their attention came to a focus on Daniel 8:14, and the words, "For two thousand and three hundred evenings and mornings; then the sanctuary shall be restored to its rightful state." In the Authorized, or King James, Version of the Bible then in common use the last clause reads, "then shall the sanctuary be cleansed."

These dedicated students of the prophecies discovered that the 2300 "evenings and mornings" of Daniel 8:14 represent 2300 years of literal time.[8] But they searched Daniel 8 in vain for any clue to enable them to correlate this long period of time with any known events of history. Eventually, a comparison of the eighth chapter with the ninth led to the conclusion that the latter continues and completes the explanation begun, but not completed, in the former, notably with respect to the problem of the 2300 "days" (King James Version). This close relationship became evident to them from the following considerations:

## Ninth Chapter Explains the Eighth

1. The vision of chapter 8:2-14, about the ram, the he-goat, and the little horn, is fully explained in verses 15-26, with the single exception of the 2300 "evenings and mornings" of verse 14. In verses 26 and 27 Gabriel began to explain "the evenings and the mornings," but broke off his explanation because Daniel "fainted, and was sick certain days" (King James Version).

2. During the interval before Gabriel's next visit, Daniel turned to the writings of Moses and Jeremiah for a clearer understanding of the divine purpose in the Babylonian captivity, particularly with respect to the reasons for it and the length of time assigned to it. In chapter 9:2 he mentions Jeremiah's prediction that the exile in Babylon would last for seventy years, and in verses 11-14 Moses' warning a thousand years before, that national apostasy would result in captivity. The seventy years were now nearly at an end, and the time of the restoration of Israel foretold by Jeremiah was approaching.[9]

3. Daniel specifically mentions that he did not understand "the vision of the evenings and the mornings," the 2300 "days," and appears to have concluded that it implied an extension of the captivity and the continued desolation of the sanctuary.[10] He well knew that the promised restoration was conditional upon sincere repentance, and his erroneous conclusion that the vision of chapter 8 implied an extension of the seventy years of exile led to the fear that his people, still in exile, had not yet truly repented and returned to God—as his importunate prayer recorded in chapter 9:3-19 makes evident.[11] In this prayer he intercedes most earnestly for God's forgiveness, for the return of the exiles, and for the restoration of the sanctuary in Jerusalem. The prayer closes with a reiteration of his plea that God will "forgive" Israel's sins and not "defer" (King James Version) the promised restoration.[12] A careful comparison of the prayer of chapter 9 with the unexplained problem of chapter 8 convinced these earnest students of prophecy that Daniel had the problem of the 2300 "days" in mind as he prayed.

4. In answer to Daniel's prayer Gabriel, who had been commissioned to explain the vision of chapter 8 and whose explanation had been interrupted when Daniel fainted and fell ill, came to Daniel and greeted him with the announcement, "O Daniel, I have now come out to give you wisdom and understanding"— obviously with respect to what Daniel had specifically said he did not understand, "the vision of the evenings and the mornings."[13] Furthermore, Daniel specifically associates the vision of chapter 9 with that of chapter

8 when he identifies Gabriel as the very angel whom he "had seen in the vision at the first."[14]

5. Gabriel's explanation in chapter 9:24-27 is Heaven's reply to Daniel's prayer, as Gabriel explicitly states in verse 23, and thus the inspired solution to the problem concerning which he had been praying. Note carefully the sequence: Gabriel had been commissioned to explain the vision of chapter 8; he had already explained all of it except the 2300 "days"; Daniel says he did not understand the unexplained portion; he prays about the matter; Gabriel returns and announces, "I have now come out to give you wisdom and understanding; . . . therefore consider the word and understand the vision"—obviously that of chapter 8. If chapter 9 does not complete the explanation of chapter 8, then the Bible leaves the 2300 "days" a mystery, and the angel Gabriel never complied fully with his commission to explain the vision to Daniel.[15]

## The 70 Weeks and the 2300 Days

The context, these students of prophecy concluded, makes certain beyond any reasonable doubt that the angel's communication of chapter 9:24-27 continues and amplifies the explanation begun in chapter 8:15-26, and thus explains the 2300 days. Accordingly, they turned to Daniel 9:24-27 for Gabriel's explanation of the 2300 "days" of chapter 8:14. The angel begins with the announcement, "Seventy weeks of years are decreed concerning your people." They found "Seventy weeks of years" to be a Hebrew expression meaning "seventy sevens of years," that is, 70 times 7, or 490 years.[16] This 490-year period, says the angel, is to be reckoned from "the going forth of the word to restore and build Jerusalem," which still lay in ruins.

As a matter of fact, three royal decrees by as many Persian kings were necessary before Jerusalem was fully restored. Cyrus issued the first of these in 537 B.C., Darius the second about 520 B.C., and Artaxerxes the third in 457 B.C.[17] The very fact that a second and finally a third decree proved necessary is evidence that the first two did not fully accomplish their objective, the restoration of Jerusalem. For this reason they took the third, effective decree as the one from which to reckon the 490 years of Daniel 9. This was promulgated in the late spring of 457 B.C. and went into effect a few months later when Ezra reached Jerusalem.

From the late summer or early autumn of 457 B.C., 490 years would extend to A.D. 34.[18] After 69 of the 70 "weeks"—483 of the 490 years—"an anointed one, a prince" was to come. As we have seen, this was the promised Messiah, the Christ.[19] The 483 years would take us to A.D. 27. In that year Christ was "anointed ... with the Holy Spirit and with power" and entered upon His earthly ministry.[20] Three and a half years later, at Passover time in the spring of A.D. 31, in the middle of the final "week" of the 70, He was crucified.[21]

When Christ died on the cross, an unseen hand rent the curtain that veiled the inner sanctuary of the Temple in Jerusalem from view, thereby indicating that the death of the Lamb of God on the cross rendered the Temple sacrifices, which foreshadowed the Messiah's death, pointless and no longer valid in God's sight.[22] The true Sacrifice had now been offered, "once

for all." Thus "sacrifice and offering," which had been
offered continuously throughout the first 69½ of the
70 "weeks" assigned to the Jews as God's chosen people, ceased to be effective for the remission of sins during the last half of the seventieth week, as Daniel had
said. About A.D. 34, terminal point of the 490 years,
Christians in Jerusalem and the surrounding region
experienced their first great persecution—at the hands
of their fellow Jews—and were at that time driven
from the city.[23]

In the precise fulfillment of the prophecy of Daniel
9 in the earthly ministry of Christ and the termination
of the "seventy weeks of years" assigned to the Jewish
nation, the Bible students of the great Second Advent
Movement of the nineteenth century found assurance
of the reliability of their interpretation of the 2300
"days" of Daniel 8:14 also. In fact, Gabriel had
specifically stated that the fulfillment of the shorter
period of 490 years would confirm the reliability of the
longer period of 2300 years.[24]

The angel said that the seventy "weeks," or 490
years, were "decreed" for the Jews as God's people.
The word translated "decreed" occurs in late Hebrew
with the meaning "to cut off." If this is the sense in
which the word is used in chapter 9:24, as the general
context implies, the 490 years must then have been
"cut off" from a longer period of time. Inasmuch as
Gabriel presents the 490 years as an explanation of
the 2300 years of Daniel 8, it is logical to conclude
that the 490 years were to be "cut off" from the 2300
years. Both periods would thus begin at the same point
of time, 457 B.C.

This gave these students of prophecy the beginning date for the 2300 years. Counting 2300 years from 457 B.C., they arrived at A.D. 1844,[25] the time at which the angel had said the sanctuary would be cleansed. But what was involved in the cleansing of the sanctuary? they wondered. Thus far they had been following the Bible with great care. Now they jumped to the conclusion, wholly without Scriptural evidence, that the cleansing of the sanctuary here foretold meant the purification of the earth by fire at the second coming of Christ, as set forth in such passages as 2 Thessalonians 1:8 and 2 Peter 3:7-12.

## A Great Disappointment

But of course Christ did not return to earth in 1844, as William Miller and the others so earnestly believed. When the time passed and their Lord did not appear, many became discouraged and gave up the hope of His soon return. Others, however, turned to the prophecies with even greater earnestness than before, to discover, if possible, the reason for their disappointment. Carefully restudying the great 2300-year prophecy step by step, they became convinced that there had been no error in reckoning the terminal date, 1844. If, then, their error had not been in the *time,* it must be in the *nature* of the event foretold, they reasoned.

These students of prophecy took consolation in the fact that Jesus' disciples had suffered a similar disappointment when, instead of claiming the throne of David as they expected, He meekly made His way to the cross.[26] Their bitter disappointment took place in spite of the fact that they had been with Jesus for

some three and a half years, and that for a number of
months He had been instructing them particularly
with respect to His imminent death on the cross.[27] In
fact, they were still laboring under their mistaken idea
of His mission the day He ascended to heaven.[28]

Of course, the disciples were altogether correct in
their belief that it was *time* for the Messiah to appear.
Their mistake and disappointment were due to a mis-
understanding of the *nature* of His first mission to
earth. They expected Him to accomplish at His first
advent what He had reserved for His second advent.
While Jesus was still with them, they went forth
preaching the message He told them to preach—"The
kingdom of heaven is at hand"[29]—fully believing that
He was about to reign as King of Israel and the world.
But their mistaken expectation and the bitter disappointment that resulted from it, unfortunate though
they were, *did not invalidate* either their discipleship
or their message. The blessing of heaven attended their
mission, and in God's own time they came to understand the reason for their disappointment.

In the same way, the fact that William Miller and
his associates had been mistaken as to the precise nature of the event ordained to take place in 1844, did
not invalidate either their mission or their message,
nor did it alter the fact that the great 2300-year
prophecy had, indeed, terminated in that year. In the
parable of the ten maidens awaiting the coming of the
bridegroom, the advent believers found that Christ
had warned of an unexpected delay in His return.[30]
They also took comfort from the word of the Lord to
the prophet Habakkuk: "The vision awaits its time;

it hastens to the end—it will not lie. If it seem slow, wait for it; it will surely come, it will not delay. . . . The righteous shall live by his faith."[31]

## The Great "Sanctuary" in Heaven

Turning again, therefore, to Daniel 8:14, the disappointed advent believers read once more, "Unto two thousand and three hundred days; then shall the sanctuary be cleansed."[32] They checked and rechecked their reckoning of the 2300 "days" and concluded that there could be no error in their understanding of this aspect of the prophecy. But what was "the sanctuary," and in what sense was it to be "cleansed"? They now found, to their amazement, that the Scriptures nowhere refer to this earth as "the sanctuary," as they had assumed. What, then, was the sanctuary?

As they searched the Scriptures further, they discovered that the term *sanctuary,* literally "holy place," originally applied to the portable structure Moses built at the time of the Exodus from Egypt, and later to the Temple in Jerusalem, which replaced it.[33] They found, further, that the original sanctuary, and later the Temple, had been built "after the pattern" God revealed to Moses on Mount Sinai.[34] After noting that the sanctuary had been made "according to the pattern" God gave Moses, the writer of the Book of Hebrews explains that the priests and their ritual ministry served as "a copy and shadow of the heavenly sanctuary," of "the true tent" which was "set up not by man but by the Lord," and in which Christ ministers as our great "high priest." In other words, the earthly was a finite representation of the infinite.[35]

Finally, they found the writer of the Book of Hebrews emphatically declaring that since the cross Christ's ministry in heaven above had replaced that of the earthly sanctuary.[36] Here, then, was the Bible's own inspired answer to their question. That which was to be cleansed in 1844 was the sanctuary in heaven above, where Christ ministers the merit of His infinite sacrifice on Calvary and to which He invites us to "draw near" by faith in order "that we may receive mercy and find grace to help in time of need."[37]

## The Annual Cleansing of the Earthly Sanctuary

But why would the heavenly sanctuary need to be cleansed? they wondered. Remembering the fact that the earthly sanctuary and its services were a "pattern" or "copy" of the greater sanctuary and the infinite ministry of Christ in heaven above, they turned to a more thorough study of the former.[38]

As the writer of the Book of Hebrews points out, the ancient sanctuary service was divided into two principal phases. First, there was a *daily* ritual that represented the release of repentant sinners from their sins and the figurative transfer of the guilt, or responsibility for these sins, to the sanctuary. In and of themselves, of course, the ancient sacrifices could not atone for sin. Only as the worshiper saw beyond the outward form and fixed his eye of faith on the perfect Lamb of God yet to be offered on Calvary was there release from sin.[39]

Second, there was an *annual* ritual on the Day of Atonement, in late September or during October, that represented the removal from the sanctuary of the guilt and responsibility for confessed and forgiven sins that had, figuratively, accumulated there during the past year, and thus its cleansing or restoration to its original, sinless state.[40] The daily service centered in the first apartment, or "holy place," of the sanctuary, and the annual service in the inner apartment, or "most holy place." There the sacred ark containing the tables of the law was kept.[41]

It is not necessary, here, to enter into a detailed description of the sanctuary or its ritual services. It is important to an understanding of the 2300 years of Daniel 8:14 and the judgment-hour message of Revelation 14:6, 7, however, to note briefly the nature and significance of the ritual that took place on the Day of Atonement each year. The special services for that day required two goats, one of which was "for the Lord" and the other "for Azazel."[42] The Lord's goat was sacrificed as a sin offering, and traces of its blood were sprinkled before the ark in the inner sanctuary "to make atonement" for it, because of the confessed and forgiven sins of the people that had, in figure, been transferred to the sanctuary day by day throughout the past year. Traces of the blood were also presented in the outer sanctuary and at the altar of sacrifice in the courtyard.

Having thus "cleansed," or made an atonement, for the entire sanctuary, the high priest placed his hands on the live goat, the one "for Azazel," confessing all the sins of Israel for the year and transferring them, figuratively, from the sanctuary to it. It is important to note that this did not represent a transfer of guilt

from the people to the goat "for Azazel," but from
the sanctuary to the goat. Accordingly, this transfer
of guilt did not represent the release of the individual
sinner from his guilt. That had already taken place day
by day during the year. To the contrary, it represented
the final and permanent eradication of sin from the
universe. When this figurative transfer of guilt had
been completed, the live goat was permanently banished to "a solitary land," thus representing the permanent disposal of the confessed and forgiven sins that
had accumulated in the sanctuary during the year.

## A Work of Judgment

Throughout the ancient Day of Atonement the Hebrew people were to "afflict" themselves, to see that
all had been made right between them and God. Anyone who neglected to do so was to be "cut off" from
Israel. As they observe the Day of Atonement, modern
Jews still consider it a day of judgment. Contemporary
Jewish writers commonly refer to it as a day when
"all mankind passes before . . . [God] like a flock of
sheep," each to have his destiny inscribed and sealed.[43]

That there is a corresponding work of judgment,
or separation of the righteous from the wicked, at the
end of time is clearly evident in several of the parables
Jesus told—for instance, the one about the separation
of the sheep from the goats.[44] When that process is
complete, He says to the righteous, "Come, O blessed
of my Father, inherit the kingdom prepared for you
from the foundation of the world," and to the wicked,
"Depart from me, you cursed, into the eternal fire
prepared for the devil and his angels."[45]

On another occasion He represented the work of the gospel by a dragnet that "was thrown into the sea and gathered fish of every kind," and the separation of the righteous from the wicked by the sorting of edible fish from those that were inedible. "So," He said, "it will be at the close of the age. The angels will come out and separate the evil from the righteous, and throw them into the furnace of fire."[46] The same process is illustrated again in the parable of the weeds, or tares, in which at harvesttime—"the close of the age"—the weeds are bound into bundles to be burned and the wheat is gathered in.[47]

Clearest of all, perhaps, is the parable about a man who came to a royal wedding reception without the prescribed wedding costume. Before festivities could proceed, the king entered the hall to examine his guests. Their eligibility to attend the feast, which represents the joy of Christ's eternal kingdom, was determined by whether they were wearing the specified attire—the figurative garment of Christ's righteous character. John explains that "the fine linen" worn by the saints represents their "righteous deeds."[48] Only after this inspection, or judgment of the guests, did the wedding festivities proceed. The unworthy guest was cast out "into the outer darkness."[49] We have already noted many literal statements in Scripture that predict this work of judgment at the end of the age.[50]

## The Cleansing of the Heavenly Sanctuary

Each year's round of services thus constituted a conspectus, in miniature, of the entire plan of salvation. The daily service in the ancient sanctuary represented Christ's redemptive ministry throughout the long day of salvation—the once-for-all atonement provided on Calvary, and its day-by-day dispensation to individual repentant sinners. The yearly service represented the final process in the great drama of salvation, a process of judgment, during the course of which the curse of sin is permanently eradicated from the universe.[51]

When we confess our sins, Christ assumes responsibility for them and releases us from their guilt, thus in figure transferring them to the sanctuary in heaven above. It is for this reason that the sanctuary in heaven, like its earthly counterpart, needs to be "purified," or "cleansed"—figuratively of course—as the writer of the Book of Hebrews explicitly states in chapter 9:23, 24. As the blood of the Lord's goat "made atonement" for the earthly sanctuary, or "cleansed" it from the figurative accumulation of confessed sins, so the precious blood of Christ atones for, or cleanses the heavenly sanctuary from, the confessed sins of God's people in all ages.

As we have found, 2300 years were to elapse before the sanctuary in heaven above would finally "be cleansed," or "restored to its rightful state,"[52] and, as applied to Christian times, this period terminated in 1844.[53] Accordingly, those who had expected Christ to appear in 1844 at last realized that the act of cleansing foretold in Daniel 8:14 pointed forward to the concluding phase of Christ's ministry in the heavenly sanctuary, which began in that year.

At best, human language and earthly examples are inadequate to represent the infinite ministry of Christ in heaven above, but God has seen fit to present these great eternal truths in the setting of the ancient sanctuary service. The writer of the Book of Hebrews does so, and then invites us, "with a true heart in full assurance of faith," to "draw near to the throne of grace" in order "that we may receive mercy and find grace to help in time of need," and thus be able to "hold fast the confession of our hope without wavering."[54]

As human language can best express it, then, there is now going forward in heaven an examination of the life records of all who have ever lived, particularly to verify the names of those who have accepted salvation in Christ and remained true to Him. We are not to understand that God is dependent on this examination of the records to find out who is eligible to enter heaven. Not at all. All things are open to Him, and He already knows who have accepted and who have rejected His offer of mercy.[55] But like every aspect of the plan of salvation, from first to last, this procedure is for the benefit of all intelligent beings in the universe—that all may realize, and be convinced, that justice has been done. Throughout eternity this conviction will stand as a perpetual safeguard against evil ever rising again to plague the universe. It is for our sakes, not for His, that He examines our individual records.

Thus in 1844 the examination of eligible subjects for the kingdom of heaven, from the days of Adam down to the present, began. We are now living in that great final day of judgment concerning which the Scriptures speak so often and clearly. Solemn thought! When the threefold gospel message of Revelation 14 has gone to earth's remotest bounds, and when every man has made his final decision to accept or to reject Heaven's gracious invitation, then Christ will bring His work in the great sanctuary above to a close. Then the end will come and He will return to this earth in power and glory as He promised, to redeem His own and to cleanse the universe of every trace of sin.

## NOTES

1. Daniel 12:4, 7-10; see pages 158, 188.
2. See page 166.
3. Jeremiah 15:16.
4. Revelation 10:11.
5. Revelation 10:7; compare 11:15.
6. See pages 261, 262.
7. Daniel 7:8-14, 21, 22, 25-27.
8. See page 167.
9. See Deuteronomy 28:58-66; Jeremiah 25:11.
10. See Daniel 8:15-17, 26, 27; 9:19.
11. See Jeremiah 18:6-10; see also pages 114, 157.
12. See especially Daniel 9:17, 19.
13. Compare Daniel 8:27 with chapter 9:22, 23.
14. Compare Daniel 9:21 with chapter 8:16.
15. Daniel 8:15, 16.
16. The key to the expression "weeks of years" lies in the meaning of the Hebrew word translated *weeks*. This word, *shabua'*, literally means "seven" or a "unit of seven." It is closely related to the more common Hebrew word for "seven," which is *sheba'*. The difference between the two words is this: *sheba'* means "seven" by actual count, whereas *shabua'* is a sort of chronometrical yardstick with seven subdivisions. Ancient Jews used it as a convenient term for measuring off longer periods of time, somewhat as we sometimes count by decades or centuries, or by dozens or scores. The Jews reckoned the week with its seven *days* as a complete unit of time, its seventh day, the Sabbath, being a holy day. The "Feast of Weeks" came exactly seven *weeks* after

the Passover. The law of Moses also recognized seven-*year* cycles, each cycle being a discrete unit, and observed every seventh year as a sabbatical year. See Exodus 34:22; Leviticus 25:3-12; Deuteronomy 16:9, 10; Ezekiel 45:21. *Shabua'* might thus refer either to a unit of seven days or to one of seven years, and ancient Jewish writers used it of both. In the Bible *shabua'* more commonly denotes a period of seven consecutive days. The Hebrew of Daniel 10:2 reads specifically "weeks *of days*"—probably to make clear that "weeks" of years are not intended.

In other ancient Jewish writings, such as the Book of Jubilees and the Mishnah, it denotes a period of seven consecutive years; and this apparently is the sense in which Daniel uses it in chapter 9:24-27. Seventy literal weeks—490 days, or about a year and four months—would obviously be far too short a time for the Jews to return from Babylon and rebuild Jerusalem, and for all the other specified events to take place. In verse 24 the Hebrew reads simply "seventy weeks," the phrase "of years" having been supplied by the translators in order to make Daniel's intended meaning clear to English readers.

A few ancient Hebrew manuscripts actually do read "weeks of years" here, and the Jewish scholars who translated the Old Testament into Greek two centuries or so before Christ so rendered it. The expression in chapter 9:24 could thus be translated more intelligibly, perhaps, as "seventy sevens of years," that is, 70 times 7 or 490 years, which, as the angel declared, were to be reckoned from the restoration decree soon to be issued.

17. According to Ezra 1:1, Cyrus issued the first of these three decrees in his first year, which would be between the spring of 538 B.C. and that of 537 B.C. The decree of Darius is mentioned in Ezra 6:1-12, but no exact date is given. The year was probably about 520 or 519 B.C. According to Ezra 7:7-11, the third decree was issued by Artaxerxes in the seventh year of his reign. Some have assigned Artaxerxes' seventh year to 458 B.C. However, Ezra probably reckoned Artaxerxes' seventh year from the fall of 458 B.C. to that of

457 B.C. Ancient papyri found at Elephantine, Egypt, particularly Kraeling No. 6 of the Brooklyn Museum Papyri, show that Jews in Ezra's time were using the Jewish fall-to-fall calendar reckoning, according to which the seventh year would be 457 B.C., instead of the Persian spring-to-spring reckoning, which would place it in 458 B.C.

18. The decree was dated about midpoint of the year 457 B.C., which would be 456½ full years "before Christ." Christ probably began His ministry during the year A.D. 27, which would be approximately 26½ full years "after Christ." Thus, 483 years from 457 B.C. would be A.D. 27.

19. See note 9, page 169.

20. Compare Acts 10:38 with Matthew 3:16, 17.

21. The astronomical evidence for the date of the crucifixion is about equally divided between A.D. 30 and A.D. 31. The date A.D. 31 seems to accord more exactly with all the Biblical evidence.

22. Matthew 27:51.

23. Acts 8:1-4.

24. Daniel 9:24.

25. See note 18. A date midpoint of 457 B.C. would be 456½ full years before Christ, and a similar date in 1844 would be 1843½ full years after Christ—a total of 2300 years.

26. Luke 24:15-21; 19:11; John 6:14, 15.

27. Matthew 16:21-23; 20:17-19.

28. Acts 1:6, 7.

29. Matthew 10:7.

30. Matthew 25:1-13.

31. Habakkuk 2:3, 4.

32. This is the translation of Daniel 8:14 as it appears in the Authorized, or King James, Version of the Bible, which was almost universally used in the English-speaking world of that time. The King James Version here follows the ancient Greek and Latin translations of the Hebrew Old Testament, whereas the Revised Standard Version follows the Hebrew text more closely.

33. Exodus 25 to 40; 2 Chronicles 2 to 4.

34. Exodus 25:8, 9, 40.

35. Hebrews 8:1-5.

36. Hebrews 7:11, 12; 8:1-6; 9:8-15, 23-28; see pages 182, 261.

37. Hebrews 4:16.

38. See notes 34, 35.

39. Hebrews 10:1-22.

40. See note 25.

41. Hebrews 9:1-5. For a more detailed description, see Exodus 25 to 40. The first fifteen chapters of the Book of Leviticus describe the daily services of the earthly sanctuary; but chapter 16 outlines the annual Day of Atonement ritual in great detail.

42. Leviticus 16:8, 15-19.

43. Philip Birnbaum, *High Holyday Prayer Book: Yom Kippur* (New York: Hebrew Publishing Company), pp. 506, 508; compare p. 282. See also *Rosh Hashanah* 16 b in *The Babylonian Talmud.*

44. Matthew 25:32-46.

45. Matthew 25:34, 41.

46. Matthew 13:47-50.

47. Matthew 13:24-30.

48. Revelation 19:8.

49. Matthew 22:1-14.

50. See page 288.

51. Romans 8:34; Hebrews 4:14-16; 9:11-14, 24; 10: 21, 22; 1 John 2:1; see page 311.

52. See note 32.

53. See pages 167, 306, 307.

54. Hebrews 4:15, 16; 10:22, 23.

55. Hebrews 4:13.

# *The Remnant Church*

THERE ARE more than two hundred and fifty denominations in the United States today. Each believes, or at some time in the past has believed, itself to be, in some special and distinctive way, a more authentic witness to the Christian faith than the others. Sooner or later a church that could offer no valid reason for existing separately would doubtless cease to do so. Perhaps, in part at least, this has been the real reason for so many church mergers in recent years. Does Christ have a people on earth today, as in ancient times, whom He uniquely claims as His own and to whom He has entrusted His last message of warning to a judgment-bound world? Or are all the churches, each in its own way, God's "remnant"? Does the Bible have an answer to this question?

When the long era of persecution foretold by Daniel, Christ, and John came to a close about A.D. 1798, "the dragon" was still "angry with the woman, and went off to make war on the rest of her offspring, on those who keep the commandments of God and bear testimony to Jesus." Here John presents the church in modern times and Satan's final effort to destroy it. The word translated *rest*—"the *rest* of her offspring"—means "remaining ones," or "remnant."[1]

Throughout the Scriptures the "remnant" of God's people has always been a small group that survived such national calamities as pestilence, famine, exile, war, or apostasy, and was mercifully spared to continue in the role of God's chosen people. They remembered the true God and chose to be loyal to Him.[2] After one great catastrophe that nearly annihilated the Hebrew nation, an inspired writer promised that "the surviving remnant of the house of Judah" would "again take root downward, and bear fruit upward," and that this "remnant" would "go forth" to declare God's glory among the Gentiles.[3]

The faithful remnant was always exclusive heir to the sacred promises, privileges, and responsibilities of the covenant, and through it God purposed to work out His plan to save the world. In Revelation 12:17 we come to the last "remnant," the last link in God's chosen line of faithful ones down through the centuries, against whom Satan now goes forth to wage war. "Remnant" is thus John's designation for God's loyal representatives on earth in modern times. Is it possible to identify this remnant, on the basis of clues John and the other Bible writers provide? Let us see.

John gives three distinctive marks by which to identify the modern "remnant." It is composed, he says, of "those who keep the commandments of God and bear testimony to Jesus." They are the ones into whose hands God entrusts the proclamation of His great final appeal to the world, the three angels' messages of Revelation 14.[4] In verse 12 of that chapter he identifies them as people "who keep the commandments of God and the faith of Jesus." Here, then, are

11

three noteworthy characteristics of those who belong
to God's faithful "remnant" people in the last days of
earth's history: They "keep the commandments of
God," they "keep . . . the faith of Jesus," and they
"bear testimony to Jesus." Let us now examine each
of these characteristics more closely, beginning with
the second of the three.

## "The Faith of Jesus"

What is "the faith of Jesus"? The faith *of* Jesus
might mean the same faith that Jesus had as a man
here on earth, His own confidence and trust in God the
Father. Or it might mean our faith *in* Jesus as the
Messiah of prophecy, the divine Son of God who
came into the world. The Greek may be understood
either way. In view of the fact that John and the other
apostles constantly stress the importance of faith *in*
Christ, in this sense, it is reasonable to conclude that
the same is true in Revelation 14:12. Implicit belief,
or faith, in the deity of Jesus Christ as the preexistent
Son of God; in His historical reality as a human being;
and in His virgin birth, vicarious death, literal resurrection, and bodily ascension to heaven is thus one
clear mark of God's remnant people today. Any
church that denies these basic facts of the Christian
faith does not measure up to John's specifications.[5]

Faith in Jesus would also include faith in the aton-
ing power of His death upon the cross for salvation
from sin. In Revelation 1:5 John declares that Jesus
has, indeed, "freed us from our sins by his blood."
Elsewhere he wrote that "the blood of Jesus . . .
cleanses us from all sin" and that Jesus "is the expia-

tion for our sins."[6] The "remnant" of which John wrote will therefore believe in the blood atonement.

Faith in Jesus will lead to sincere acceptance of the things Jesus taught. To profess belief in Jesus but to reject His teachings is a hopeless contradiction of ideas. Faith in Jesus will lead a person to read and meditate on the inspired record of His life and teachings while He was here on earth, and as reflected later in the writings of the apostles.

Faith in Jesus implies acceptance of the entire Bible as the inspired authority in matters of faith and doctrine, and as the norm of Christian conduct.[7] This includes the Old Testament as well as the New, for Jesus Himself believed its writers to be God's chosen penmen. They all "bear witness to me," He said. Following His resurrection He patiently chided the unbelieving disciples: "O foolish men, and slow of heart to believe all that the prophets have spoken!" Then, "beginning with Moses and all the prophets, he interpreted to them in all the scriptures the things concerning himself." Paul similarly believed "everything laid down by the law or written in the prophets."[8]

Faith in Jesus will lead to an earnest study of the prophecies of Daniel and the Revelation. The latter book John calls "the revelation of Jesus Christ," and says, "Blessed are those who hear, and who keep what is written therein."[9] God's remnant people will not, like a majority of professed Christians today, neglect and disparage it as a sealed book, as one that cannot be understood. The angel specifically told John, "Do not seal up the words of the prophecy of this book."[10] Faith in Jesus' teachings will naturally result in believing His interpretation of the prophecies of Daniel, which we have considered at some length in this book.

Faith in Jesus will lead, finally, to confidence in His promise to return to earth a second time, personally and visibly. "I will come again and will take you to myself," Jesus promised His disciples, "that where I am you may be also." He who returns to earth will be "this Jesus," the very same person "who was taken up" from earth "into heaven." Furthermore, "all the tribes of the earth . . . will *see* the Son of man coming on the clouds of heaven with power and great glory."[11]

In the Book of Revelation John refers again and again to Jesus' second coming. In fact, the book closes with a repetition of Jesus' promise, "Surely I am coming soon," and John's impassioned response, "Come, Lord Jesus!" God's remnant people will be eagerly waiting for him.

God's last remnant church will be proclaiming the full, everlasting gospel about salvation by faith in Christ, including the good news that He is coming again soon. It will be warning men that the hour of God's judgment has come. It will have a world vision and a world mission, for God's last message of mercy is to go "to every nation and tribe and tongue and people."[12] It will be an active, missionary-minded church.

## "The Commandments of God"

Faith in Jesus automatically excludes the possibility of attaining to righteousness by one's own deeds, or works, whether by a scrupulous observance of the ritual requirements of the ceremonial regulations of ancient times, or by a legalistic attempt to earn salvation through a meticulous compliance with the precepts of the Decalogue, or by any other device that is supposed to win merit or favor with God. "By grace you have been saved through faith," Paul wrote to the believers at Ephesus, "and this is not your own doing, it is the gift of God."[13] Salvation is not earned; it is a free gift.

But faith does not release a man from obedience to any part of God's revealed will. A man who has already found salvation by faith in Christ will want to obey Him in all things. Jesus said that only the man who, when he "hears these words of mine," actually "does them," that is, "does the will of my Father who is in heaven," will ever "enter the kingdom of heaven." Genuine faith in Jesus automatically presumes a sincere intent to follow His example in all things. "He who says he abides in . . . [Christ] ought to walk in the same way in which he walked."[14]

It is worthy of note that John twice mentions the keeping of God's commandments as an identifying characteristic of His remnant people.[15] In principle and in practice they will recognize the continuing validity of all that God has commanded, including all ten precepts of the Decalogue, His unchanging moral law. Most of the Christian world accepts nine of the ten—all, that is, except the fourth. For this reason, to honor the nine would not constitute an identifying characteristic, whereas to honor the fourth—literally, as it reads—would do so.

"If you keep my commandments," Jesus said, "you will abide in my love." "He who says 'I know him' but disobeys his commandments is a liar, and the truth is not in him; but whoever keeps his word, in him truly love for God is perfected."[16] The fact that a man has been saved by faith in Christ does not release him from obeying Christ, any more than a boy whose father has forgiven him for disobedience is thereby released from obeying his father in the future. Furthermore, a lad who sincerely loves his father will *delight* to obey him. Thus it will be with us and our heavenly Father.

## "Testimony to Jesus"

In the Greek the expression translated *bear testimony to Jesus*[17] reads literally, "have the testimony of Jesus," which may also and with equal validity be rendered, "the testimony that comes from Jesus." Testimony borne *to* Jesus would be the witness borne by the church to its faith in Him, while the testimony that comes *from* Jesus would be messages borne by His spokesmen, the prophets, to the church. John's meaning here may thus be either that this "remnant" bears a faithful witness concerning God's Word already revealed, or that it is itself the recipient and custodian of messages from God, or possibly both.

In Revelation 19:10, however, John defines "the testimony of Jesus" as "the spirit of prophecy," that is, the gift of prophecy by which holy men of old were divinely qualified to receive and transmit messages from God. The spirit of prophecy is one of the "gifts" of the Holy Spirit.[18] The emphasis in Revelation 12: 17 is thus that God's last "remnant" will be the direct recipient of inspired messages to guide them in their last great struggle with the powers of evil, though it is certainly also true that they will bear a faithful witness to the world concerning their faith in Him.

Beyond question, the canon of Scripture closed with the writings of the apostles, but the New Testament nowhere suggests that the gift of prophecy was to cease with the apostolic church. To the contrary, Paul declares that together with the other gifts of the Spirit he lists in Ephesians 4:11-13 it was to continue "until we all attain to the unity of the faith and of the knowledge of the Son of God, to mature manhood, to the measure of the stature of the fulness of Christ." Obviously that time has not yet come.

All the other gifts of the Holy Spirit are still needed in the church, and men and women are still qualified by the Spirit for these tasks. Why should the prophetic office be considered an exception? Furthermore, the Bible writers name many genuine prophets, both men and women, whose inspired messages, both oral and written, never found a place in the sacred canon.[19] Apparently God has spoken to His people as truly by men and women whose messages are not on record in the Bible, as by those whose messages are recorded there.

There have ever been counterfeit manifestations of the prophetic gift, alongside the true, and in His great discourse outlining the dangers through which His people must pass, Christ warned that the church would be troubled by *false* prophets, particularly as the time for His second advent should draw near.[20] This warning against a false manifestation of the prophetic gift prior to His second coming argues strongly that there would also be a genuine manifestation of the gift. Otherwise, He would simply have warned the church against *all* prophets. "Do not despise prophesying," says the Apostle Paul, "but test everything; hold fast what is good." "Do not believe every spirit," wrote John, in similar vein, "but test the spirits to see whether they are of God."[21]

We therefore conclude that another identifying mark of God's remnant people in the last days is the presence among them of the true gift of prophecy, not, to be sure, as an addition to the sacred canon of Scripture, but to provide the special counsel and guidance the church needs in its last mighty conflict with "the dragon." At no time has the appearance of the prophetic gift replaced or minimized the importance of what the prophets have already written. Rather, each new, authentic manifestation of the gift calls men back to what former prophets have already declared to be God's will. The gift is imparted, not to reveal a new way of salvation, but to confirm the everlasting gospel and to help God's people to apply its principles intelligently to their own circumstances. It ever leads men to understand, appreciate, and be loyal to the Bible. If the church ever needed direct divine guidance keyed to its contemporary plight, that time is now, just before the great final crisis breaks like a thermonuclear bomb on the world.

Would you like to find God's "remnant" today? Then look for a group of people who, among other things, have a living faith in Jesus, who keep all God's commandments, including the fourth, who are bearing a consistent witness to the great saving truths of the everlasting gospel, and to whom God has entrusted the prophetic gift to prepare them for the crucial events soon to take place.

## Reflecting the Character of Christ

John declares that there will be "a hundred and forty-four thousand" who measure up in a special way to His ideal of character in the last days of earth's history, and who belong to His remnant people.[22] In the seventh chapter he says that these 144,000 have been "sealed . . . upon their foreheads" with "the seal of the living God." In the fourteenth chapter he says that they have the names of Christ and the Father "written on their foreheads." He saw them "clothed in white robes" made "white in the blood of the Lamb," and was told that they had "come out of great tribulation," evidently the great final time of trouble.[23]

"A hundred and forty-four thousand" is doubtless an ideal, symbolic number representing *all* the "remnant" who go through the last great crisis, rather than their actual number by count. For there to be precisely twelve thousand from each of the twelve tribes, no more and no less, would suggest arbitrary selection on God's part. Furthermore, consistency requires that if the *number* is to be taken literally, then the people themselves should all be considered literal Jews. But, as we have seen, God's elect at the end of time, those who accept His call to come out of Babylon and who go through the last crisis, are from every nation on earth.[24]

What is God's seal? In chapter 7 the 144,000 are said to have this "seal" in their foreheads, but in chapter 14, the names of Christ and the Father. Apparently God's "name" and his "seal," or divine signature, are the same thing. It is noteworthy that God's seal is affixed to the forehead, indicating that the person receiving it has made an intelligent commitment to Him. Unlike the mark of the beast, it is not affixed to a person's right hand. A formal compliance, in contrast with a thoroughgoing dedication of mind and heart, will not satisfy the divine requirements.

A signature, or seal, affixed to a document attests its authenticity and indicates that its contents meet the approval of the one who signs or seals it. God's name represents His character.[25] Figuratively affixed to the foreheads of the saints, it attests that by the grace of Christ they meet His approval and are found worthy to become subjects of His eternal kingdom. They "have not defiled themselves with women, for they are chaste," says John.[26] They have refused to drink the wine of the harlot Babylon. They are pure because they "keep the commandments of God," including the fourth along with the other nine, and are loyal to "the faith of Jesus." Their lives reflect His character.

## God Calls for You

Are you looking for God's remnant people in the world today? Then make these heaven-appointed distinguishing marks your guide. Today God calls *you* to the stage of action. Contrary to all appearances, the complicated play and counterplay of human events is still under His control, and He is overruling all for the accomplishment of His purposes. Amid the strife and tumult of history His unseen hand still guides the affairs of earth. The increasingly lawless state of society and the mounting unrest among the nations testify that we are standing on the threshhold of great and solemn events, that the world is on the verge of a stupendous crisis, that something great and decisive is about to take place.

As in ancient times, God has a people on earth today who have chosen to love and serve Him, people whose lives are fully committed to His honor and to service for their fellowmen. Through them it is His purpose to proclaim the knowledge of a crucified, risen, and soon-coming Saviour to the world. "This gospel of the kingdom will be preached throughout the whole world, as a testimony to all nations; and then the end will come."[27]

God calls *you* to be a part of His remnant people.

## NOTES

1. See page 206.
2. Genesis 45:7; 2 Chronicles 30:6; Ezra 9:13, 14; Isaiah 10:20, 22; Jeremiah 42:2; 44:14; Ezekiel 6:8, 9; 7:16; 14:22; etc. See page 177.
3. 2 Kings 19:30, 31; Isaiah 37:31, 32; 66:19.
4. Revelation 12:17; 14:6-12; see chapter entitled "Last Countdown."
5. See Matthew 16:16, 17; Acts 4:12; 1 Timothy 3:16; 2 Peter 1:16, 17; 1 John 1:1-3; 2:23; 4:2, 3, 15; 5:10-12; etc.
6. 1 John 1:7; 2:1, 2; see also Revelation 5:9.
7. See chapter entitled "A Light in the Dark."
8. John 5:39; Luke 24:25-27, 44; Acts 24:14.
9. Revelation 1:3; 22:7.
10. Revelation 22:10.
11. Matthew 24:30; John 14:1-3; Acts 1:11.
12. Revelation 14:6, 7; compare 10:11.

13. Ephesians 2:8.

14. Matthew 7:21, 24; 1 John 2:6.

15. Revelation 12:17; 14:12.

16. John 15:10; 1 John 2:4.

17. Revelation 12:17.

18. 1 Corinthians 12:10; Ephesians 4:11.

19. Exodus 15:20; Judges 4:4; 2 Kings 22:14; 1 Chronicles 29:29; 2 Chronicles 11:2; Acts 21:8, 9.

20. Matthew 24:11, 24.

21. 1 Thessalonians 5:20, 21; 1 John 4:1.

22. Revelation 7:3, 4.

23. Revelation 7:2-4, 9-14; 14:1-5.

24. Revelation 7:13, 14; 14:3, 6; see pages 182-184.

25. Exodus 34:5-7.

26. Revelation 14:4.

27. Matthew 24:14.

# Grapes of Wrath

OR TWENTY centuries earnest hearts have been praying, "Thy kingdom come, thy will be done, on earth as it is in heaven." They have been longing for the time when "the kingdom of this world" will "become the kingdom of our Lord and of his Christ." It was an ardent desire for the realization of this agelong hope that prompted the disciples, who mistakenly "supposed that the kingdom of God was to appear immediately," to ask Jesus, "When will this be, and what will be the sign of your coming and of the close of the age?" This is the great question to which serious-minded men and women in our time, observing conditions in the world, would like an answer.[1]

In reply to the disciples' question, Jesus explained that His coming and the close of the age must wait until "this gospel of the kingdom" has been "preached throughout the whole world, as a testimony to all nations." Only then, He said, will "the end" come. He could not return, and the kingdom could not be set up, before all men everywhere should have an opportunity to hear and to heed the good news of salvation. Much remained to be done, and Jesus entrusted the doing of it to His disciples. "Go therefore and make disciples of all nations," He commanded them, and then promised, "Lo, I am with you always, to the close of the age." Thus, in a sense, the answer to the question lay in their own hands, and their faithfulness in carrying out the assigned task might conceivably hasten, or possibly even delay, His return.[2]

But the disciples did not as yet fully understand the import of Jesus' words, and a few weeks later they were asking again, "Lord, will you at this time restore the kingdom to Israel?" Jesus replied, "It is not for you to know times or seasons which the Father has fixed by his own authority," and again He told them, "You shall be my witnesses in Jerusalem and in all Judea and Samaria and to the end of the earth." Only when they had done so would the long day of salvation draw to a close, and what the Bible writers call "the great day of the Lord" begin. Only then would God intervene to bring the present order of things to an end and to inaugurate His own universal reign of righteousness.[3]

## The Close of Human Probation

In the seventh chapter of the Book of Revelation the Apostle John relates that he "saw four angels standing at the four corners of the earth, holding back the four winds of the earth, that no wind might blow on earth or sea or against any tree."[4] In Bible prophecy wind is the usual symbol for war, and four winds would indicate universal strife.[5] Similarly, the four angels represent divine restraint on the forces that would precipitate this great time of trouble. According to Hebrews 1:13, 14, angels are "ministering spirits

sent forth to serve, for the sake of those who are to obtain salvation."

In the Revelation John repeatedly speaks of great
strife and confusion on earth immediately preceding
Christ's return in power and glory. Satan would be
angry with the church and would set out to make war
on it. The nations, too, would be angry, and "the kings
of the whole world" would be preparing "for battle on
the great day of God the Almighty." In fact, when
Christ appears, "the kings of the earth with their
armies" would be "gathered to make war against him
. . . and against his army."[6] But the four angels of
Revelation 7 are to hold the four winds in check until
the news of Christ's coming has gone to all the world.

In Revelation 7 John's attention next turns to "another angel ascend[ing] from the rising of the sun,
with the seal of the living God." This angel calls with
a loud voice to the four angels holding the four winds,
"Do not harm the earth or the sea or the trees, till we
have sealed the servants of our God upon their foreheads."[7] As we have seen, the seal of God is His name,
or signature, figuratively affixed to those who by the
grace of Christ meet His approval and are eligible for
admission to His kingdom.[8] When this angel has
sealed all who are qualified to receive it, the four
angels will loose the winds of the last day to blow
upon the earth. Evidently the sealing angel collaborates closely with the three angels of chapter 14 and
the mighty angel of chapter 18:1-4, into whose hands
God has entrusted His last message of grace.[9] The
winds of strife would interfere with this closing work
of the gospel if permitted to blow prematurely.

But finally the fateful moment arrives when the last man in the most remote corner of earth hears and heeds, or rejects, the gospel call. When he has either been sealed in his forehead, or has received the mark of the beast, a solemn voice from the throne of God announces the close of human probation: "Let the evildoer still do evil, and the filthy still be filthy, and the righteous still do right, and the holy still be holy."[10] This solemn decree reflects the fact that, by his own choice, every man's character has been fixed for eternity. The sun of divine mercy sets, the long day of salvation comes to a close, God withdraws His Spirit from the earth, mercy no longer pleads with hard hearts, and human probation is at an end.

When that time comes, every living person will have made the great, irrevocable choice, and all humanity will be divided into but two classes. Only when men have thus chosen sides for the last great battle of the agelong conflict between good and evil will the four angels loose their hold and permit the unprecedented strife and confusion of the last days to cover the earth. In the fifteenth to the nineteenth chapters of Revelation John presents a vivid picture of the fearful events that will take place when that time comes. To a consideration of these events we now turn.

## The Seven Last Plagues

As we have seen, the third angel of Revelation 14: 9-11 warns those who choose to worship the beast and its image that one day they will have to "drink the wine of God's wrath," which is to be "poured unmixed into the cup of his anger."[11] According to Revelation 15:1, "the wrath of God is ended," or reaches its climax, in "seven plagues, which are the last." These, which we may properly designate "the seven last plagues," John describes one by one in chapter 16. The seven last plagues are reminiscent of the ten great plagues God visited upon ancient Egypt because Pharaoh refused to permit the people of Israel to leave for the Promised Land.[12] Those terrible visitations of divine displeasure left the valley of the Nile all but desolate.

John saw the seven plague-bearing angels leaving the temple of God in heaven to visit His retributive justice on unrepentant sinners. As he departs, each angel is given a figurative bowl containing his particular plague. The fact that henceforth "no one could enter the temple until the seven plagues of the seven angels were ended" indicates that divine forbearance is at an end.[13] A command from the throne to the seven angels to "go and pour out on the earth the seven bowls of the wrath of God" sends them forth on their fateful mission.[14]

## The First Three Plagues

"The first angel went and poured his bowl on the earth, and foul and evil sores came upon the men who bore the mark of the beast and worshiped its image." The numerical designation of the angels implies that the seven plagues fall successively, one after another and, as we shall see, with cumulative effect. The word translated *sore* means "ulcer" or "suppurating wound." For this malignant sore, science will have no remedy.

Furthermore, the vaunted miracle-working power of the evil spirits now cooperating with apostate Christianity proves unavailing, thus demonstrating the falsity of its pretentious claims.[15]

Then "the second angel poured his bowl into the sea, and it became like the blood of a dead man, and every living thing died that was in the sea." For people living along the seacoast this plague would be a fearful scourge. It would be fatal to all forms of marine life. This fact forces upon the mind a gruesome picture of loathsome bloated creatures covering the surface of a foul ocean.[16]

The third plague is identical in nature, but affects a different locality. "The third angel poured his bowl into the rivers and the fountains of water, and they became blood." The effects of this plague must be immediate and serious, for man's supply of water for drinking, cooking, bathing, and irrigation is affected. This plague resembles the first of those visited upon the land of Egypt, which affected the water in the Nile River.[17]

## How Can a Just God So Afflict Men?

John heard "the angel of water," that is, the one whose plague affects the waters, make a deposition vindicating God, in view of these terrible judgments. "Just art thou in these thy judgments," he says, "for men have shed the blood of saints and prophets." Now God gives them "blood to drink," for "it is their due!" The punishment fits the crime. The plagues that fall upon these rebellious ones are not an arbitrary, vindictive act on God's part.[18]

Those who have "conquered the beast and its image" John represents as standing victorious before the throne of God in heaven and ascribing praise to Him. "Great and wonderful are thy deeds, O Lord God the Almighty!" they exclaim as the plagues are poured out. "Just and true are thy ways, O King of the ages!" They exclaim, "Who shall not fear and glorify thy name, O Lord? For thou alone art holy. All nations shall come and worship thee, for thy judgments have been revealed."[19] They have remained loyal to God through earth's last great crisis. They have experienced the worst that Satan and his evil legions can bring against them. Now they affirm God's justice in visiting these terrible judgments upon a race of unrepentant rebels.

Isaiah speaks of the retributive judgments of God in the earth as His "strange . . . deed." Never before have men witnessed "God's wrath, poured unmixed into the cup of his anger."[20] Heretofore in all His dealings with men His wrath has been tempered with mercy, but not so now. "Not wishing that any should perish, but that all should reach repentance," God is by nature "forbearing" to sinful men.[21] He is not a vengeful tyrant.

During the long day of salvation men have witnessed His mercy and forbearance, but the time eventually comes when those who resolutely resist His grace will experience His stern, unmitigated justice. These retributive judgments demonstrate God's hatred of sin, and its awful results. If God permitted rebellion to go unrebuked forever, men would conclude that it makes little difference whether they obey God or not.

It is likewise an act of mercy on His part finally to eradicate sin and sinners from the universe. God's resolute but just dealings with unrepentant sinners will forever safeguard the universe against the reentry of sin.

## The Fourth and Fifth Plagues

Next, relates John, the fourth angel "poured his bowl on the sun, and it was allowed to scorch men with fire."[22] Heretofore the sun has been man's benefactor, supplying, as it does, the light, warmth, and energy that make life on earth possible. Now it seems to turn against him. Doubtless, one result of this plague will be the most severe drought and famine the world has ever known.

Men at last begin to realize that these fearful plagues are not ordinary visitations of nature, but are supernatural. As John watched men suffer under the intense heat of the fourth plague, "they cursed the name of God who had power over these plagues, and they did not repent and give him glory."[22] Often, adversity and disaster have led men to repent of their evil ways. But this is not so now—clear proof that those who suffer under the plagues are confirmed in their spirit of revolt against God. The plagues reveal that they are utterly and irremediably perverse at heart, prove them to be what they are in fact—devoted servants of Satan and rebels against God. They refuse to admit that they are in the wrong, even in the face of judgments that would lead honest, contrite men to repent and mend their ways. Their hard hearts are unsusceptible alike to divine mercy or severity.

Then "the fifth angel poured his bowl on the throne of the beast," with the result that "its kingdom was in darkness." This darkness was so intense that "men gnawed their tongues in anguish and cursed the God of heaven for their pain and sores, and did not repent of their deeds."[23] The severe heat of the fourth plague is suddenly replaced by the intense and penetrating cold that accompanies prolonged darkness. The absence of light and heat is all the more impressive and painful in contrast with the intense light and heat of the preceding plague.

In a previous chapter we identified "the beast" as the papacy, and its "seat" (King James Version), or headquarters, as the city of Rome.[24] We have noted also that in the great final crisis Satan will have succeeded in uniting the world under his control. Accordingly, at that time the beast's "kingdom" will embrace the entire world. Apparently, then, the entire world will be enveloped in a pall of darkness for the duration of this plague. God sends men literal darkness to remind them of the gross spiritual darkness that has already enshrouded their unrepentant hearts.

## The Sixth Plague

The sixth and the seventh plagues are closely related, in the sense that the one is preparatory to, and leads into, the other. "The sixth angel poured his bowl on the great river Euphrates," and under the seventh "the great city . . . Babylon" is shattered and drinks "the cup of the fury of . . . [God's] wrath." As we have seen, "Babylon" is John's designation for apostate Christianity, particularly during earth's last days.[25]

Historically and geographically, the ancient city of Babylon was situated on the literal Euphrates River. In view of the fact that in the Revelation the term *Babylon* is dissociated completely from the ancient city of that name, we conclude that the same is true of the term *Euphrates.* Both are used in a figurative, or symbolic, sense. Except for the waters of the Euphrates River the environs of ancient Babylon would have been an arid desert. The city was dependent upon the river for its very existence. Furthermore, in the symbolic language of the Revelation, *waters* represent "peoples and multitudes and nations and tongues." Accordingly, the *Euphrates* would be people who support Babylon the great. The great harlot of Revelation 17, "Babylon the great," is figuratively pictured as being "seated upon many waters"—the peoples of earth over whom she bears sway.[26]

When "the sixth angel poured his bowl on the great river Euphrates, . . . its water was dried up, to prepare the way for the kings from the east."[25] According to ancient accounts of the fall of old Babylon to the forces of Cyrus the Great in 539 B.C., he diverted the waters of the Euphrates River temporarily from the riverbed above the city into the surrounding countryside.[27] As a result, the Persian army was able to make its way unopposed to the very heart of the city, bypassing its supposedly impregnable walls. John here builds his figurative description on the ancient historical narrative.

Comparably, the drying up of the "waters" of the mystical Euphrates River would be the removal of mystical Babylon's support and defenses, thus preparing the way for its downfall. This aspect of events John describes in Revelation 17, where the nations and people who have heretofore championed the cause of mystical Babylon, the harlot, now hate her, turn on her, "make her desolate and naked, and devour her flesh and burn her up with fire."[28] They withdraw their support. The world will be united behind Babylon the great during the future crisis, but when men eventually realize that the fearful seven last plagues have fallen upon them as punishment for adhering to her policies, they will desert her and turn in vindictive wrath upon her.

As the drying up of the ancient Euphrates prepared the way for Cyrus, a king who literally came from the east, to conquer Babylon and release God's people, so the drying up of its modern, mystical counterpart prepares the way for "the kings from the east" to conquer mystical Babylon and deliver God's beleaguered people held captive by Babylon the great.

## How "the Euphrates" Is "Dried Up"

In Revelation 16:13, 14 John describes the process by which "the great river Euphrates" is "dried up." He tells of seeing "three foul spirits like frogs" "issuing from the mouth of the dragon and from the mouth of the beast and from the mouth of the false prophet," and going "abroad to the kings of the whole world, to assemble them for battle on the great day of God the Almighty." As the three angels of Revelation 14 figuratively proclaim God's last message to earth, so these "three foul spirits" go forth with Satan's last summons to marshal his forces for their last battle.

"The dragon" here referred to is doubtless that of chapter 12, "the beast" that of chapter 13:1-10, and "the false prophet" another designation for the third Satanic power, the image to the beast of chapter 13:11-17. In chapter 19:20 John says that this false prophet "worked the signs" by which the second beast successfully "deceived those who had received the mark of the [first] beast and those who worshiped its image." This evil trio—the dragon, the beast, and the false prophet—are the component parts of Babylon the great.[29]

The apostate religious powers of earth go forth to assemble the "kings," or political powers, of earth to the last great battle, here spoken of as the battle that takes place "on the great day of God the Almighty." Now, at long last, the kings of earth "are of one mind and give over their power and authority to the beast" for a brief period of time to "make war on the Lamb," Christ, in the person of His saints on earth. This universal religiopolitical combine aspires to rule the world in defiance of God.[30]

The kings of the earth, says John, were assembled by the three unclean spirits "at the place which is called in Hebrew Armageddon." So far as is known, no geographical locality ever bore the name "Armageddon." Inasmuch as John uses "Babylon" and "Euphrates" in a symbolical, not a geographical, sense, we conclude that the same is true of "Armageddon." Armageddon appears to be a combination of two Hebrew words meaning "the mountains of Megiddo." Now, the region of Megiddo in ancient Palestine witnessed a succession of major military encounters.[31]

Some of the ancient battles fought there, particularly that of Judges 4:4 to 5:31, were decisive in the history of ancient Israel, and brought deliverance from formidable foes. By specifying that *Armageddon* is a Hebrew term John doubtless purposed to remind his readers of those glorious victories over the enemies of ancient Israel, in which deliverance came through the signal manifestation of divine power. So it will be in earth's last great battle.

## The Seventh Plague

But the battle is not actually joined under the sixth plague. John closes his description of that plague with the statement that the kings of the earth and their armies were "assembled . . . at the place which is called . . . Armageddon." Immediately, "the seventh angel poured his bowl into the air, and a great voice came out of the temple, from the throne, saying, 'It is done!'" Following this proclamation "there were flashes of lightning, loud noises, peals of thunder, and a great earthquake," one "such as had never been since men were on the earth." As a result, "the great city [Babylon] was split into three parts, and the cities of the nations fell." As we have seen, the great city Babylon is an evil trio composed of the major religious powers of earth, listed by name in verse 13, while "the cities of the nations" are the political powers, or the "kings of the whole world," as mentioned in verse 14.[32]

The effect of the seventh plague is thus to shatter the great religiopolitical combine through which Satan purposed to rule the world, the moment it is poised to strike the deathblow against God's people. A death decree has been issued against them, and it appears that they are about to fall before their enemies.[33] God permits the plot to progress to the very verge of success, only to intervene at the last moment. The arch-villain is thus caught in the very act of committing the crime and can offer no alibi. Such is the significance of the proclamation, "It is done!" It is at this point that "the kings of the earth with their armies" turn on the harlot Babylon—their erstwhile religious leaders—making her "desolate and naked" and devouring "her flesh" and burning "her up with fire."

Obviously it would take a figurative "earthquake" to shatter the symbolic city called "Babylon the great." Never before has there been a single, unified, world-wide religiopolitical organization such as the one here pictured, and the divine stroke that shatters it is, appropriately, also the greatest of all time. The nations of earth have gathered to "make war on the Lamb" (Christ), but He "will conquer them, for he is Lord of lords and King of kings, and those with him are called and chosen and faithful."[34] This figurative earthquake is the agency by which He overpowers them.

In highly figurative language chapter 18 describes at some length this fearful judgment that overtakes Babylon. God shatters the religiopolitical union at one fell blow, and Babylon the great drains the dregs from the cup of God's fury. Doubtless a literal earthquake also rends the earth itself apart at the same time, for "every island fled away," John says, "and no mountains were to be found." Simultaneously "great hail-stones, heavy as a hundredweight, dropped on men from heaven, till men cursed God for the plague of the hail, so fearful was that plague."[35]

## Christ Smites the Nations With a Rod of Iron

The time has come for Christ "to smite the nations" and to "rule them with a rod of iron."[36] In chapter 19: 11-21 John describes the gory conflict that now takes place. Here, again in highly figurative language, he tells of seeing Christ, mounted on a white horse, descend visibly to earth in power and glory to champion the cause of His beleaguered people. "In righteousness he judges and makes war," says John, and "he is clad in a robe" figuratively "dipped in blood," the blood of the rebels He has come to scatter and slay.

This picture is highly reminiscent of the fearful scene described in Revelation 14:18-20 where, at the coming of Christ, blood flows from "the great wine press of the wrath of God," and also that of Isaiah 63: 1-6, where the Lord comes "in crimsoned garments," as if He had been treading an ancient winepress. Here Isaiah reports the Lord as saying, "I have trodden the wine press alone; . . . I trod . . . [my enemies] in my anger and trampled them in my wrath; their lifeblood is sprinkled upon my garments, and I have stained all my raiment. For the day of vengeance was in my heart, and my year of redemption has come. I looked, but there was no one to help; I was appalled, but there was no one to uphold; so my own arm brought me victory, and my wrath upheld me. I trod down the peoples in my anger, I made them drunk in my wrath, and I poured out their lifeblood on the earth."

In the great battle scene of Revelation 19:11-21 "the armies of heaven" follow Christ as He descends from heaven to earth in His role as "King of kings and Lord of lords." Like a mighty warrior of old He issues a challenge to the kings, the captains, the valiant men of earth, and all who have rejected His mercy. No sooner is battle joined, however, than "the beast was captured, and with it the false prophet" and the two of them "were thrown alive into the lake of fire that burns with brimstone." Simultaneously, John saw the kings of the earth and their armies "slain by the sword of him who sits upon the horse, the sword that issues from his mouth; and all the birds were gorged with their flesh."

## Victory

God's people witness this conflict, but do not actually participate in it. To encourage them in this, their hour of supreme crisis, God sends a message of comfort: "Lo, I am coming like a thief! Blessed is he who is awake, keeping his garments that he may not go naked and be seen exposed!" The phraseology here used is remarkably like that Christ and the apostles often used to describe our Lord's return. Unexpectedly, when the peoples of earth least anticipate it, Christ returns to execute judgment upon them. The garments represent character.[37]

According to Revelation 12:12, at the cross the inhabitants of heaven rejoiced at the defeat of Satan and his legions.[38] Then the devil went to make war upon the remnant of God's people on earth, a theme that is developed through chapters 13 to 19 of the book. Now that his plot against them has failed, they too rejoice: "Rejoice over her, O heaven, O saints and apostles and prophets, for God has given judgment for you against her!" "Babylon the great city" is thus "thrown down with violence, and shall be found no more."[39]

Then, in response to the command to rejoice at the final defeat of the forces of evil, John heard "what seemed to be the mighty voice of a great multitude in heaven, crying, 'Hallelujah! Salvation and glory and power belong to our God, for his judgments are true and just; he has judged the great harlot who corrupted the earth with her fornication, and he has avenged on her the blood of his servants.'"[40]

Next, John "heard what seemed to be the voice of a great multitude, like the sound of many waters and like the sound of mighty thunderpeals, crying, 'Hallelujah! For the Lord our God the Almighty reigns. Let us rejoice and exult and give him the glory.'" Now, at long last, "the kingdom of this world has become the kingdom of our Lord and of his Christ, and he shall reign for ever and ever."[41] The power of Satan and his evil legions is forever at an end.

### NOTES

1. Matthew 6:10; 24:3; Luke 19:11; Revelation 11:15.
2. Matthew 24:14; 28:19, 20.
3. Acts 1:6-11; 1 Thessalonians 5:2, 3; 2 Peter 3:10.
4. Revelation 7:1.
5. See page 141.
6. Revelation 12:17; 13:1-17; 16:14; 17:14; 19:18, 19.
7. Revelation 7:2, 3.
8. See pages 329, 330.

9. See page 295.

10. Revelation 22:11. See pages 282, 283, 329, 330.

11. See pages 292, 293.

12. For an account of the plagues on the land of Egypt read Exodus, chapters 7 to 12.

13. Revelation 15:8.

14. Revelation 16:1.

15. See Revelation 13:12-14.

16. Revelation 16:3.

17. Revelation 16:4; compare Exodus 7:17, 19.

18. Revelation 16:5-7.

19. Revelation 15:2-4.

20. Isaiah 28:21; Revelation 14:10.

21. 2 Peter 3:9 (compare Exodus 34:6); Romans 2:4; 1 Peter 3:20.

22. Revelation 16:8, 9.

23. Revelation 16:10, 11.

24. See pages 232-234.

25. Revelation 16:12-21; see pages 289-292.

26. Revelation 17:1, 15.

27. See page 103.

28. Revelation 17:16.

29. Revelation 16:13, 14.

30. See page 345.

31. See Judges 4:4 to 5:31, especially chapter 5:31; 6: 33 to 7:25; 1 Kings 18:36-40; Psalm 83.

32. Revelation 16:16-21. See page 291.

33. See Revelation 13:15-17.

34. Revelation 17:14.

35. Revelation 16:19, 21.

36. Revelation 19:15; compare chapter 12:5; see page 206.

37. Revelation 16:15; 19:8. See 1 Thessalonians 5:2, 4; 2 Peter 3:10; Revelation 3:3; compare Matthew 24:42-46.

38. See page 209.

39. Revelation 18:20, 21.

40. Revelation 19:1, 2.

41. Revelation 19:6, 7; 11:15.

# Rendezvous in Space

AS THE few short years of His earthly ministry drew to a close, Jesus told His disciples, "I go to prepare a place for you," but "I will come again and will take you to myself, that where I am you may be also." When the time finally came for Him to return to the Father, He retired with them to a quiet spot on the Mount of Olives, half an hour's walk from Jerusalem.

There, "as they were looking on, he was lifted up, and a cloud took him out of their sight. And while they were gazing into heaven as he went, behold, two men stood by them in white robes"—two angels— "and said, 'Men of Galilee, why do you stand looking into heaven? This Jesus, who was taken up from you into heaven, will come in the same way as you saw him go into heaven." Among those who saw Jesus ascend and who heard the promise of His return was John, who later declared, "He is coming with the clouds, and every eye will see him." Of that grand event, which he calls "our blessed hope," the Apostle Paul wrote, "The Lord himself will descend from heaven."[1]

Down through the centuries these promises have burned brightly in the hearts of all true believers. Jesus *will* return. He will return *in person.* He will *descend from heaven.* He will descend *in the same way* that He ascended. People will *see* Him descend. Clearly, the Scriptures leave no room here for a secret, imaginary, figurative, or impersonal advent.

Some have supposed that when the Bible writers speak of Jesus' second coming and the establishment of His kingdom, they refer to the conversion or the death of individual Christians or to the gradual betterment of the world. But Jesus and the apostles evidently believed in a real, literal, personal, visible return. When General Douglas MacArthur, upon leaving the Philippine Islands early in World War II, announced, "I will return," friend and foe alike understood him to mean that he would return literally and personally—as in fact he did a little more than three years later. The writer of the Book of Hebrews declares that Christ, "having been offered once to bear the sins of many, will appear a second time."[2] His second coming will be as real and literal an event as His first coming was.

The second advent of our Lord will also be a spectacular event, for He will come "with power and great glory," and "all the angels with him." It will be as readily visible, He said, as when "lightning comes from the east and shines as far as the west." No one will have to be told about it, because every living person will see Him with his own eyes. He will not appear mysteriously, in secret, somewhere. In fact, Jesus specifically warned His disciples against rumors to the effect that He has already come and may be seen "here" or "there."[3]

Furthermore, at His second coming Jesus will not set foot on the earth as He did the first time, for Paul declares that those who love the Lord will all "be caught up together . . . to meet the Lord in the air; and so," he says, "we shall always be with the Lord." But there will be no "secret rapture," as some have imagined, for the Bible makes plain that all men will see Him when He comes back to earth again.[4] Clearly, neither Christ nor the apostles believed in a "secret rapture," in which the saints are snatched away one by one prior to the end of the age. No, Paul assures us, all the righteous of all ages will be taken to heaven at the same time—when Jesus appears—and not before.

## The Resurrection of the Righteous

In his first letter to the believers in Thessalonica Paul vividly describes the events that are to take place when Christ and the myriads of holy angels appear in the sky above the earth. "The Lord himself will descend from heaven with a cry of command, with the archangel's call, and with the sound of the trumpet of God," he wrote, "and the dead in Christ will rise first." These "dead in Christ," he explains, are the righteous dead of all ages who have been "asleep" in the grave. Our Lord similarly spoke of death as a "sleep."[5]

Thus, according to the Bible, when Jesus returns to earth, the righteous dead are not in heaven. They are still here on earth in their graves, asleep in Jesus. The Scriptures know nothing of a conscious, disembodied soul that supposedly returns to heaven at death. That which constitutes man a conscious, intelligent, feeling, personal being remains in the grave from the time of death to that of the resurrection. The righteous dead are not on some far-off planet, mute witnesses to the terrible course of evil upon earth, to the sickness, suffering, jealousy, hatred, crime, war, and disaster that are so familiar to all of us. They "sleep in Jesus" (King James Version) and know nothing until Christ awakens them on the resurrection morning. God in mercy lays them to rest, and they sleep peacefully until the resurrection morn. "We believe that Jesus died and rose again," says Paul, and "even so, through Jesus, God will bring with him," that is, with Jesus from the grave, "those who have fallen asleep."[6]

As for those "who are alive, who are left until the coming of the Lord," Paul continues, they "shall not precede those who have fallen asleep." Nor, for that matter, will those who have fallen asleep in Jesus precede the living. "The dead in Christ will rise first; then we who are alive, who are left, shall be caught up *together* with them in the clouds to meet the Lord in the air; and so we shall always be with the Lord."[7] Could language be more plain?

The great apostle describes this same glorious scene in the fifteenth chapter of his first letter to the believers at Corinth, which has appropriately been called the great resurrection chapter of the Bible. Here he firmly maintains the reality of the resurrection. "Christ died," "he was buried," "he was raised on the third day," Paul begins, and was seen by hundreds of witnesses, a number of whom he names and most of whom were still living at the time he wrote. If there is no such thing as a resurrection from the dead, Paul reasons logically, then Christ could not actually have come forth from the tomb. "If the dead are not raised, then Christ has not been raised." It is as simple and uncomplicated as that. And "if Christ has not been raised, your faith is futile," and "those also who have fallen asleep in Christ have perished." If there is to be no resurrection of the righteous dead, the Christian faith is pointless. From this line of argument Paul concludes that "those who belong to Christ" will certainly "be made alive"—"*at his coming.*"[8]

## Immortality Bestowed

In the same chapter Paul goes on to explain that when the trumpet of the Lord sounds on the resurrection day, the righteous dead and the righteous living will "all be changed, in a moment, in the twinkling of an eye," and that "this perishable nature must put on the imperishable, and this mortal nature must put on immortality."[9] If the righteous receive the gift of immortality *then,* it is obvious that they were not in possession of it *before* that glorious moment arrives.[10] Beyond any doubt or quibble, Paul here teaches that no person who has ever lived, however righteous he may have been, has immortality now. In fact, elsewhere the apostle specifically declares that at present God "alone has immortality."[11]

Contrary to popular belief, the Bible writers nowhere set forth the idea that man, by nature and in his present state, has, or is, an "immortal soul." Christ "brought life and immortality to light through the gospel," Paul wrote to Timothy. John declares that

"God gave us eternal life" in Christ, and that only "he who has the Son has life." "Your life is hid with Christ in God," Paul wrote to the Colossians, and "when Christ who is our life appears, *then* you also will appear with him in glory."[12]

Christ appears. Those who "sleep in Jesus" (King James Version) are raised from the grave. The saints of all ages are vested with immortality. Then Christ "will send out his angels with a loud trumpet call, and they will gather his elect from the four winds, from one end of heaven to the other." They will "be caught up together . . . in the clouds to meet the Lord in the air" and so "always be with the Lord."[13] Hasten on, glad day!

The righteous thus enter upon their eternal reward. When Christ comes with His angels and in the glory of His Father, "*then* he will repay every man for what he has done," said Jesus. "You will be repaid at the resurrection of the just," He promised on another occasion. That is the time when God "will give eternal life" to all "those who by patience in well-doing" in this life "seek for glory and honor and immortality." "I am coming soon, bringing my recompense, to repay every one for what he has done," Jesus promised John in vision many years later.[14]

Just before his execution in Rome the Apostle Paul wrote, "I am already on the point of being sacrificed; the time of my departure has come. I have fought the good fight, I have finished the race, I have kept the faith. Henceforth there is laid up for me the crown of righteousness, which the Lord, the righteous judge, will award to me *on that Day,* and not only to me but also to all who have loved his appearing." No, Paul did not expect to enter upon his eternal reward at death, but simultaneously with "all who have loved his appearing"—"on that Day."[15]

## A Thousand Years With Christ

As we have seen, Jesus promised His disciples, "I will come again and will *take you to myself.*" Paul wrote that at the resurrection all the saints of all ages will be "caught up together" from the earth "to meet the Lord in the air," and so "always *be with the Lord.*" The righteous dead "came to life," says John, in what he calls "the first resurrection," and "reigned *with Christ* a thousand years"—not on this earth, but in heaven.[16] Clad in immortality, the righteous saints ascend to heaven at the beginning of the thousand years to be with Christ.

How will the saints spend this thousand years "with Christ"? John says that he "saw thrones, and seated on them were those to whom judgment was committed." The Apostle Paul doubtless had this in mind when he told the believers at Corinth that "the saints will judge the world." Yes, "the world is to be judged by you," he wrote, and "do you not know that we are to judge angels?"[17] Apparently, during the thousand years the redeemed participate with Christ and the angels in examining the life records of those who have adamantly resisted God's love and mercy, and who have gone to Christless graves.

What could be more fair than to grant all who are eternally lost the right to have their cases reviewed, in absentia (for they are all dead), by a jury of their peers? Furthermore, the privilege of examining all the evidence on record in heaven concerning one's relatives and friends who are lost will erase forever any possible doubt as to God's justice in barring them from heaven. This conviction, based on direct, personal access to the official records made by the angels, will be an eternal safeguard to the stability of the divine government.

## The Earth Depopulated and Desolate

John vividly describes the terror that overwhelms the wicked when they see Christ descending amid the clouds of heaven. "The kings of the earth and the great men and the generals and the rich and the strong, and every one, slave and free," he says, "hid in the caves and among the rocks of the mountains, calling to the mountains and rocks, 'Fall on us and hide us from the face of him who is seated on the throne, and from the wrath of the Lamb; for the great day of their wrath has come, and who can stand before it?'" Christ said that "all the tribes of the earth will mourn" when in that fearful reckoning day they "see the Son of man coming on the clouds of heaven with power and great glory."

John again describes this scene in the nineteenth chapter of Revelation. There he figuratively pictures Christ as riding forth from heaven on a white horse, in His role as Commander of "the armies of heaven" (the angels), to deliver His people from their bloodthirsty foes ("the kings of the earth with their armies"), who have "gathered to make war against him who sits upon the horse and against his army."[18]

At the end of the thousand years, then, the wicked dead come forth in a second resurrection, the one Christ called "the resurrection of judgment."[23] "Their number is like the sand of the sea," John goes on to say, "and they marched up over the broad earth and surrounded the camp of the saints and the beloved city." In connection with events at the close of the millennium John also relates that he saw "the holy city, new Jerusalem, coming down out of heaven from God."[24]

In view of the fact that in Revelation 20:9 John specifically locates the New Jerusalem on this earth during events that take place immediately at the close of the thousand years, and calls it "the camp of the saints," it is evident that the city and the saints have descended again to earth prior to the events of verses 9 to 15, and are on earth during the scene there described. When Christ descended to earth at the beginning of the thousand years, the living wicked had been "gathered to make war against him."[25] Now, at the close of the thousand years, they take up life where they had left it, and set out again to attack Christ and the saints.

John then relates that he "saw a great white throne and him who sat upon it," and "the dead, great and small, standing before the throne."[26] The "books" which contained the records of their wayward lives "were opened," and "another book was opened, which is the book of life." The former lists the names of the wicked, and the latter those of the righteous.[27] Those whose names are registered in the book of life have already been judged, and their cases do not come up for review at this time.[28] But the wicked are now "judged by what was written in the books, by what they had done."[29]

## The Annihilation of the Wicked

Those who have despised God's mercy stand speechless as the divine indictment is read. Not a man among them has an excuse to offer. All plead guilty and acknowledge God's justice.[30] There is a long moment of awful silence, and then the fateful sentence is pronounced. Immediately, says John, "fire came down from heaven," and "if any one's name was not found written in the book of life, he was thrown into the lake of fire." This John calls "the second death," in contrast with the first death, which is the natural lot of all men.[31] It is the "hell fire" of which Christ frequently spoke.[32]

The fires of hell are not burning now, but when ignited, at the close of the thousand years, the great holocaust that results will cover the face of the earth. It will thoroughly burn up every trace of sin and sinners, everything that would mar the peace and the security of God's eternal, righteous kingdom. "In flaming fire," as the Apostle Paul wrote, God will inflict "vengeance upon those who do not know God and upon those who do not obey the gospel of our Lord Jesus." They are to "suffer the punishment of eternal destruction and exclusion from the presence of the Lord."[33]

Christ declared that God will "destroy both soul and body in hell."[34] Contrary to popular belief, there is nothing in the Greek word here translated *soul* that even remotely implies an immortal, conscious entity supposedly able to survive the body at death. The word means simply "breath" or "life," and refers to that part of man's being which constitutes him a living organism—the life principle. In no instance do Bible writers use the word to refer to a conscious entity capable of existence apart from the body. As Christ said, both soul and body will be *destroyed* by the fires of hell which, as we have seen, are to burn here on earth at the close of the thousand years.[35] The Greek word translated *destroy* means "to annihilate," "to demolish," "to do away with," "to abolish." Anything that is thus destroyed ceases to exist. It is annihilated—reduced to nothingness.

## The Vengeance of Eternal Fire

"The smoke of their torment," John continues, "goes up for ever and ever."[36] Grammatically, this statement may mean either that the process of burning goes on forever and that the smoke is therefore ascending perpetually, or that the fire burns until it has consumed everything consigned to it, and that when the smoke ascends, it does so once for all. If a continuous act is indicated, the fire burns on endlessly throughout eternity, but if a completed act, emphasis is on the permanence of the results. The first would denote a continuous act, the second a completed fact. The latter would be a fire that cannot be quenched until its task is complete, a fire from which there is no respite, one which will burn until it has consumed everything combustible, but no longer. Which of these two mutually exclusive ideas do the Scriptures teach?

The figure of smoke ascending "forever" is doubt-less drawn from Isaiah 34:9, 10, where the prophet describes the desolation of Edom: "The streams of Edom shall be turned into pitch, and her soil into brimstone; her land shall become burning pitch. Night and day it shall not be quenched; its smoke shall go up for ever." That the prophet did not envi-sion an eternal inferno, however, becomes evident immediately, for he describes the land of Edom *after* the conflagration as a desolate waste, to be inhabited only by wild beasts. Here, clearly, the expression, "its smoke shall go up for ever," does not mean that the smoke was to continue rising endlessly throughout eternity, but that the *results* of the conflagration would be permanent. The divine act of punishment on Edom would never need to be repeated.

The Apostle Jude similarly declares that God pun-ished the ancient cities of Sodom and Gomorrah with what he calls "eternal fire," and specifically cites their fate as "an example" of the great inferno of the last day. Obviously, however, the "eternal fire" that de-stroyed those wicked cities is not burning today. But its results *are* eternal. Fire obliterated them, and they are extinct. In fact, the flames went out "for ever" nearly four thousand years ago. The fire itself was not permanent, but its results have been, and will continue to be—"for ever."[37]

Christ said that the conflagration of the last great day is "prepared for the devil and his angels."[38] Con-tinuing his account of the final punishment of the wicked, John says, in Revelation 20, that "fire came down from heaven and *consumed*" Satan and all the obdurately impenitent, and "tormented [them] day and night for ever and ever." The form of the Greek word translated *consumed* denotes a completed, not a continuous, action. John calls this "the second death."

## Eternal Death Not a Painful Form of Eternal Life

Now death is the opposite of life. "The wages of sin is *death*," wrote the Apostle Paul, "but the free gift of God is eternal *life* in Christ Jesus our Lord." Christ told Nicodemus that "whoever believes in him should not *perish* but have eternal *life*." For those who accept the gift of salvation Jesus "abolished *death* and brought *life* and immortality to light." "God gave us eternal life, and this life is in his Son. He who has the Son has life; he who has not the Son has not life," wrote John. Outside of Christ and the gospel is *death*, otherwise described as "eternal destruction and exclusion from the presence of the Lord." Eternal *life* is reserved exclusively for those who are "in Christ."[39]

Thus, according to the Bible, the rewards of the righteous and of the wicked are not two kinds of eternal life—one amid the bliss of heaven and the other immersed in the tortures of hell—but eternal *life* and eternal *death*. These two fates are opposite and mutually exclusive. Eternal death is not a painful form of eternal life.

According to Revelation 20:9, the fires of hell will rage *on this earth*. But when everything has been consumed that can be consumed, those flames will go out. Of this fact the prophet Malachi wrote, "Behold, the day comes, burning like an oven, when all the arrogant and all evildoers will be stubble; the day that comes shall *burn them up,* says the Lord of hosts, so that it will leave them neither root nor branch."[40] Obviously, the prophet here describes a completed act of utter annihilation, or destruction—not a perpetual, endless process of destroying.

## No Ever-burning Hell

The Bible writers knew nothing of an ever-burning hell, and when they used expressions like "eternal," "everlasting," and "for ever" to describe its flames, they referred to the permanence of their *effect,* not to the flames themselves as burning on and on throughout eternity. For that matter, what joy could heaven possibly hold for us if loved ones were forever suffering the torments of hell? Under such circumstances the mental torment of heaven would be at least equal to the physical torture of hell. No, the wicked will "suffer the punishment of eternal destruction and exclusion from the presence of the Lord and from the glory of his might."[41] God is not a vengeful tyrant. He is not pleased or honored by the suffering of His creatures.[42]

It is thus evident that when the great fires of the last day have completed their fearful work, sin and sinners will cease to exist. Not only so, but even "Death and Hades [the grave]" are to be "thrown into the lake of fire."[43] Hell will be a very real place of torment, but it does not exist now. The Bible makes plain beyond a quibble or a doubt that the fires of hell will burn on this earth, and that they will burn until sin and sinners have been consumed—"for ever."

The Apostle Peter wrote, "The heavens will pass away with a loud noise, and the elements will be dissolved with fire, and the earth and the works that are upon it will be burned up." On the great day of God "the heavens will be kindled and dissolved, and the elements will melt with fire! But according to his promise we wait for new heavens and a new earth in which righteousness dwells." Purged thus by flames that have obliterated every trace of sin, and with "all the arrogant and all evildoers" burned up so completely as to "leave them neither root nor branch," the earth now awaits the touch of the Creator's hand to restore it to the beauty and perfection of Eden.[44]

## NOTES

1. John 14:1-3; Acts 1:9-11; Titus 2:13; 1 Thessalonians 4:16; Revelation 1:7.

2. Hebrews 9:28.

3. Matthew 16:27; 24:23-27, 30; 25:31.

4. 1 Thessalonians 4:16, 17; compare John 14:3; see Matthew 24:30; Hebrews 9:28; Revelation 1:7; 6:15-17.

5. 1 Thessalonians 4:13-17; John 11:11-14.

6. 1 Thessalonians 4:14; compare chapter 1:10; Hebrews 13:20.

7. 1 Thessalonians 4:14-17.

8. 1 Corinthians 15:1-23.

9. 1 Corinthians 15:51-53.

10. Compare 1 Corinthians 15:22, 23 with verses 51-55.

11. 1 Timothy 6:16.

12. 2 Timothy 1:10; 1 John 5:11, 12 (compare John 1:4; 3:16); Colossians 3:3, 4.

13. Matthew 24:31; 1 Thessalonians 4:17.

14. Matthew 16:27; Luke 14:14; Romans 2:5-8; Revelation 22:12.

15. 2 Timothy 4:6-8.

16. John 14:3; 1 Thessalonians 4:17; Revelation 20:4, 5.

17. Revelation 20:4; 1 Corinthians 6:1-3; Matthew 19:28.

18. Revelation 6:15-17; Matthew 24:30 (compare Revelation 1:7); Revelation 19:11-21.

19. Revelation 19:13-15, 21; compare 14:14-20. See page 347.

20. 2 Thessalonians 2:8; 1:6-8.

21. Revelation 20:5; Acts 24:15; John 5:28, 29.

22. Revelation 20:2, 3, 5, 7, 13.

23. John 5:28, 29.

24. Revelation 20:5-9; 21:2; compare Zechariah 14:1-4.

25. Revelation 19:19; compare 17:14. See pages 343-348.

26. See Revelation 20:9-12.

27. Revelation 20:12; see Philippians 4:3; Revelation 3:5; 13:8; 17:8; 21:27; 22:19.

28. See page 315.

29. Revelation 20:11, 12.

30. Romans 14:11; Philippians 2:10, 11.

31. Revelation 20:9, 14, 15.

32. Revelation 20:14; see Matthew 5:22 (King James Version); 10:28; compare Matthew 25:46.

33. 2 Thessalonians 1:7-9.

34. Matthew 10:28.

35. See Revelation 20:8, 9.

36. Revelation 14:11.

37. Genesis 19:24-29; Jude 6, 7.

38. Matthew 25:41.

39. John 3:16; Romans 6:23; 2 Timothy 1:10; 1 John 5:11, 12; 2 Thessalonians 1:9, 10; 1 Corinthians 15:18-22; 1 Thessalonians 4:16; compare Romans 2:6-8.

40. Malachi 4:1.

41. 2 Thessalonians 1:9, 10.

42. Ezekiel 33:11; 2 Peter 3:9.

43. Revelation 20:14.

44. 2 Peter 3:10-13; Malachi 4:1.

# Your World Beyond Tomorrow

A FUTURAMA depicting what designers think cities and homes, automobiles and highways, communications facilities and space travel will be like a decade or two in the future appeals to our natural curiosity to know in what ways life will be better tomorrow than it is today. Tomorrow is the time when the science fiction dreams of today will come true. What do the Scriptures have to say about that wonderful world beyond tomorrow, when the all-consuming fires of the last great day have finally subsided and the embers have grown cold?

"The elements will be dissolved with fire," wrote the Apostle Peter, "and the earth and the works that are upon it will be burned up," but "according to his promise we wait for new heavens and a new earth in which righteousness dwells."[1] The surface of this old world will be reduced to its primal elements, and the last traces of the long and dreary reign of sin will be erased. But the Apostle John also tells of seeing "a new heaven and a new earth," after "the first heaven and the first earth had passed away," and of hearing God's voice proclaim, "Behold, I make all things new."[2] John's inspired preview of the perfection, the beauty, and the opportunities of that wonderful world beyond tomorrow assures us that the reality will far surpass our fondest dreams today. Purified by fire, and with the blight of sin removed forever, the earth will be restored to its Edenic beauty, and upon all things, small and great, perfection will rest once more.

On the wings of inspired poetry the prophet Isaiah revels in the beauty and perfection of that better land: "The wilderness and the dry land shall be glad, the desert shall rejoice and blossom; like the crocus it shall blossom abundantly, and rejoice with joy and singing. The glory of Lebanon shall be given to it, the majesty of Carmel and Sharon." "Waters shall break forth in the wilderness, and streams in the desert."[3]

The Bible writers make clear beyond a doubt that the new earth will be a very real place inhabited by real people with a capacity for enjoying life, friendship, and interesting and satisfying activities far surpassing those of this mortal life. The Apostle Paul assured his converts in the ancient city of Corinth that the people who dwell in the new earth will have real bodies, perfect and immortal, to be sure, but nonetheless real. We will recognize our friends and see one another "face to face."[4] Immortality will remove the limitations imposed by sin and will open to the saved a pathway of infinite opportunity and advancement.

## No Sickness, Suffering, Pain, or Death

The inhabitants of the earth made new will enjoy perpetual health and vigor, and the flush of youth will ever be upon their faces. They will never become weary or exhausted. The sickness, suffering, and physical defects that have made the lot of so many in this life one of misery and pain will all be gone. Think of it! Never again will feebleness and old age cripple the powers of body and mind. There will be no heart attacks to steal away our loved ones, no malignant cancer to deplete the vital energies, no cerebral palsy or muscular dystrophy or multiple sclerosis or poliomyelitis to paralyze the body, no migraine headaches and no neuritis, arthritis, or rheumatism with their excruciating pain, not even the passing nuisance of a common cold. But best of all, there will be no grim funeral trains wending their forlorn way out to the silent city of the dead.

In that better land "the eyes of the blind shall be opened, and the ears of the deaf unstopped; then shall the lame man leap like a hart, and the tongue of the dumb sing for joy." Immortalized, they "shall renew their strength, they shall mount up with wings like eagles, they shall run and not be weary, they shall walk and not faint." No one will ever say, "I am sick." God "will wipe away every tear from their eyes, and death shall be no more, neither shall there be mourning nor crying nor pain any more, for the former things have passed away."[5]

"Then he showed me the river of the water of life, bright as crystal, flowing from the throne of God and of the Lamb through the middle of the street of the city; also, on either side of the river, the tree of life with its twelve kinds of fruit, yielding its fruit each month; and the leaves of the tree were for the healing of the nations."[6] Privileged to eat again of the fruit of the tree of life, men express gratitude for God's gracious gift of life eternal. Its elixir stimulates their vital forces and prevents dissolution and death.

## Permanent Peace and Security

The lot of most men in practically all ages and lands of earth has been one of uncertainty and insecurity. How often large-scale warfare has disrupted, and then taken, the lives of millions! In how many parts of the world, even today, are revolution, civil war, guerrilla raids, political unrest, and comparative anarchy accepted as a more or less normal way of life. How many millions of displaced persons, political refugees, and war orphans there are!

Even in lands where stable government generally prevails, how many thousands of people are crippled or killed as a result of violent crime and accident! How often the great jetliners of the sky, and speeding trains on the ground, carry multiplied scores and hundreds to sudden death! How often hurricanes, tornadoes, earthquakes, and floods leave disaster in their wake! Even at its best, life on this earth is fraught with uncertainty. Breathes there a man who would not exchange it all for eternal peace and security, if he could?

Again in the rapturous language of poetry Isaiah describes the universal peace and security of that better land beyond tomorrow: "The wolf shall dwell with the lamb, and the leopard shall lie down with the kid, and the calf and the lion and the fatling together, and a little child shall lead them. The cow and the bear shall feed; their young shall lie down together; and the lion shall eat straw like the ox. The sucking child shall play over the hole of the asp, and the weaned child shall put his hand on the adder's den. They shall not hurt or destroy in all my holy mountain; for the earth shall be full of the knowledge of the Lord as the waters cover the sea." Elsewhere he wrote, "No lion shall be there, nor shall any ravenous beast come up on it; they shall not be found there, but the redeemed shall walk there."[7]

Thank God! The time is coming when men of peace and goodwill can live happily together under a universal government where there will be security, opportunity, prosperity, and justice for all.

## Peace of Heart and Mind

Inner peace of heart and mind are even more important than the outer peace in the world about us. But for so many this life is full of heartaches, blighted friendships, family quarrels, and broken homes. All too often parents go astray, and their children follow them. But in that world beyond tomorrow there will be no selfishness, no jealousy, no hatred, no desire for revenge. In fact, "there shall no more be anything accursed," wrote John. "Nothing unclean shall enter" that wonderful land of beginning again, "nor any one who practices abomination or falsehood, but only those who are written in the Lamb's book of life."[8]

In that land beyond tomorrow there will be no disappointments or defeats, no frustrations or loneliness to produce neurotic syndromes, maladjusted personalities, social misfits, and suicides. There will be no frayed nerves or brittle tempers, no inhumanity of man toward his fellowmen. Brilliant careers will not be cut short by circumstances beyond one's control. There will be no slaves to monotonous drudgery at home or the office. There will be no alcoholics or drug addicts, no people with split personalities who have taken flight from the world of reality, yet who turn this world into a living hell for those who cannot escape from *them*. Never again, in that land beyond tomorrow, will we ever hear "the sound of weeping and the cry of distress." We will "not build and another inhabit," nor will we "plant and another eat," for the saved will "long enjoy the work of their hands."[9]

Home budgets will never get out of balance, and there will be no arguments about family finance. The banks will never close, the stock market will never drop, business ventures will never go into bankruptcy, there will be no foreclosures. Rent and installment payments and taxes will never come due. There will be no fast business deals to trap the unwary, and no need to sue at law.

## An Eternal Adventure

Let no one think that better world beyond tomorrow will be a place of idleness and inactivity, however. The fortunate people who live there will spend eternity making their grandest dreams come true. They will "build houses and inhabit them," they will "plant vineyards and eat their fruit."[10] They will raise flowers, fruit, crops, and cattle. With never-failing delight they will contemplate the wonders of God's creative power. They will revel in observing birds and beasts, flowers, trees, and fields unmarred by sin. Unfettered by finite limitations they will explore the marvels of the universe—suns, stars, and galaxies. They will investigate the properties of light and magnetism, of atomic energy and radiation. They will study the mysteries of the human body, such as how man's built-in electronic computer operates to gather, store, and use information, how the genes and chromosomes transmit individual characteristics, how the chemical reactions of the body take place, and how the marvelous coordination of the various organs is effected.

In a very real and literal sense, that world beyond tomorrow will be a thing of joy forever. No one will ever get tired of the earth made new. The grandest enterprises can be carried forward and the highest ambitions realized. All the treasures of the universe will be open to the study and investigation of the saved. With unutterable delight they will enter into the wisdom and the joy of unfallen beings.

"The ransomed of the Lord shall return, and come to Zion with singing; everlasting joy shall be upon their heads; they shall obtain joy and gladness, and sorrow and sighing shall flee away." In God's presence there will be "fulness of joy," and at His right hand "pleasures for evermore."[11] Realizing that God's goodness and love have made all this possible, they will turn to Him in heartfelt appreciation and praise. Adopted into the heavenly family, they will be sons and daughters of the Infinite One who created and redeemed them. He "will dwell with them, and they shall be his people."[12]

God's original design for this old earth is at last realized. In the long ago God gave man "dominion over the works of . . . [His] hands," but because of sin man forfeited his right to rule. Now he is restored to his long-lost kingship. As Daniel prophesied, "the kingdom and the dominion and the greatness of the kingdoms under the whole heaven shall be given to the people of the saints of the Most High; their kingdom shall be an everlasting kingdom, and all dominions shall serve and obey them."[13] They are heirs forever of the wonderful place the Saviour promised to prepare for them. "Come, O blessed of my Father," He will say, "inherit the kingdom prepared for you from the foundation of the world."[14]

## An Appreciation of God's Infinite Goodness

What a joy it will be to see the Saviour face to face and to listen to His voice! Throughout eternity the redeemed of earth will thrill with an ever-deepening appreciation of the love and grace that prompted the gift of God's only Son for their salvation. John relates that he "heard every creature in heaven and on earth and under the earth and in the sea, and all therein, saying, 'To him who sits upon the throne and to the Lamb be blessing and honor and glory and might for ever and ever!' "[15]

Throughout eternity the only reminder of the terrible results of sin, and the infinite cost of salvation, will be the marks of the nails in the hands of the Saviour.[16] The agelong conflict between good and evil portrayed in figure and symbol by Daniel and John is ended, and the universe is forever free from the blight of sin. All is once more harmony and peace. "From the minutest atom to the greatest world, all things, animate and inanimate, in their unshadowed beauty and perfect joy, declare that God is love."[17]

## Will You Be There?

"Since all these things"—the world as we know it today—"are thus to be dissolved," exclaims the Apostle Peter, "what sort of persons ought you to be in lives of holiness and godliness, waiting for and hastening the coming of the day of God, because of which the heavens will be kindled and dissolved, and the elements will melt with fire! But according to his promise we wait for new heavens and a new earth in which righteousness dwells. Therefore, beloved, since you wait for these, be zealous to be found by him without spot or blemish, and at peace." As the Apostle John expresses it, "Every one who thus hopes in him purifies himself as he is pure."[18] Christ has gone to prepare a place for us, and He invites us individually to prepare a place for Him in our hearts and lives. He calls us to cooperate with Him here and now, so that we will fit into His plan for a perfect universe then.

It is not enough to know about these things. "If you know these things," Christ said, "blessed are you if you do them."[19] A knowledge of truth calls us to forsake this world, to make a personal commitment to Christ, and to set out on a lifelong journey for that better land beyond tomorrow. It calls us to action. A mental assent to truth will save no one; God expects the life to be brought into harmony with the principles of heaven—here and now. "Not every one who says to me, 'Lord, Lord,' shall enter the kingdom of heaven,"

warned Christ, "but he who does the will of my Father
who is in heaven." "If you love me," He said, "you
will keep my commandments."[20]

To illustrate the importance of doing God's will
and obeying His commands, as well as believing,
Christ once gave the following illustration: "Every
one then who hears these words of mine and does
them will be like a wise man who built his house upon
the rock; and the rain fell, and the floods came, and
the winds blew and beat upon that house, but it did
not fall, because it had been founded on the rock. And
every one who hears these words of mine and does not
do them will be like a foolish man who built his house
upon the sand; and the rain fell, and the floods came,
and the winds blew and beat against that house, and
it fell; and great was the fall of it."[21]

## Grace to Follow in Christ's Footsteps

May God give us the grace to follow in the footsteps of the Master, first to the cross, and then in the
straight and narrow way He has marked out for us
through life, all the way into the earth made new. He
calls us to "live by faith in the Son of God, who loved
. . . [us] and gave himself for" us. He calls us "to live
sober, upright, and godly lives in this world." "Do not
be conformed to this world," appeals the Apostle Paul,
"but be transformed by the renewal of your mind, that
you may prove what is the will of God, what is good
and acceptable and perfect."[22]

"Blessed is he who reads aloud the words of the
prophecy, and blessed are those who hear, and who
keep what is written therein." "Behold, I am coming

soon," is Christ's message to men in the space age. May our response echo that of the Apostle John, who closes the Book of Revelation and the canon of Holy Scripture with the earnest prayer, "Come, Lord Jesus!" Let us eagerly await the soon coming of our Lord and Saviour on that glorious day when He will award the "crown of righteousness . . . to all who have loved his appearing." Let us endure to the end, and be among those who hear Him say, "Well done, . . . enter into the joy of your master."[23]

"Yet a little while," wrote the author of the Book of Hebrews, "and the coming one shall come and shall not tarry." But there is still time to anchor our souls in the harbor of infinite grace and to prepare for His soon return. "Blessed are those who wash their robes, that they may have the right to the tree of life and that they may enter the city." "Let him who is thirsty come, let him who desires take the water of life without price."[24]

Will you be ready to meet your Lord and Master in peace?

"Think of—
  Stepping on shore, and finding it Heaven!
  Taking hold of a hand, and finding it God's hand.
  Breathing a new air, and finding it celestial air.
  Feeling invigorated, and finding it immortality.
  Passing from storm and tempest to an unbroken calm.
  Waking up, and finding it Home."[25]

## NOTES

1. 2 Peter 3:10-13.
2. Revelation 21:1, 5; compare Isaiah 65:17.
3. Isaiah 35:1, 2, 6.
4. 1 Corinthians 15:35-41; 13:12.
5. Isaiah 35:5, 6; 33:24; 40:31; Revelation 21:4.
6. Revelation 22:1-5.
7. Isaiah 11:6-9; 35:9; 65:19.
8. Revelation 22:3; 21:27.
9. Isaiah 65:19, 22.
10. Isaiah 65:21.
11. Isaiah 35:10; compare 65:18.
12. Psalm 16:11; Revelation 21:7, 3; 22:3, 4.
13. Psalm 8:6; Daniel 7:27; John 14:1-3.
14. Matthew 25:34.
15. Revelation 5:13.
16. Zechariah 13:6.
17. Ellen G. White, *The Great Controversy Between Christ and Satan,* p. 678.
18. 2 Peter 3:11-14; 1 John 3:3.
19. John 13:17.
20. Matthew 7:21; John 14:15.
21. Matthew 7:24-27.
22. Galatians 2:20; Titus 2:12; Romans 12:2.
23. Revelation 1:3; 22:7, 20; Hebrews 9:28; 2 Timothy 4:8; see Hebrews 6:19, 20; Matthew 24:13; 25:21.
24. Hebrews 10:37; Revelation 22:14, 17.
25. Author Unknown.